Lucian,

On the Death of Peregrinus

C. T. Hadavas

Lucian, *On the Death of Peregrinus*

An Intermediate Ancient Greek Reader
Ancient Greek text with vocabulary and commentary

First Edition

© 2014 by C. T. Hadavas

The Greek text is the edition of A. M. Harmon, first published in 1936 by Harvard Univ. Press and William Heinemann.

ISBN-13: 978-1500303099
ISBN-10: 1500303097

Published by C. T. Hadavas

Cover Design: C. T. Hadavas

Cover Image: "Vulture in Flight" (photo designed by C. T. Hadavas, consisting of sky/background by C. T. Hadavas and "Soaring" [vulture] by K. W. Sanders); cf. *On the Death of Peregrinus* 39 and 40.

Fonts: (English) Times New Roman; (Greek) Αρισταρχος

hadavasc@beloit.edu

TABLE OF CONTENTS

How To Use This Book

The reader is assumed to have a basic acquaintance with Ancient Greek grammar. All vocabulary found in the passage of *On the Death of Peregrinus* on the left page, with the exception of the verb "to be" and personal pronouns, is given on the facing page. For many verbs, only the first person singular present active indicative form is given. For verbs with unusual forms (e.g., verbs with deponent futures, second aorists, or with futures and aorists from unrelated stems) the first person singular active forms of the present, future, and aorist are given. For -μι verbs, the second aorist active and the perfect active, where warranted, are also provided. After a word appears five separate times in the Vocabulary lists it does not appear again (though it will be found, along with all pronouns, in the **GLOSSARY** at the end of this book).

On the understanding that most students who will use this text have either just finished the first year of college Ancient Greek or are returning after a hiatus of some time from their study of the language, I have provided at the bottom of the text page rather detailed grammatical and syntactical notes. Lucian's works, with their numerous historical, biographical, and literary references, allusions, and appropriations, were written for the educated elite of his time, who had an easy familiarity with nine centuries of Greek history, literature and culture. I have, therefore, also included notes that provide much (not all!) of the necessary background information for appreciating Lucian's sophisticated (and often sophistic) use of such material.

LUCIAN

More than 80 works have come down to us with the name of Lucian (*c.* 120 – after 180 CE) as their author (around 70 of which are considered authentic). And although some of these texts are either ostensibly autobiographical (*The Dream, or Lucian's Career*) or contain autobiographical information (*Twice Accused*), our knowledge of Lucian's life is quite limited. The reasons for this are twofold: (1) the external biographical evidence about Lucian is almost non-existent; (2) even though Lucian can appear quite open about important autobiographical details in such works as *The Dream*, he is a notoriously unreliable source, employing allegory and literary allusion in the construction of the narratives that recount the most significant turning points in his life.[1]

What little we do know about Lucian is that he was born sometime near the beginning of the reign of the Roman emperor Hadrian (117 – 138 CE) in Samosata, a Syrian city (now in modern-day Turkey) on the banks of the Euphrates river.[2]

Though Lucian's native language may have been Aramaic, he most likely learned Greek as a schoolboy. He spent his early years as a sophist (see **INTRODUCTION** and **LUCIAN AND THE SECOND SOPHISTIC** below), teaching rhetoric, pleading in court, and performing oratorical displays in Asia Minor, Athens, and Gaul. Becoming disillusioned with such work, he gave it up around the age of 40 and moved to Athens where he composed many different literary pieces, including his influential "parody of mendacious travel writing,"[3] *A True Story*.

---

[1] Hopkinson 1, 93-7.

[2] Samosata was the former capital of the small Hellenistic kingdom of Commagene, which became a Roman province in 72 CE. It was the homebase to two Roman legions as well as a flourishing commercial center in the 2nd century CE.

[3] The phrase is Hopkinson's (3). *A True Story* has influenced, among others, Rabelais and Swift. Its combination of satire and science fiction – it is often considered to be the first work of science fiction – also makes it a predecessor to Douglas Adams' *The Hitchhiker's Guide to the Galaxy* radio drama/series of books.

INTRODUCTION

Lucian's *On the Death of Peregrinus* (hereafter simply *Peregrinus*) is mostly read today for its references to both Jesus and the Christians of the 2nd century CE. This is not surprising, since this text, written in the form of a letter to a friend named Cronius, contains some of the earliest and most interesting comments made by a member of the Greco-Roman educated elite on that particular religion in its second century of existence (see **LUCIAN AND CHRISTIANITY** below). However, this aspect of the text is only one part of what makes the *Peregrinus* such a fascinating work.

The narrative's nature and purpose are simple enough: Lucian's literary epistle is a hatchet job designed to destroy the postmortem reputation of a certain Cynic philosopher named Peregrinus (*c.* 95/100 – 165 CE), a man depicted as a glory-obsessed impostor who is determined at all costs to establish a new religious cult to himself. To counteract Peregrinus' propaganda and prevent him from achieving his goal, the text recounts – often in a sensationalistic manner – Peregrinus' (supposed) character flaws, moral failings, and criminal actions.[4]

Not so simple, however, are Lucian's narratological methods, and in particular his use of various authorial perspectives (see **LUCIAN, "LUCIAN," AND "LUCIAN'S DOUBLE"** below). In addition, the work's mixing of different genre elements contributes to its somewhat ambiguous nature: is the *Peregrinus* primarily a satirical narrative posing as a friendly letter to a friend? Or is it fundamentally a journalistic exposé – serio-comic to be sure – that employs satirical elements in order to better convince readers of its author's message?

---

[4] Lucian's predecessor in the "hatchet job genre" was the comic playwright Aristophanes (cf., e.g., his *Clouds*, one of whose main targets is the philosopher Socrates). Lucian learned much from Aristophanes in terms of both technique and as a source for ideas, words, and phrases that he might allude to and rework (e.g., in 29 and 30 of *Peregrinus*, Lucian makes use of material drawn from Aristophanes' *Knights* and *Lysistrata*).

Venturing beyond the narratological and genre questions, one finds a Lucian who, as a representative of the most important cultural movement of his time, sophistry, is clearly engaging in a dialogue with his audience of fellow educated elites. Lucian does this through the "language" that they share – literally in terms of the long-dead spoken dialect of Greek in which he writes, Attic (see LANGUAGE below), and figuratively in terms of his use of quotations from, allusions to, and repurposings of "classic" texts from the archaic and classical periods of Greek history (see LITERARY STYLE below).

Despite his former career as a practicing sophist, and his continuing use throughout his written works of sophistic techniques, ideas, and discourse, Lucian is among the greatest critics and satirists of sophists since Plato. In fact, in the *Peregrinus* Lucian expands the already multivalent definition of sophist (see LUCIAN AND THE SECOND SOPHISTIC below) to include contemporaries like Peregrinus (described in 32 as "the death-fixated sophist") as well as a long-deceased non-Greek speaker from Palestine (described in 13 as "that crucified sophist"). In Lucian's eyes, the former was a shameless self-promoter and performer who desperately craved the world's attention, while the latter was guilty of promising his followers immortality but offering them no real proof that he could make good on such a promise. For Lucian, then, such works as the *Peregrinus* clearly reveal that sophistry was not simply something that was practiced by certain educated elites for the intellectual delectation of other educated elites – the primary understanding of sophistry in Lucian's world – but also something that was being employed by so-called wonderworkers to manipulate and delude foolish simpletons through carefully orchestrated "miracles" and empty promises of healing and resurrection. Such charlatans, Lucian apparently believed, were sophists of a particularly dangerous nature, and, for that reason, they must be fought wherever and whenever they appeared.[5]

---

[5] Another work in which Lucian aggressively attacks a contemporary for the fraudulent schemes that he perpetrates on all and sundry is his *Alexander, or the False Prophet*. In this work his loathing for a certain Alexander of Abonouteichos, who established a well-regarded oracular shrine that housed an enormous prophetic snake, surpassed even his hatred for Peregrinus.

PEREGRINUS-PROTEUS-PHOENIX

What's in a name? In the case of the subject of Lucian's *On the Death of Peregrinus* (whose neutral-sounding title belies its nature as "an abusive obituary"[6]), quite a lot. Peregrinus (perhaps his given name) is a Latin noun meaning "foreigner," "traveler." And travel Peregrinus did: from his hometown of Parium on the Black Sea, to Armenia, Palestine, Asia Minor, Alexandria, Rome, Athens, and Olympia (on four different occasions). His second name, Proteus, which he has already assumed at the beginning of Lucian's text, references Homer's "Old Man of the Sea", a minor divinity in the *Odyssey* famous for his shape-shifting abilities and oracular powers. Our Proteus will change character several times thoughout his life, from young parricide to pederast, leader of the Christian Church, Cynic philosopher, cult leader (inflected with Brahmanic elements), and celebrated suicide. Even after his death his protean spirit will lay claim to a series of new incarnations: a so-called divine guardian of the night, an oracular shrine, and statues of him set up in his honor throughout the eastern Roman Empire. At Olympia in 165 CE, Peregrinus-Proteus takes on his final name, Phoenix, as he builds his own funeral pyre in imitation of the mythical phoenix's nest of cremation and resurrection – though in this instance his "rebirth" from the ashes will be due entirely to Lucian's satirical imagination.

In the face of this name-changing, shape-shifting dynamo, Lucian aggressively sets out to destroy the pre-suicide reputation of Peregrinus in order to prevent the growth of his cult that had sprung up immediately after his self-immolation.[7] But was Peregrinus really the impostor that Lucian's text makes him out to be?

---

[6] Macleod 7. The word translated here as *death* (Τελευτῆς), in the Greek title of the work, Περὶ τῆς Περεγρίνου Τελευτῆς, can also mean *completion, accomplishment,* or *end.*

[7] Although the date of the central event described in the text – Peregrinus' suicide – is secure (165 CE), the date of the work's composition is unknown. Most scholars posit a date shortly after the event (e.g., Jones 169), though Macleod is skeptical (4) and thinks that certain indications point to a period after the cult of Peregrinus had begun to take root and spread (Macleod 11, 274).

TWO OTHER PERSPECTIVES ON PEREGRINUS

Nearly all of our knowledge of Peregrinus' life is derived from Lucian's text. Even the few words ostensibly spoken by Lucian's Peregrinus (33, 36) or the speech in praise of him by his second-in-command, Theagenes (4-6), may be – either partially or wholly – Lucian's invention. However, there do exist two other references to Peregrinus that supplement Lucian's version in interesting ways.

The first of these is by Aulus Gellius (*c.* 125 – after 180 CE), a contemporary of Lucian, who describes how, while residing in Athens, he regularly visited Peregrinus (12.11):

> When I was at Athens, I met a philosopher named Peregrinus, who was later surnamed Proteus, a man of dignity and fortitude (*virum gravem atque constantem*), living in a hut outside the city. And visiting him frequently, I heard him say many things that were in truth helpful and noble. Among these I particularly recall the following:
>
> He used to say that a wise man would not commit a sin, even if he knew that neither gods nor men would know it; for he thought that one ought to refrain from sin, not through fear of punishment or disgrace, but from love of justice and honesty and from a sense of duty. If, however, there were any who were neither so endowed by nature nor so well disciplined that they could easily keep themselves from sinning by their own will power, he thought that such men would all be more inclined to sin whenever they thought that their guilt could be concealed and when they had hope of impunity because of such concealment. "But," said he, "if men know that nothing at all can be hidden for very long, they will sin more reluctantly and more secretly." Therefore he said that one should have on his lips these verses of Sophocles, the wisest of poets:
>
> > See to it lest you try aught to conceal;
> > Time sees and hears all, and will all reveal.
> > (J. C. Rolfe, trans.)

Gellius' account, though limited to the period when Peregrinus was in Athens (tellingly, Peregrinus had not yet acquired his new name of Proteus), provides us with a snapshot of a serious Cynic philosopher (even if some of his philosophical ideas seem to be warmed-over sentiments taken from Plato's Socrates). Gellius says that he repeatedly visited Peregrinus, implying that he may have been his "student" for a time, and perhaps this bias contributed to his particular view of the man. The most striking phrase in Gellius' brief narrative is his description of Peregrinus as *virum gravem atque constantem*. At first glance this clearly distinguishes Gellius' Peregrinus from that of Lucian's, for Gellius considers Peregrinus to be a "serious/dignified" (*gravem*) man in possession of "fortitude/ resolve/steadfastness" (*constantem*). But the latter quality is also one that Lucian's Peregrinus (now calling himself Proteus) promises to demonstrate for mankind by means of his forthcoming immolation: δεινήν τινα τὴν καρτερίαν ὑπισχνούμενος (*promising a certain incredible* [sc. display of] *endurance/fortitude*, 21; cf. also 23 and 25). The most significant difference between the two accounts, then, is that Lucian believes such *constantia*/καρτερία is not, in fact, what Peregrinus will be displaying through his suicide, but cowardice (*But what he should have done, I think, was first and foremost to wait for death and not to run away from life*, 21).

The second mention of Peregrinus is by Philostratus (*c.* 172 – *c.* 250 CE), who, in his *Lives of the Sophists*, recounts the following anecdote that took place between the fabulously wealthy Athenian sophist Herodes Atticus (101 – 177 CE) and Peregrinus (71.10-22):

> But how strongly he (Herodes) bore himself in the face of this abuse will appear also from what was once said by him to the Cynic Proteus at Athens. For this Proteus was one of those who philosophize so courageously that he even threw himself into a fire at Olympia; and he used to follow Herodes closely and publicly insult him in a semi-barbaric language. And so Herodes turned around and said, "It's O.K. that you publicly insult me, but why do you do it in such a way [i.e., with such bad Greek]?" And when Proteus was assaulting him with additional accusations, he said, "We have grown old: you in publicly insulting me and I in hearing you." Pointing out, of course, that though he was hearing what he said, he was mocking him because he believed that false insults reach no further than the ears.

Though he disapproves of the rude manner in which Peregrinus spoke to Herodes Atticus, Philostratus nevertheless attributes his suicide to "philosophical courage." Like Gellius' description of Peregrinus as a man of fortitude, this too confirms another aspect of Lucian's characterization of Peregrinus, who says in his own voice in the *Peregrinus* that this was the point he was trying to make with his suicide: "I wish to benefit mankind by showing them how one must despise death." (33). Lucian, of course, believes this was simply a lie (most likely intentional, though also possibly in part delusional), and views the act itself both as one of cowardice and as a last-ditch effort to reclaim some of the glory Peregrinus had known earlier in his career (33-42).

Both Aulus Gellius and Philostratus can thus be seen to corroborate essential components of Lucian's portrait of Peregrinus – they only do so from a perspective that regards such characteristics from a far more sympathetic point of view.

In the end, though, it was Lucian's openly hostile take on Peregrinus' character and the motivations for his actions that won out – not only in terms of how we view him today, but also how the majority of those in the ancient world came to understand the Cynic philosopher's attempt to leave behind some lasting legacy of himself and his ideas. As Jones (130) notes, "Peregrinus and his followers seem to have been far less successful than other religious innovators like Alexander [of Abonouteichos], and though his memory lived on for centuries, the cult is only mentioned within a few years of his death. This hybrid of Cynicism and popular religion was perhaps too monstrous to survive." Jones' observations leave out one possible contribution to the quick demise of the cult of Peregrinus-Proteus-Phoenix: the effectiveness of Lucian's "abusive obituary."[8]

---

[8] Contrast the fates of Socrates and Peregrinus after their deaths. The former, though strongly satirized by Aristophanes in his lifetime (a thing which Plato's Socrates claims was one of the causes of his trial [*Apology* 18b-e]), ended up becoming a philosophical martyr – something that was due in no small part to a group of disciples (e.g., Plato, Antisthenes, Xenophon) that greatly extolled their friend and teacher in their writings. The latter, shortly after his death, although he also had disciples, failed to establish any kind of lasting memory outside of his spectacular suicide at the Olympic Games in 165 CE – an event that Lucian aggressively strips of any notion of "philosophical courage."

LUCIAN AND CHRISTIANITY

During the peace and prosperity that reigned throughout the Roman Empire for much of the second century CE, Christianity, which began its existence a century ago as an offshoot of Judaism, began moving out of the shadows and into the consciousness of pagan educated elites such as Lucian and his contemporaries.[9]

Although Lucian possibly conflates Christian and Jewish ideas (cf., e.g., *Head of the synagogue*, 11), that may be due more to the similarity the two closely related religions exhibited to outsiders at the time than to his own ignorance.[10] In fact, Lucian's knowledge of Christianity is generally quite accurate for an outsider (see 13 and notes ad loc.). What he does do when commenting on Christianity, understandably enough, is see it through Greek-tinted lenses.[11] Indeed, Lucian's main reason for criticizing the Christians was that they "accepted such things [i.e., beliefs, teachings] without any definite proof" (13).[12] This made them susceptible in his eyes not only to the faith-based promises of a Jesus, but also to the machinations of any con-artist like Peregrinus who came along prepared to exploit the opportunity such "foolish simpletons" (13) easily presented to them.

---

[9] Jones (121) notes that Christianity at this time had "recently reached the age of intellectual maturity. The behavior of its adherents is noted by several of Lucian's contemporaries, among them Galen, Aelius Aristides, Fronto, Marcus Aurelius, and correspondingly the new sect had now begun to produce its first great crop of intellectual defenders or "apologists." It was already possible for cultured Greeks to be attracted to the new faith, and both Tatian and the great Justin were converts from Greek philosophy."

[10] Before the Bar Kokhba revolt (132–136 CE), many (the majority?) of the Christian communities in Palestine and Syria were made up of Jewish Christians with strong ties to Judaism. Peregrinus seems to have been a Christian in Palestine sometime during the period of *c.* 120 – *c.* 135 BCE (cf. Bagnani 112).

[11] Jones 122.

[12] This is a common theme throughout Lucian's works. Cf., for example, Sidwell 113: "In general, Lucian mocks those gullible enough to substitute for sound rationality a superstitious credulity."

Many scholars thus believe that although Lucian's attitude toward Christianity appears dismissive, it "is not particularly hostile, as his worst strictures were reserved for those who behaved badly and failed to practise what they preached. To Lucian the Christians are merely poor fools, accepting their beliefs 'without any sure proof', but, despite his intellectual contempt for them, his description of them is surprisingly accurate and compares favourably with that of his contemporary Fronto."[13]

This may be correct, but one should note that in Lucian's text both Jesus and the Christians share the same descriptors as Lucian's principal target, Peregrinus: Jesus and Peregrinus are both labeled as "sophists" (σοφιστής; 13, 32; see LUCIAN AND THE SECOND SOPHISTIC below); the Christians and Peregrinus are both described as "possessed by an evil spirit," "wretches" (κακοδαίμων, 1, 13, 42). In addition, both the Christians and those impressed by Peregrinus' rants against the Roman emperor are called "ignorant fools" (ἰδιώτης; 13, 18) – a particularly disdainful insult from an intellectual elitist.

———————

Lucian's relationship with later Christians was decidedly mixed. Though Christians in Late Antiquity and the Middle Ages enjoyed his satirical attacks on the pagan gods, they had issues with his depiction of themselves in the *Peregrinus*.[14] Nevertheless, his entire corpus was copied assiduously (and often with annotations), by Byzantine monks and scholars thoughout the Middle Ages. Renaissance humanists discovered Lucian *c.* 1400 and immediately employed him in the classroom. Soon thereafter Lucian became an inspirational model of irreverent wit for the satirical works that had begun to be produced in the 15th century. Lucian's popularity, however, did hit a minor roadblock in 1559 when several of his works, including the *Peregrinus*, were placed on the Catholic Church's newly created *Index Librorum Prohibitorum* ("Index of Prohibited Books").[15]

———————

[13] Macleod 270. Cf. also Allinson 205 and Costa 74.

[14] See Jones 22.

[15] By 1590 all of Lucian's works had been placed on the *Index*. In 1966, more than four centuries after its creation, the *Index* was abolished by Pope Paul VI.

LUCIAN AND THE SECOND SOPHISTIC

Lucian was active during a period that, thanks to the (self-promoting) phrase coined by Philostratus (*c.* 172 – *c.* 250 CE), an Athenian sophist and biographer of sophists, is now known as the Second Sophistic.[16] Lasting approximately two centuries (*c.* 60 CE – *c.* 230 CE), the Second Sophistic was a cultural movement at the center of which were performing superstars known as sophists, "high class teacher[s] of rhetoric, traveling around giving displays of [their] rhetorical skill to audiences and charging high fees."[17] These displays consisted of epideictic speeches performed in character before educated audiences who could appreciate the sophists' strategic deployment of rhetorical tropes, apt use of literary quotations, and clever repurposings of the words of classic authors (see **LITERARY STYLE** below).[18] Successful sophistic performances combined such verbal dexterity with acting prowess into a single, seamless whole.[19]

The linguistic component of this verbal dexterity, however, did not consist of the common Greek spoken by the masses at the time (known as Koine). Instead, the educated elite employed an imitative recreation of the vocabulary, syntax, style, and contents of Classical Greek literature, most of it Athenian from *c.* 425 BCE – *c.* 300 BCE (see **LANGUAGE** below).

---

[16] Philostratus created the phrase "Second Sophistic" to simultaneously distinguish it from the so-called "First Sophistic" of the Classical period (*c.* 450 – *c.* 375 BCE) as well as "claim a link between the sophists of the Classical period and those nearer to his own times who were noted for their public performances or outstanding rhetorical abilities." (Hopkinson 5)

[17] Macleod 2. The best brief account of a 2nd-century CE sophist can be found in W. C. Wright, *Philostratus and Eunapius: The Lives of the Sophists*. London: 1922, xv-xxii. Though sophistic performances took place throughout the Roman Empire, they were largely a Greek phenomenom primarily cultivated by the educated elite in the cities of the eastern Mediterranean.

[18] Lucian himself was a traveling sophist, at least until around the age of 40, after which he gave up performance for full-time writing and administrative posts.

[19] Whitmarsh 6-10 provides a succinct overview of the Second Sophistic and of the current schools of academic thought concerning it.

To the sophists and sophistic writers of Lucian's era, the gatekeepers on either end of this linguistic-literary period were the historian Thucydides (*c.* 460 – *c.* 395 BCE) and the orator Demosthenes (384 – 322 BCE), with its star, the philosopher Plato (428/427 – 348/347 BCE), occupying center stage. Honorary guests included the epic poet Homer (*c.* 700 BCE), the Ionian historian Herodotus (*c.* 484 – 425 BCE), the tragic playwright Euripides (*c.* 480 – 406 BCE), the historian Xenophon (*c.* 430 – 354 BC), orators such as Aeschines (389 – 314 BCE), and comic playwrights such as Aristophanes (*c.* 446 – *c.* 386 BCE) and Menander (*c.* 341 – *c.* 290 BCE). In a fundamental way, sophistry, whether in verbal or written form, was an attempt by its practioners, and the audiences who fueled their growth, to recapture the spirit of classical Greece as embodied by that period's language, literature, and culture – a spirit that for the most part imagined a world in which the reality of Rome did not exist.

The word "sophist," however, was not limited in Lucian's day to the new meaning it had recently acquired of "a highly educated Attic Greek speaker-performer/teacher of rhetoric." In fact, the word had existed with different meanings before the two periods to which Philostratus attached the name (and, as we will shortly see, even the sophists of the "First Sophistic" were themselves somewhat different from the teachers of rhetoric and showmen in Lucian's time).

In the classical period (*c.* 475 – *c.* 400 BCE), a sophist was a "master of one's craft," an "expert," and the word was used of poets, musicians, and diviners. It is also the word employed by Herodotus (1.29) to describe the Seven Sages of the 6th century BCE as "wise men," i.e., "men who were prudent" or "statesmanlike."

From *c.* 450 – *c.* 375 BCE (the so-called "First Sophistic") the word was applied to a revolutionary group of itinerant scholars (e.g., Protagoras, Prodicus, Gorgias, and Hippias). Renowned for their intellectual and pedagogical skills in grammar, rhetoric, literary studies, linguistics, politics, and ethics, these sophists both created and commercialized higher education. Although these men flourished under the Athenian democracy, they were feared by many Athenians, since the advantages that the wealthy could attain by learning the necessary rhetorical skills taught by many sophists were particularly applicable to the realm of democratic politics. Under the influence of

Aristophanes and Plato, each of whom had issues with the ethically problematic teachings of many of these new scholars, the word sophist came to take on the pejorative meaning that it retains to this day: "a person who reasons with clever but fallacious arguments."

With the *Peregrinus*, Lucian contributed to the various meanings of the word sophist that were active in the 2nd century CE.[20] In Lucian's narrative the word appears twice: once in reference to Jesus (13), and a second time in reference to Peregrinus (32). Neither of these individuals fit the standard definition of sophist in Lucian's time as "a highly educated Attic Greek speaker-performer/teacher of rhetoric"; nor do they match up neatly with any earlier meaning of the word. What both Jesus and Peregrinus apparently represent to Lucian is a new category of sophist – the itinerant charlatan who, promising much based on unreasoning faith, attempts to dupe others in his delusional quest for glory and a divine afterlife.

---

[20] Cf. Whitmarsh 14-19, who concisely explicates the elusive definitional aspects of the word sophist during the period of the Second Sophistic.

Lucian, "Lucian," and "Lucian's Double"

As sophists performed various roles on stage, Lucian did the same in his texts. Perhaps the greatest of Lucian's roles are those in which he played himself. In the *Peregrinus* three different "Lucians" are evident.

The first is the historical Lucian, the author of the *Peregrinus*. About this individual we know far too little (see **Lucian** above). He is the man behind the curtain, manipulating his characters (including those of himself) and their words in order to manipulate his readers.

The second Lucian is more interesting. This character, whom I call "Lucian," begins the narrative with his own name in an epistolary greeting, a rarity in the Lucianic corpus.[21] After providing a breathless summary of the events that have "recently" transpired (1), "Lucian," employing the first-person,[22] plunges into the narrative proper by presenting himself as an innocent bystander who just happened to be present at Theagenes' speech in praise of Peregrinus' person and his decision to commit suicide (3). Although "Lucian" tells us that he is surprised by this news (5), later in the narrative we are informed that four years earlier Peregrinus had publicly disclosed to the world that he was planning to commit suicide at the next Olympics (21). It seems quite improbable, then, that "Lucian" would not have known this. However, a surprised reaction at this point in the story allows him to be present at the suicide "accidentally" in the persona of an individual who is largely ignorant of what Peregrinus' life entailed. This guise allows "Lucian" to take on the part of "curious educated individual," someone whose function is to provide a rationalist's perspective on irrational human behavior. "Lucian" can even play the role of hero, risking his life by calling Peregrinus' actions idiotic before a crowd of the latter's followers (2), or drawing their anger after Peregrinus' suicide by angrily telling them as they linger dejectedly around the funeral pyre to go home and no longer inhale the burning stench of their master's flesh (37). What "Lucian"

---

[21] Lucian rarely names himself, even in works in which he employs a first-person narrator (cf. Whitmarsh 83).

[22] Cf. Whitmarsh 82, who notes: "Lucian's 'I' is devious and elusive."

cannot do is furnish his readers with the salacious details and insulting comments designed to utterly destroy Peregrinus' pre-suicide reputation. To pull this off as effectively as he might, Lucian created a second authorial voice under the guise of an unnamed double (hereafter called "Lucian's Double").[23]

If "Lucian" is depicted as mostly ignorant of Peregrinus' life, "Lucian's Double" is (strangely) well-informed about all of its un-savory and ignominious details. And if "Lucian" is a mostly sober, intelligent, and heroic rationalist, thus functioning as a psychological foil to the crazed Cynics of the text, then "Lucian's Double", who is responsible for much of the heavy lifting in terms of thoroughly besmirching Peregrinus' character, employs several of these same Cynics' qualities that are on display in the *Peregrinus*: exaggeration, bombast, innuendo, and invention.

In fact, "Lucian's Double" is a problematic narrator in several ways. First of all, the sources he cites for his information about Peregrinus in 8 appear (at best) quite questionable:

> And so that you might know what sort of thing is this sacred image that is about to be burned up, listen to me, a person who from the beginning (sc. of Peregrinus' career) carefully watched over his character and observed closely his career. And I have learned some things from his fellow citizens and from those people to whom it was necessary to know him thoroughly.

His main narration is thus based on the rather hard to believe idea that he has been closely following Peregrinus from the start of the latter's career. Since Peregrinus is *c.* 65-70 years of age when he commits suicide, "Lucian's Double" would have had to be doing this for at least three to four decades! He then adds that this careful observation has been supplemented by "some things" he has learned from Peregrinus' fellow citizens and from the conveniently unnamed (and rather absurdly described) "people to whom it was necessary to know

---

[23] Lucian is quite fond of creating pseudonymous doubles of himself in his works. Among many such stand-in characters is one named Parrhessiades ("Son of Frankness," *The Fisherman* 19), a figure who clearly represents his own beliefs (cf. Macleod 11).

him thoroughly." Since Peregrinus left his hometown at a young age and only returned once (14-15), his "fellow citizens" from Parium cannot have known much about him outside of the "story" that he had murdered his father (10). The ridiculous phrase "people to whom it was necessary to know him thoroughly" is such an impossibility the less said about it the better.

And even when a source is named, which "Lucian's Double" does with regard to the Sybilline oracle reputedly spoken by Theagenes about Peregrinus that he reports in 29, the validity of it is undermined by the number of chains in the link: "Lucian's Double" claims to have heard it from one of his friends, who quoted it from memory after hearing it from Theagenes earlier, who in turn claims that he heard it from the prophetic Sybil. This Chinese-nesting-box game of "I heard it from a friend who heard it from someone who etc." can be extended when we recall that our author Lucian is reporting this story in an account that his character "Lucian" heard from an unnamed speaker (i.e., "Lucian's Double") who claims that he heard it from a friend who in turn heard it from Theagenes who supposedly heard it from the Sybil.

With respect to the general nature of the speech of "Lucian's Double" (7-31), which takes up more than half of the work, Jones (120) observes that it contains certain charges that "are so hackneyed that they seem designed to provoke amusement [in the original audience] rather than indignation."[24] This does not seem a concern to "Lucian's Double," who is apparently a proponent of the proposition "fight fire with fire." It is his job in the text to provide the defamatory comments about Peregrinus' life that our other narrator, "Lucian," cannot (or will not) lay claim to. At the very end of the narrative (43-44), however, the two narrators become one as "Lucian" partakes of the methods of "Lucian's Double" by narrating three incidents about Peregrinus (sexual perversion [43], cowardice [43], and gluttony [44]) that are of a similar nature as those told by his unnamed doppelgänger throughout 9-31.

---

[24] Concerning the allegations of sexual perversion, Hopkinson 119 notes that such charges "are commonplace in law-court oratory as well as in satire."

If Second Sophistic writing had one element around which everything else revolved, it was "novelty" (καινότης). But this novelty was not based on inventing new genres or entirely new forms of expression. Instead, it was more focused on clever and inventive ways of repurposing the genres and words of the past, from Homer to the dawning of the Hellenistic period, into a new, witty, and sophisticated whole. It was thus, paradoxically it might appear, a novelty based on nostalgia (genuine, affected/ironic, or both), especially that felt for the Greek past before the advent of Rome. Lucian was a master of mixing the materials of such "old masters" as Homer, Herodotus, Thucydides, Aristophanes, Plato, Demosthenes, Menander, and Menippus[25] into something new through quotations, parodies, and adaptations of their words, ideas, and literary forms.[26]

Compare, for example, the opening line of hexameter verse of the unnamed speaker's oracle in 30 (itself a witty riposte to Theagenes' "Sibylline" oracle in 29 on the forthcoming afterlife of his master Peregrinus):

ἀλλ' ὁπόταν Κυνικὸς πολυώνυμος ἐς φλόγα πολλὴν

But whenever the many-named Cynic (shall leap) into a great flame...

These words echo the first line of Homer's *Odyssey* both metrically (each verse consists of all dactyls) and lexically:

ἄνδρα μοι ἔννεπε, μοῦσα, πολύτροπον, ὃς μάλα πολλὰ

Sing in me, Muse, of the man of many twists and turns, who very many...

Through means of such allusive adaptation Lucian is simultaneously displaying his own sophistic credentials − look at how clever I am at

---

[25] Menippus (*fl.* 3rd century BCE) was a Cynic writer of satiric diatribes.

[26] Cf. Macleod 11-14; Sidwell 114-17.

reworking famous lines! – and having his unnamed speaker make a comparison between Peregrinus and Odysseus, a master liar and deceiver. Indeed, this is actually the second reference to Odysseus' "poly(tropic)" nature in the text, since the connection of Peregrinus to Odysseus had already been even more clearly made by "Lucian" at the very beginning of his work in his description of the Cynic philosopher as μυρίας τροπὰς τραπόμενος (*twisting himself in countless twists and turns*, 1).

Sometimes Lucian's repurposing is so sophisticated that it appears to work on several levels. Compare, for example, how in 33 the original intention of Peregrinus' words are very differently understood by Lucian and his intended audience. In this section we are told by "Lucian" that among the final things Peregrinus said before committing suicide was that he wanted χρυσῷ βίῳ χρυσῆν κορώνην ἐπιθεῖναι (*on a golden life "a golden crown to put"*). This phrase is an allusion to and adaptation of the second half of *Iliad* 4.111, χρυσέην ἐπέθηκε κορώνην, words which are part of the description of the elaborately constructed bow of the Trojan ally Pandarus. Peregrinus' pun is both on the word κορώνη (which can mean both *tip of the bow* [on which the bowstring was hooked] and *seal, end, crown*) and on the word βίος (*life*, and with a different accent, βιός, *bow*). "Lucian" states that these words were spoken by Peregrinus, but whether they are his or Lucian's own invention we will never know. In any case, as Macleod (274) notes, the sophistic allusion works in two additional ways: "Peregrinus is pleased with his pun because his exemplar Heracles was famous for his bow, and Lucian is contemptuous of it, expecting his audience to think of the treacherous Pandarus" (who breaks the truce between the Greeks and the Trojans in pursuit of individual glory).

LANGUAGE

In Lucian's day there existed primarily two forms of Greek: (1) Koine (ἡ κοινὴ διάλεκτος, *the common dialect* [sc. of Greek]), the common language of spoken discourse and of written communication employed by Greek speakers in the eastern half of the Roman Empire; (2) Atticizing Greek, a movement by the educated elite to return to the Attic Greek used by writers of the fifth and fourth centuries (in prose especially that of Thucydides, Plato, and Demosthenes; in verse, Euripides, Aristophanes and Menander).

Koine Greek developed in the years following the conquests of Alexander the Great (d. 323 BCE) from the Attic Greek of the fifth and fourth centuries. It shared certain elements with non-Attic dialects (especially Ionic), and had developed many (mostly minor) grammatical, syntactical, and lexical differences from Attic Greek in its linguistic evolution from that language. Koine was the language of literary texts as diverse as those of the biographer and essayist Plutarch (*c.* 46 – 120 CE) and the various works that make up the New Testament (*c.* 51 – *c.* 100 CE). It was also the language of government and day-to-day life as revealed by such surviving materials as imperial decrees, legal contracts, and personal letters.

Atticism was an attempt to purify the Koine of its non-Attic elements and reintroduce long-lost aspects of the grammar, syntax and vocabulary of Attic literary discourse. Atticists ranged from extremists, who banished all deviant lexical forms and grammatical constructions, to those who wrote very good Attic prose with an occasional admixture of Koine elements. Lucian, who satirized the extremists for their obsession with linguistic purity, wrote excellent Attic Greek, only occasionally deviating from earlier usages.[27]

---

[27] The majority of Lucian's non-Attic elements involve vocabulary, approximately 20% of which is non-Attic, with the majority of these being either new compounds formed by attaching prefixes and suffixes to standard Attic words, or of the occasional word that was used either by poets of the classical age or in writers of the Hellenistic period. Chabert is the standard work regarding Lucian's linguistic relationship to Attic Greek. Allinson xxx-xlii provides a convenient listing of the main differences and/or unusual features that distinguish Lucian's prose from Attic Greek.

A BRIEF NOTE ON MONETARY VALUES

It is quite challenging to ascertain the value of money in the ancient world in contemporary terms, since both the type of labor and the things people purchased were often valued quite differently than they are today. What I have done in the notes when such amounts are listed is give equivalents based on the value of silver (all amounts in the text are understood to be denominated in talents of silver) in the year of the publication of this book – 2014. However, the hyperbolic tendencies of Lucian's characters in the *Peregrinus* seem to suggest that the reader can multiply the numbers found in the notes by a factor of 10 and still be within the realm of possibility regarding the essential value of these amounts in 2nd-century CE terms.

BIBLIOGRAPHY

Anderson, G., *Lucian: Theme and Variation in the Second Sophistic*, Mnemosyne Suppl. 41 (Leiden, 1976).

──────. *Studies in Lucian's Comic Fiction*, Mnemosyne Suppl. 43 (Leiden, 1976).

Bagnani, G. "Peregrinus Proteus and the Christians", *Historia: Zeitschrift für Alte Geschichte*, Bd. 4, H. 1 (1955), 107-112.

Baldwin, B. *Studies in Lucian*. Hakkert: Toronto, 1973.

Bowersock, G. W., *Greek Sophists in the Roman Empire*. Oxford: Clarendon, 1969.

Branham, R. Bracht. *Unruly Eloquence: Lucian and the Comedy of Traditions*. Harvard Univ. Press: Cambridge, Mass., and London, 1989.

Chabert, S. *L'atticisme de Lucien*. Paris, 1897.

Clay, D. "Lucian of Samosata: Four Philosophical Lives (Nigrinus, Demonax, Peregrinus, Alexander Pseudomantis)," *ANRW* II.36.5, 3406-3450.

Edwards, M. J. "Satire and Verisimilitude: Christianity in Lucian's "Peregrinus"," *Historia: Zeitschrift für Alte Geschichte*, Bd. 38, H. 1 (1st Qtr., 1989), 89-98.

Hall, J. A. *Lucian's Satire*. Arno Press: New York, 1981.

Hopkinson, N. *Lucian: a selection*. Cambridge Univ. Press: Cambridge and New York, 2008.

Jones, C. P., *Culture and Society in Lucian*. Harvard Univ. Press: Cambridge, Mass., and London, 1986.

Levy, H. *Lucian: Seventy Dialogues*. University of Oklahoma Press: Norman, 1976.

Sidwell, K. *Lucian: Selections*. Bristol Classical Press: Bristol, 1986.

Smyth, H. W. *Greek Grammar*, rev. G. M. Messing. Harvard Univ. Press: Cambridge, Mass., 1956.

Swain, S., *Hellenism and Empire*. Oxford: Clarendon, 1996.

Whitmarsh, T. *The Second Sophistic*. Oxford Univ. Press: Oxford, 2005.

EDITIONS WITH COMMENTARY

Though somewhat old, two editions of the Greek text with commentary are still of much value (the second is written in Dutch):

Allinson, F. C. *Lucian: Selected Writings*. Ginn & Company: Boston, 1905.

Plooij, D. and J. C. Koopman. *Lucianus: de Dood van Peregrinus*. G. J. A. Ruys: Ultrecht, 1915.

THE TEXT

The text used in this edition is:

Harmon, A. M. *Lucian* (Loeb Classical Library), vol. V. Harvard Univ. Press: Cambridge, Mass., and William Heinemann: London, 1936, 1-51.

For a more scholarly edition (with apparatus criticus), the reader should consult:

Macleod, M. D. *Luciani opera III: libelli 44–68*. (Oxford Classical Texts). Oxford Univ. Press: Oxford, 1980.

ENGLISH TRANSLATIONS

Casson, L. *Selected Satires of Lucian.* W. W. Norton & Company: New York, 1968.

Costa, D. C. *Lucian: selected dialogues.* Oxford Univ. Press: Oxford, 2005.

Harmon, A. M. *Lucian* (Loeb Classical Library), vol. V. Harvard Univ. Press: Cambridge, Mass., and William Heinemann: London, 1936.

Macleod, M. D. *Lucian: a selection.* Aris & Philips: Warminster, 1991.

ABBREVIATIONS

acc.(usative)
act.(ive voice)
adj.(ective)
adv.(erb)
aor.(ist)
c. circa
cf. compare (Latin *confer*)
ch.(apter)
comp.(arative)
conj.(unction)
d.(ied)
dat.(ive)
dep.(opent)
dir.(ect)
fem.(inine)
fl. floruit: the period in which an individual lived, worked, or was most active
fut.(ure)
gen.(itive)
gen.(itive) abs.(olute)
impera.(tive)
imperf.(ect)
indecl.(inable)
indic.(ative)
indir.(ect)
inf.(initive)
masc.(uline)
mid.(dle voice)
neut.(er)
n.(ote)
nom.(inative)
obj.(ect)
opt.(ative)
p./pp. page(s)
part.(iciple)
pass.(ive voice)
perf.(ect)
pl.(ural)
pluperf.(ect)
pres.(ent)
pron.(oun)
rel.(ative) pron.(oun)
sc. = supply or understand
sing.(ular)
subj.(ect)
subju.(nctive)
superl.(ative)
voc.(ative)

Περὶ τῆς Περεγρίνου Τελευτῆς

On the Death of Peregrinus

Περὶ τῆς Περεγρίνου Τελευτῆς

Λουκιανὸς Κρονίῳ εὖ πράττειν.

[1] ὁ κακοδαίμων Περεγρῖνος, ἢ ὡς αὐτὸς ἔχαιρεν

ὀνομάζων ἑαυτόν, Πρωτεύς, αὐτὸ δὴ ἐκεῖνο τὸ τοῦ

Ὁμηρικοῦ Πρωτέως ἔπαθεν· ἅπαντα γὰρ δόξης ἕνεκα

γενόμενος καὶ μυρίας τροπὰς τραπόμενος, τὰ τελευταῖα

ταῦτα καὶ πῦρ ἐγένετο· τοσούτῳ ἄρα τῷ ἔρωτι τῆς δόξης

εἴχετο. καὶ νῦν ἐκεῖνος ἀπηνθράκωταί σοι ὁ βέλτιστος

Λουκιανὸς Κρονίῳ εὖ πράττειν: Lucian's text takes the form of a
letter to a certain Cronius. Epistolary greetings nearly always employ the
inf. as a verbal noun in the acc. (the regular inf. in such greetings was,
naturally, χαίρειν, *greetings*); sc. λέγει, of which Λουκιανὸς is the subj.
and Κρονίῳ the indir. obj. The phrase εὖ πράττειν was, according to
Lucian himself (*A Slip of the Tongue in Greeting* 4), the manner in which
Plato (*c.* 428/427 – 348/347 BCE) began his letters, and so marks Cronius
as a Platonist. Cf. also the concluding words of Plato's *Republic*: εὖ
πράττωμεν (*let us fare well* or *be successful*; *let us do well*). To paraphrase
Lucian's greeting: *Lucian wishes his Platonist friend Cronius success in all
of his actions.*   **αὐτὸ δὴ ἐκεῖνο τὸ**: *that very thing itself, the one
(thing).*   **Πρωτέως**: a sea divinity most famous for his appearance in
Homer's *Odyssey* (4.454-59), where he attempts to free himself from
Menelaus' grasp by transforming himself into the forms of a lion, a serpent,
a leopard, a boar, water and a tall tree.   **τροπὰς τραπόμενος, τὰ
τελευταῖα ταῦτα**: note the cognate wordplay (τροπὰς τραπόμενος,
making twists and turns) – a rhetorical trope known as *figura etymologica*,
in which a verb or part. governs its related noun – and heavy alliteration.
τὰ τελευταῖα ταῦτα: *this last time.*   **ἀπηνθράκωταί**: 3rd
sing. perf. mid./pass. indic. < ἀπανθρακόω; this verb, which only occurs
here, is apparently a Lucianic coinage.   **εἴχετο**: 3rd sing. imperf.
pass. indic. < ἔχω. The agent of a pass. verb is expressed either by ὑπό +
gen. (regularly in the case of a person) or simply with the dat. (here
τοσούτῳ, τῷ ἔρωτι; regularly in the case of a thing).   **σοι ὁ
βέλτιστος**: σοι is either an ethical dat. (i.e., *you see* or *let me tell you*) or
a dat. expressing possession (i.e., *your*); ὁ βέλτιστος is ironic.

2

Vocabulary

ἄπας, ἄπασα, ἄπαν, *all*; *every*; *whole*

ἀπανθρακόω, *burn to a cinder, carbonize*

ἄρα, particle, *after all, so*; *therefore*

αὐτός, -ή, -ό, (intensive adj.) *-self, -selves*; (adj.) *same*; (pron. in gen., dat., acc.) *him, her, it, them*

βέλτιστος, -η, -ον, *best, very good*; (as mode of address) *(my) good friend*

γίγνομαι, γενήσομαι, ἐγενόμην, *become*

δή, particle, *indeed*; *in fact*; *then, therefore, now*

δόξα, ἡ, *reputation, honor, glory*; *notion, expectation*; *opinion, judgment*

ἑαυτοῦ, ἑαυτῆς, ἑαυτοῦ, (reflex. pron. in gen., dat., acc.) *himself, herself, itself*

ἐκεῖνος, -η, -ό, *that*; (pl.) *those*

ἕνεκα, prep. (+ preceding gen.), *for the sake of, because of*

ἔρως, -ωτος, ὁ, *love, desire, passion*

εὖ, adv., *well*

ἔχω, ἕξω, ἔσχον, *have*; *hold*; (mid. + gen.) *hold onto*

ἤ, conj., *or*; (with comparatives) *than*

κακοδαίμων (gen., κακοδαίμονος), *possessed by an evil spirit, unlucky, wretched*

μυρίος, -α, -ον, *numberless, countless*

νῦν, adv., *now*

Ὁμηρικός, -ή, -όν, *Homeric*

ὀνομάζω, *name, call*

οὗτος, αὕτη, τοῦτο, *this*; (pl.) *these*

πάσχω, πείσομαι, ἔπαθον, *experience*; *suffer, undergo*

περί, prep. (+ gen.), *about, concerning, on (the topic / matter of)*

πράττω, πράξω, ἔπραξα, *do, act*

πῦρ, πυρός, τό, *fire*

τελευταῖος, -α, -ον, *last*; τὰ τελευταῖα (adv.), *the last time, finally, in the end*

τελευτή, ἡ, *end, end of life* (i.e., *death*)

τοσοῦτος, -αύτη, -οῦτον, *so much, so great*; (pl.) *so many*

τρέπω, τρέψω, ἔτρεψα, (Epic and Ionic have 2nd aor. ἔτραπον), *turn* X; (mid.) *turn* X *(for oneself / one's own benefit)*, *turn oneself*

τροπή, ἡ, *turn, turning*; *change, transformation*

χαίρω, χαιρήσω, ἐχάρην, *rejoice, be glad*; (+ pres. part.) *be in the habit of, accustomed to*

ὡς, adv., *as*

3

κατὰ τὸν Ἐμπεδοκλέα, παρ᾽ ὅσον ὁ μὲν κἂν διαλαθεῖν

ἐπειράθη ἐμβαλὼν ἑαυτὸν εἰς τοὺς κρατῆρας, ὁ δὲ γεννάδας

οὗτος, τὴν πολυανθρωποτάτην τῶν Ἑλληνικῶν πανηγύρεων

τηρήσας, πυρὰν ὅτι μεγίστην νήσας ἐνεπήδησεν ἐπὶ

τοσούτων μαρτύρων, καὶ λόγους τινὰς ὑπὲρ τούτου

εἰπὼν πρὸς τοὺς Ἕλληνας οὐ πρὸ πολλῶν ἡμερῶν τοῦ

τολμήματος.

Ἐμπεδοκλέα: a pre-Socratic philosopher from Agrigentum, Sicily, Empedocles (*c.* 490 – *c.* 430 BCE) was most famous for his theory that everything in the universe was constructed of four indestructible elements (earth, air, fire, water), which combine and separate in various degrees at different times through the power of "Love" and "Strife." The most popular versions of his death, which quickly entered the realm of legend, are collected in Diogenes Laërtius' (*fl. c.* 3rd century CE) mini biography of Empedocles (*Lives of the Philosophers* 8.68-75). Among these is related the best known of the legends – that Empedocles threw himself into Mount Etna (an active volcano in Sicily) so that people would believe his body had vanished and he had turned into a god. In Lucian's fantasy tale *Icaromenippus*, Menippus encounters Empedocles on the moon, with the latter describing his attempted suicide thus (13-14): *When I threw myself with great energy into the crater, the smoke, having snatched me up from Etna, brought me up here; and now I live on the Moon, spending much of my time thinking deep thoughts, and for food I partake of dew.*   **ὁ μὲν**: i.e., Empedocles.   **κἂν**: crasis of καί ἄν; here, as a strengthened καί, intensifies διαλαθεῖν (though English usage prefers to place the emphasis on the main verb); i.e., = *he* (i.e., Empedocles) *also / at least tried* **to escape notice.**   **ἐπειράθη**: 3rd sing. aor. pass. (mid. in sense) indic. < πειράομαι.   **ὁ δὲ γεννάδας οὗτος**: i.e., Peregrinus; like ὁ βέλτιστος above, γεννάδας οὗτος is heavily ironic.   **ὅτι**: ὅτι or ὡς + superlative = "super superlative," i.e., *as X as possible*.   **ὑπὲρ τούτου**: i.e., his reasons for committing suicide by jumping into a pyre.   **οὐ πρὸ πολλῶν ἡμερῶν**: *not many days before*, i.e., *a few days before*; πρὸ also governs τοῦ τολμήματος.

Vocabulary

ἅπας, ἅπασα, ἅπαν, *all; every; whole*

γεννάδας, -ου, ὁ, *noble*

διαλανθάνω, διαλήσω, διέλαθον, *escape notice*

ἑαυτοῦ, ἑαυτῆς, ἑαυτοῦ, (reflex. pron. in gen., dat., acc.) *himself, herself, itself*

εἰς, prep. (+ acc.), *into; to; at*

Ἕλλην, -ηνος, ὁ, *Greek, Hellene*

Ἑλληνικός, -ή, -όν, *Greek, Hellenic*

ἐμβάλλω, ἐμβαλῶ, ἐνέβαλον, *throw in*

ἐμπηδάω, ἐμπηδήσομαι, ἐνεπήδησα, *leap in or into*

ἐπί, prep. (+ gen.), *before, in the presence of*

ἡμέρα, -ας, ἡ, *day*

κατά, prep. (+ acc.), *in the manner of*

κρατήρ, -ῆρος, ὁ, (pl. often = sing.) *crater, mouth of a volcano*

λέγω, ἐρῶ, εἶπον, *say, speak, tell*

λόγος, ὁ, *word, speech*

μάρτυς, μάρτυρος, ὁ, *witness*

μέγιστος, -η, -ον, *biggest, largest, greatest*

νέω, *heap, pile up*

ὅσον, adv., *so far as, as much as*

ὅτι, conj., *that, because*; (+ superlative) *as X as possible*

οὗτος, αὕτη, τοῦτο, *this*; (pl.) *these*

πανήγυρις, -εως, ἡ, *assembly, festival; national assembly or festival*

παρά, prep. (+ acc.), *except*

πειράομαι, πειράσομαι, ἐπειράθην, (mid. more common that act. πειράω) *attempt, endeavor, try* (often + inf.)

πολυάνθρωπος, -ον, *crowded, much-visited*

πολύς, πολλή, πολύ, *much*; (pl.) *many*

πρό, prep. (+ gen.), *before*

πρός, prep. (+ acc.), *to*

πυρά, ἡ, *pyre, funeral-pyre*

τηρέω, *watch for, wait for*

τις, τι, (gen. τινος) (indefinite adj.) *a certain; some; a, an*; (indefinite pron.) *someone; something; anyone; anything*

τόλμημα, -ατος, τό, *adventure, enterprise, deed of daring*

τοσοῦτος, -αύτη, -οῦτον, *so much, so great*; (pl.) *so many*

ὑπέρ, prep. (+ gen.), *on, concerning*

[2] πολλὰ τοίνυν δοκῶ μοι ὁρᾶν σε γελῶντα ἐπὶ τῇ κορύζῃ
τοῦ γέροντος, μᾶλλον δὲ καὶ ἀκούω βοῶντος οἷά σε εἰκὸς
βοᾶν, "ὦ τῆς ἀβελτερίας, ὦ τῆς δοξοκοπίας, ὦ —" τῶν
ἄλλων ἃ λέγειν εἰώθαμεν περὶ αὐτῶν. σὺ μὲν οὖν πόρρω
ταῦτα καὶ μακρῷ ἀσφαλέστερον, ἐγὼ δὲ παρὰ τὸ πῦρ αὐτὸ
καὶ ἔτι πρότερον ἐν πολλῷ πλήθει τῶν ἀκροατῶν εἶπον αὐτά,
ἐνίων μὲν ἀχθομένων, ὅσοι ἐθαύμαζον τὴν ἀπόνοιαν τοῦ
γέροντος· ἦσαν δέ τινες οἳ καὶ αὐτοὶ ἐγέλων ἐπ' αὐτῷ.

πολλά: neut. pl. acc. as adv. modifying γελῶντα.   **δοκῶ μοι**: *I
seem to myself*, i.e., *I think* or *imagine*.   **κορύζῃ**: the metaphorical
meaning of this word as *stupidity* may have originated at Plato, *Republic*
343a, where Thrasymachus, unable to defend his definition of justice from
Socrates' cross-examination, resorts to equating Socrates with a snot-nosed
child whose nanny won't wipe his nose since he is incapable of telling her
the difference between a shepherd and his sheep.   **μᾶλλον δὲ καὶ**:
and even more.   **βοῶντος**: sc. σοῦ; οἷά (neut. acc. pl.) is its dir. obj.
σε εἰκὸς βοᾶν = (ἐστι) εἰκὸς σε βοᾶν.   **βοᾶν**: pres. act. inf. <
βοάω.   **ὦ**: an exclamatory sound expressing surprise, joy, or pain;
i.e., *Oh!* or *Ah!*   **τῆς ἀβελτερίας, τῆς δοξοκοπίας, τῶν
ἄλλων**: Greek uses the gen. case for exclamations.   **τῶν ἄλλων**:
everything else.   **περὶ αὐτῶν**: *about them*; i.e., either *people like
this* or *these kinds of things/actions.*   **σὺ μὲν**: sc. λέγεις or ποιεῖς.
μακρῷ: dat. of degree of difference with a comp. adj./adv.; i.e., *far
(more...).*   **αὐτά**: i.e., τῆς ἀβελτερίας,...   **ἐνίων μὲν
ἀχθομένων**: gen. abs.

6

Vocabulary

ἀβελτερία, ἡ, *silliness, stupidity*

ἀκούω, ἀκούσομαι, ἤκουσα, *hear* (+ gen. of person)

ἀκροατής, -ου, ὁ, *listener, hearer*

ἀλλός, -ή, -ό, *another, other*

ἀπόνοια, ἡ, *loss of all sense; madness; desperation*

ἀσφαλής, -ές, *safe, secure*

αὐτός, -ή, -ό, (intensive adj.) -*self, -selves*; (adj.) *same*; (pron. in gen., dat., acc.) *him, her, it, them*

ἄχθομαι, (dep.) *be annoyed, be angry*

βοάω, βοήσομαι, ἐβόησα, *shout*

γελάω, γελάσομαι, ἐγέλασα, *laugh*

γέρων, -οντος, ὁ, *old man*

δοξοκοπία, ἡ, *thirst/hunger for fame* or *popularity*

δοκῶ, (uncontracted = δοκέω) *seem; think; expect; imagine*

εἰκός, -οτος, τό, *likely, probable, reasonable* (with or without ἐστί + inf.)

εἴωθα, (perf. with pres. meaning) *be accustomed, be in the habit*

ἔνιοι, ἐνίων, *some*

ἐπί, prep. (+ dat.), *in reference to*; (in later Greek) *at*

ἔτι, adv., *still*

θαυμάζω, *marvel, be amazed, wonder at; admire, honor, worship*

κόρυζα, -ης, ἡ, *running nose, nasal discharge; stupidity*

λέγω, ἐρῶ, εἶπον, *say, speak, tell*

μακρός, -ά, -όν, *long; large; great*

μᾶλλον, adv., *more, much more; rather, instead*

οἷος, οἵα, οἷον, *such as; what sort/kind* (of person/thing)

ὁράω, ὄψομαι, εἶδον, *see*

ὅς, ἥ, ὅ, rel. pron., *who, whose, whom, which, that*

ὅσος, -η, -ον, *as great as, as much as*; (pl.) *as many as*

οὗτος, αὕτη, τοῦτο, *this*; (pl.) *these*

παρά, (+ acc.) *beside, near, by*

περί, prep. (+ gen.), *about, concerning; around*; (+ dat.) *concerning*; (+ acc.) *around*

πλῆθος, -ους, τό, *number, multitude, crowd, throng*

πολύς, πολλή, πολύ, *much, great*; (pl.) *many*

πόρρω, adv., *far off, far away*

πρότερον, adv., *formerly, before, earlier*

πῦρ, πυρός, τό, *fire*

τις, τι, (gen. τινος) (indefinite pron.) *someone; something; anyone; anything*

τοίνυν, particle, *therefore, accordingly; moreover*

ἀλλ᾽ ὀλίγου δεῖν ὑπὸ τῶν Κυνικῶν ἐγώ σοι διεσπάσθην

ὥσπερ ὁ Ἀκταίων ὑπὸ τῶν κυνῶν ἢ ὁ ἀνεψιὸς αὐτοῦ

ὁ Πενθεὺς ὑπὸ τῶν Μαινάδων.

ὀλίγου δεῖν: literally, *to lack a little*; i.e., *practically, almost*. **τῶν Κυνικῶν**: the Cynics were followers of the philosopher Antisthenes (*c.* 445 – *c.* 365 BCE), himself a follower of Socrates (470/469 – 399 BCE). They got their name (*Dog-like*) from either the gymnasium (Κυνόσαργες, *Shining* or *Swift Dog*) in the suburbs of Athens where Antisthenes taught, or as an insult directed at them for their dog-like behavior (e.g., urinating in public). **ἐγώ σοι**: note the collocation of pronouns; σοι here means *for your sake*, i.e., as a person representing your (school of philosophy's) beliefs. **ὁ Ἀκταίων**: while hunting in the woods one day, Actaeon caught sight of the goddess Artemis bathing naked; she transformed him into a stag, and he was torn apart by his own hounds. **ὁ Πενθεὺς**: King of Thebes who, after banning the worship of Dionysus (Pentheus' cousin), was torn apart by his mother Agave and his aunts Ino and Autonoë (the mother of Actaeon) – all of whom, along with the other women of Thebes, had been driven mad by Dionysus. **τῶν Μαινάδων**: literally, *the Raving Ones*; Maenads were the female followers of Dionysus.

[3] ἡ δὲ πᾶσα τοῦ πράγματος διασκευὴ τοιάδε ἦν. τὸν μὲν

ποιητὴν οἶσθα οἷός τε ἦν καὶ ἡλίκα ἐτραγῴδει παρ᾽ ὅλον

τὸν βίον, ὑπὲρ τὸν Σοφοκλέα καὶ τὸν Αἰσχύλον. ἐγὼ δὲ ἐπεὶ

τάχιστα εἰς τὴν Ἦλιν ἀφικόμην, διὰ τοῦ γυμνασίου ἀνιὼν

ἐπήκουον ἅμα Κυνικοῦ τινος μεγάλῃ καὶ τραχείᾳ τῇ φωνῇ

ἡ δὲ πᾶσα τοῦ πράγματος διασκευὴ: note the syntactical "nesting." **τὸν μὲν ποιητὴν**: i.e., Peregrinus. **τε, καὶ**: *both... and*. **Σοφοκλέα, Αἰσχύλον**: famous Athenian tragic playwrights of the fifth century BCE. **Ἦλιν**: Elis was a city-state in the northwest part of the Peloponnese. The first Olympics was organized in Olympia, a sanctuary *c.* 16 miles south of the city of Elis, by the authorities of Elis in the 8th century BCE. **ἀνιὼν**: masc. nom. sing. pres. act. part. < ἄνειμι (this Attic fut. of ἀνέρχομαι is pres. tense in non-indic. forms).

8

Vocabulary

ἅμα, adv., *together, at the same time*; prep. (+ dat.), *together with*

ἀνέρχομαι, ἄνειμι, ἀνῆλθον, *go up*

ἀνεψιός, ὁ, *first cousin*

ἀφικνέομαι, ἀφίξομαι, ἀφικόμην, (dep.) *arrive at, come to, reach*

βίος, ὁ, *life*

γυμνάσιον, τό, *training ground, public place where athletic exercises were practiced (and philosophers and sophists would gather to peddle their "wares")*

δέω, *lack, be in need of* (+ gen.)

διά, prep. (+ gen.), *through*

διασκευή, ἡ, *stage setting, mise-en-scène; theatrical performance; rhetorical elaboration* (of a topic)

διασπάω, *tear apart, tear to pieces*

εἰς, prep. (+ acc. with ἀφικνέομαι), *at*

ἐπακούω, ἐπακούσομαι, ἐπήκουσα, *listen, hear* (+ gen. of person)

ἐπεί, conj., *after, since, when*; (+ τάχιστα) *as soon as*

ἤ, conj., *or*; (with comparatives) *than*

ἡλίκος, -η, -ον, *as big as, as great as*; (in indir. questions) *how big/great*; neut. pl. as adv., *how greatly*

Κυνικός, ὁ, *Cynic*, i.e., a follower of the philosopher Antisthenes

κύων, κυνός, ὁ or ἡ, *dog*

μέγας, μεγάλη, μέγα, *large, great*; (of sounds) *loud*

οἶδα, (perf. with pres. meaning) *know*

οἷος, οἵα, οἷον, *such as; what sort/kind* (of person/thing)

ὀλίγος, -η, -ον, *little, small*; (pl.) *few*

ὅλος, -η, -ον, *whole, entire*

παρά, (+ acc.) *along the whole course of, during*

πᾶς, πᾶσα, πᾶν, *all, every, whole*

ποιητής, -οῦ, ὁ, *poet, writer; playwright*

πρᾶγμα, -τος, τό, *matter, thing, affair*

τάχιστος, -η, -ον, *quickest, swiftest*

τις, τι, (gen. τινος) (indefinite adj.) *a certain; some; a, an*; (indefinite pron.) *someone; something; anyone; anything*

τοιόσδε, τοιάδε, τοιόνδε, *of such a kind* (as follows)

τραγῳδέω, *put on an elaborate performance* (in the style of ancient tragedy)

τραχύς, -εῖα, -ύ, *rough, sharp, harsh; hoarse*

ὑπέρ, prep. (+ acc.), *over, above, exceeding, beyond, more than*

ὑπό, prep. (+ gen. of the agent, with pass. verbs), *by*

φωνή, ἡ, *sound, noise, voice*

ὥσπερ, adv., *just as, even as*

9

τὰ συνήθη ταῦτα καὶ ἐκ τριόδου τὴν ἀρετὴν ἐπιβοωμένου καὶ

ἅπασιν ἀπαξαπλῶς λοιδορουμένου. εἶτα κατέληξεν αὐτῷ ἡ

βοὴ ἐς τὸν Πρωτέα, καὶ ὡς ἂν οἷός τε ὦ πειράσομαί σοι

αὐτὰ ἐκεῖνα ἀπομνημονεῦσαι ὡς ἐλέγετο. σὺ δὲ γνωριεῖς

δηλαδή, πολλάκις αὐτοῖς παραστὰς βοῶσιν.

ἐκ τριόδου τὴν ἀρετὴν: since street corners were locations where commoners hung out, the prep. phrase *from the street corner* came to mean *trite, hackneyed, everyday, trivial* (cf. English "trivial," from Latin *trivium* = τρίοδος); with τὴν ἀρετὴν translate as *hackneyed (conceptions of) virtue*. **ἐπιβοωμένου, λοιδορουμένου**: both modify Κυνικοῦ τινος. **ἐπιβοωμένου**: *shouting out over* (sc. *the crowd* or *din*). **αὐτῷ**: dat. of possession with ἡ βοή. **ὡς ἂν οἷός τε ὦ**: *as far as I am able, as much as I can, to the best of my ability* (Harmon); οἷός τε εἰμί is an idiom, literally meaning *and the kind of person I am*, i.e., *I am able*; ὦ is the 1st sing. pres. subju. of εἰμί; subju. after a verb of effort. **ἐλέγετο**: sc. as subj. αὐτὰ ἐκεῖνα; neut. plurals regularly take sing. verbs. **γνωριεῖς**: sc. as dir. obj. αὐτὰ ἐκεῖνα. **παραστὰς**: masc. nom. sing. 2nd aor. act. part. < παρίστημι. **βοῶσιν**: masc. dat. pl. pres. act. part. < βοάω.

---

[4] "Πρωτέα γάρ τις," ἔφη, "κενόδοξον τολμᾷ λέγειν, ὦ γῆ

καὶ ἥλιε καὶ ποταμοὶ καὶ θάλαττα καὶ πατρῷε Ἡράκλεις—

Πρωτέα: masc. acc. sing.; the dir. obj. of λέγειν, which takes two accusatives (*to call* X Y, *to say that* X [*is*] Y). As we learn from the punctuation on the next page, this long sentence is a question. **ὦ γῆ, ἥλιε, ποταμοὶ, θάλαττα, πατρῷε Ἡράκλεις**: all vocatives. **Ἡράκλεις**: an appropriate deity for the Cynic follower of Peregrinus to invoke, since Heracles was (a) the legendary founder of the Olympic Games, (b) a hero who ended his suffering on earth by having himself burned alive on a pyre, after which (in some accounts) his spirit ascended to Mt. Olympus to dwell with the gods, and (c) a sort of Cynic patron saint, viewed as an embodiment of Cynic ideals who also was responsible for bringing from Hades to earth the greatest "dog" of them all, Cerberus. The Cynic speaker will explicitly mention (b) near the end of his speech below.

Vocabulary

ἀπαξαπλῶς, *in general*

ἅπας, ἅπασα, ἅπαν, *all; every; whole*

ἀπομνημονεύω, *relate (from memory), recount*

ἀρετή, ἡ, *excellence, goodness, virtue*

αὐτός, -ή, -ό, (intensive adj.) *-self, -selves*; (adj.) *same*; (pron. in gen., dat., acc.) *him, her, it, them*

βοή, ἡ, *shout(ing), loud cry(ing)*

βοάω, βοήσομαι, ἐβόησα, *shout*

γῆ, ἡ, *earth*

γνωρίζω, γνωριῶ, *be acquainted with, recognize*

δηλαδή, adv., *quite clearly*

εἶτα, adv., *then, next; soon, presently; and so, therefore, accordingly*

ἐκ, ἐξ, prep. (+ gen.), *from, out of*

ἐκεῖνος, -η, -ο, *that*; (pl.) *those*

ἐπιβοάω, ἐπιβοήσομαι, ἐπεβόησα, *cry* or *shout out*; (mid.) *cry* or *shout out* X (acc.) *over* Y (dat.)

ἐς, εἰς, prep. (+ acc.), *(ended) in/with*

ἥλιος, ὁ, *sun*

θάλαττα, ἡ, *sea*

καταλήγω, *end, stop*

κενόδοξος, -ον, *vainglorious, conceited*

λέγω, ἐρῶ, εἶπον, *say, speak, tell*

λοιδοροῦμαι, (dep.) *abuse, revile, rebuke* (+ dat.)

οἷος, οἵα, οἷον, *what sort/kind* (of person/thing)

οὗτος, αὕτη, τοῦτο, *this*; (pl.) *these*

παρίστημι, παραστήσω, (1st aor.) παρέστησα, *present, show*; (2nd aor.) παρέστην, (perf.) παρέστηκα, *stand by, be present*

πατρῷος, -η, -ον, *of one's father, hereditary*

πειράομαι, πειράσομαι, ἐπειράθην, (mid. more common that act. πειράω) *attempt, endeavor, try* (often + inf.)

πολλάκις, *many times, often*

ποταμός, ὁ, *river*

συνήθης, -ες, *habitual, customary, usual, ordinary*

τις, τι, (gen. τινος) (indefinite pron.) *someone; something; anyone; anything*

τολμάω, *dare, be brave* or *bold enough*

τρίοδος, ἡ, *street corner, a meeting of three roads; trite, hackneyed, everyday, trivial*

φημί, φήσω, ἔφην (imperf.), ἔφησα (aor., rare), *say*

ὡς, *as; that*

11

Πρωτέα τὸν ἐν Συρίᾳ δεθέντα, τὸν τῇ πατρίδι ἀνέντα

πεντακισχίλια τάλαντα, τὸν ἀπὸ τῆς Ῥωμαίων πόλεως

ἐκβληθέντα, τὸν τοῦ Ἡλίου ἐπισημότερον, τὸν αὐτῷ

ἀνταγωνίσασθαι τῷ Ὀλυμπίῳ δυνάμενον; ἀλλ᾽ ὅτι διὰ πυρὸς

ἐξάγειν τοῦ βίου διέγνωκεν ἑαυτόν, εἰς κενοδοξίαν τινὲς

τοῦτο ἀναφέρουσιν; οὐ γὰρ Ἡρακλῆς οὕτως; οὐ γὰρ

Ἀσκληπιὸς καὶ Διόνυσος κεραυνῷ; οὐ γὰρ τὰ τελευταῖα

Ἐμπεδοκλῆς εἰς τοὺς κρατῆρας;"

Συρίᾳ: made part of the Roman Republic in 64 BCE; after being merged with the province of Judea in 135 CE, it was officially called Syria Palaestina.   δεθέντα: masc. acc. sing. aor. pass. part. < δέω; made a substantive by the article τὸν (English prefers relative clauses, i.e., who...); so too ἀνέντα, ἐκβληθέντα, ἐπισημότερον, and δυνάμενον, which are all in apposition to Πρωτέα. The repetition of τὸν at the beginning of these clauses is an example of the rhetorical figure of anaphora ("repetition").   ἀνέντα: masc. acc. sing. aor. act. part. < ἀνίημι. πεντακισχίλια τάλαντα: a very large sum of money – c. $130,000,000 in today's terms.   ἐκβληθέντα: masc. acc. sing. aor. pass. part. < ἐκβάλλω.   τοῦ Ἡλίου: gen. of comparison. αὐτῷ ἀνταγωνίσασθαι τῷ Ὀλυμπίῳ: note how the intensive adj. is separated from its noun; the speaker (syntactically) views Proteus as a true rival of Zeus.   ἀλλ᾽...ἑαυτόν = ἀλλ᾽ ὅτι διέγνωκεν ἐξάγειν ἑαυτόν [ἐκ] τοῦ βίου διὰ τοῦ πυρός.   τοῦτο: i.e., his decision to end his life. οὐ γὰρ: more anaphora, with the added joke that the verbal cognate of anaphora, ἀναφέρουσιν, precedes the first οὐ γὰρ.   οὕτως: sc. end his life.   Ἀσκληπιὸς καὶ Διόνυσος κεραυνῷ: i.e., (Were not the lives of) Asclepius and Dionysus (ended) by a thunderbolt? As Harmon (6, n. 1) notes, the cases of Asclepius and Dionysus are "not quite parallel" to that of Heracles, let alone Proteus. Asclepius, a mortal son of Apollo, after bringing back to life Hippolytus (the son of Theseus), was killed by Zeus to ensure that no mortal, once dead, could live again. It was not Dionysus, an immortal son of Zeus, who had his life ended by Zeus' thunderbolt, but Semele, Dionysus' mortal mother. She had been tricked by Zeus' jealous wife Hera, and so was incinerated by Zeus unwillingly while still pregnant with Dionysus.   εἰς τοὺς κρατῆρας: sc. leap or jump.

Vocabulary

ἀναφέρω, ἀνοίσω, ἀνήνεγκα, *ascribe, attribute*

ἀνίημι, ἀνήσω, ἀνῆκα, *let go, give up*

ἀνταγωνίζομαι, (dep.) *prove a match for, vie with; be set against*

ἀπό, prep. (+ gen.), *from, away from; by*

αὐτός, -ή, -ό, (intensive adj.) *-self, -selves;* (adj.) *same;* (pron. in gen., dat., acc.) *him, her, it, them*

βίος, ὁ, *life*

δέω, *bind, tie, enchain; put in prison*

διά, prep. (+ gen.), *through*

διαγιγνώσκω, διαγνώσομαι, διέγνων, *resolve, decide* (+ inf.)

δύναμαι, (dep.) *be able, can* (+ inf.)

ἑαυτοῦ, ἑαυτῆς, ἑαυτοῦ, (reflex. pron. in gen., dat., acc.) *himself, herself, itself*

εἰς, prep. (+ acc.), *to; into*

ἐκβάλλω, ἐκβαλῶ, ἐξέβαλον, *throw* or *cast out*

ἐν, prep. (+ dat.), *in, by, by means of, among*

ἐξάγω, ἐξάξω, ἐξήγαγον, *lead out, take from*

ἐπίσημος, -ον, *notable, remarkable; notorious*

Ἥλιος, ὁ, *Helios* (the sun-god), *sun*

κενοδοξία, ἡ, *vanity, conceit*

κεραυνός, -οῦ, *thunderbolt*

κρατήρ, -ῆρος, ὁ, (pl. often = sing.) *crater, mouth of a volcano*

Ὀλύμπιος, -ον, *Olympian;* ὁ Ὀλύμπιος, *Zeus*

ὅτι, conj., *that, because*

οὗτος, αὕτη, τοῦτο, *this;* (pl.) *these*

οὕτως, adv., *so, thus; as follows*

πατρίς, πατρίδος, ἡ, *one's fatherland/country*

πεντακισχίλιοι, -αι, -α, *five thousand*

πόλις, πόλεως, ἡ, *city, city-state*

πῦρ, πυρός, τό, *fire*

Ῥωμαῖος, -α, -ον, *Roman*

τάλαντον, -ου, τό, *talent* (a weight and a sum of money = 6,000 drachmas)

τελευταῖος, -α, -ον, *last;* τὰ τελευταῖα (adv.), *finally, in the end*

τις, τι, (gen. τινος) (indefinite pron.) *someone; something; anyone; anything*

[5] ὡς δὲ ταῦτα εἶπεν ὁ Θεαγένης — τοῦτο γὰρ ὁ κεκραγὼς

ἐκεῖνος ἐκαλεῖτο — ἠρόμην τινὰ τῶν παρεστώτων, "τί

βούλεται τὸ περὶ τοῦ πυρός, ἢ τί Ἡρακλῆς καὶ Ἐμπεδοκλῆς

πρὸς τὸν Πρωτέα." ὁ δέ, "οὐκ εἰς μακράν," ἔφη, "καύσει

ἑαυτὸν ὁ Πρωτεὺς Ὀλυμπίασιν." "πῶς," ἔφην, "ἢ τίνος

ἕνεκα;" εἶτα ὁ μὲν ἐπειρᾶτο λέγειν, ἐβόα δὲ ὁ Κυνικός,

ὥστε ἀμήχανον ἦν ἄλλου ἀκούειν. ἐπήκουον οὖν τὰ λοιπὰ

ἐπαντλοῦντος αὐτοῦ καὶ θαυμαστάς τινας ὑπερβολὰς

ὡς: + aor. indic. = *when, after.*   **ὁ Θεαγένης**: for more on Theagenes, a disciple of Peregrinus who came from Patras, see 30 below. Macleod (271) notes that he might "possibly [be] the man referred to by Galen as a well-known Cynic philosopher who conversed daily in Trajan's gymnasium in Rome." Theagenes is, perhaps coincidentally, also the name of a celebrated athlete of the 5th century BCE, credited with victories in numerous events in the Olympian, Pythian, Nemean, and Isthmian games. After his death he had a cult devoted to him on the island of Thasos, his birthplace. Lucian mentions in his *Assembly of the Gods* 12 how a statue dedicated to Theagenes on Thasos cured people with fevers (for the curing of fevers in connection to Peregrinus, see 28; for the dedication of statues to Peregrinus, see 41).   **κεκραγὼς**: masc. nom. sing. perf. act. part. < κράζω.   **τῶν παρεστώτων**: masc. gen. pl. perf. act. part. < παρίστημι.   **τὸ περὶ τοῦ πυρός** = τὸ (πρᾶγμα) περὶ τοῦ πυρός. This noun phrase is the subj. of βούλεται.   **τί Ἡρακλῆς καὶ Ἐμπεδοκλῆς**: sc. *have to do.*   **οὐκ εἰς μακράν**: *shortly, before long, fairly soon.* Hopkinson (99) suggests that the phrase is perhaps an ellipse for οὐκ εἰς μακράν ὁδόν, *not on a long road.*   **τίνος ἕνεκα**: literally, *because of what thing*; i.e., *why.*   **ἀκούειν. ἐπήκουον**: an example of the rhetorical figure known as *anadiplosis* ("double-up"), in which a word is used at the end of a clause or sentence and then used again at the beginning of the next clause or sentence.   **τὰ λοιπὰ**: sc. *of his speech.*

Vocabulary

ἀκούω, ἀκούσομαι, ἤκουσα, *hear* (+ gen. of person)

ἀλλός, -ή, -ό, *another, other*

ἀμήχανος, -ον, *difficult, hard, impossible*

αὐτός, -ή, -ό, (intensive adj.) *-self, -selves*; (adj.) *same*; (pron. in gen., dat., acc.) *him, her, it, them*

βοάω, βοήσομαι, ἐβόησα, *shout*

βούλομαι, *wish, want* (+ inf.); *mean*

ἑαυτοῦ, ἑαυτῆς, ἑαυτοῦ, (reflex. pron. in gen., dat., acc.) *himself, herself, itself*

εἰς, prep. (+ acc.; of time), *for*

εἶτα, adv., *then, next*; *soon, presently*; *and so, therefore, accordingly*

ἐκεῖνος, -ή, -ό, *that*; (pl.) *those*

ἕνεκα, prep. (+ preceding gen.), *for the sake of, because of*

ἐπακούω, ἐπακούσομαι, ἐπήκουσα, *listen, hear* (+ gen. of person)

ἐπαντλέω, *pour a flood (of words) over*

ἔρομαι (not found in pres. ind), ἐρήσομαι, ἠρόμην, *ask, inquire, question*

ἤ, conj., *or*; (with comparatives) *than*

θαυμαστός, -ή, -όν, *wonderful, marvelous*

καίω, καύσω, ἔκαυσα, *set on fire, burn up*

καλέω, *call, call in, summon*

κράζω, *scream, shriek*

Κυνικός, ὁ, *Cynic*, i.e., a follower of the philosopher Antisthenes.

λέγω, ἐρῶ, εἶπον, *say, speak, tell*

λοιπός, -ή, -όν, *remaining*; τὰ λοιπά, *the rest*

μακρός, -ά, -όν, *long*; *large*; *great*; (fem. acc. sing. as adv.) *long time*

Ὀλυμπίασι(ν), adv., *at Olympia.*

οὗτος, αὕτη, τοῦτο, *this*; (pl.) *these*

παρίστημι, παραστήσω, (1st aor.) παρέστησα, *present, show*; (2nd aor.) παρέστην, (perf.) παρέστηκα, *stand by, be present*

πειράομαι, πειράσομαι, ἐπειράθην, *attempt, endeavor, try* (often + inf.)

περί, prep. (+ gen.), *about, concerning*; *around*; (+ dat.) *concerning*; (+ acc.) *around*

πρός, prep. (+ acc.), *in reference* or *relation to*; *with*

πῦρ, πυρός, τό, *fire*

πῶς, adv., *how?, in what manner* or *way?*

τις, τι, (gen. τινος) τις, τι, (gen. τινος) (indefinite adj.) *a certain*; *some*; *a, an*; (indefinite pron.) *someone*; *something*; *anyone*; *anything*

τίς, τί, (gen. τίνος) interrog. pron. and adj., *who? which? what?*

ὑπερβολή, ἡ, *hyperbole*

φημί, φήσω, ἔφην (imperf.), ἔφησα (aor., rare), *say*

ὥστε, conj., *so that, that, with the result that*

διεξιόντος κατὰ τοῦ Πρωτέως· τὸν μὲν γὰρ Σινωπέα ἢ τὸν

διδάσκαλον αὐτοῦ Ἀντισθένη οὐδὲ παραβάλλειν ἠξίου αὐτῷ,

ἀλλ᾽ οὐδὲ τὸν Σωκράτη αὐτόν, ἐκάλει δὲ τὸν Δία ἐπὶ τὴν

ἅμιλλαν. εἶτα μέντοι ἔδοξεν αὐτῷ ἴσους πως φυλάξαι

αὐτούς, καὶ οὕτω κατέπαυε τὸν λόγον· [6] "δύο γὰρ ταῦτα,"

ἔφη, "ὁ βίος ἄριστα δημιουργήματα ἐθεάσατο, τὸν Δία

τὸν Ὀλύμπιον καὶ Πρωτέα· πλάσται δὲ καὶ τεχνῖται, τοῦ μὲν

Φειδίας, τοῦ δὲ ἡ φύσις. ἀλλὰ νῦν ἐξ ἀνθρώπων εἰς θεοὺς

διεξιόντος: masc. gen. sing. pres. act. part. < διέξειμι (this Attic fut. of διεξέρχομαι is pres. tense in non-indic. forms).　　**τὸν μὲν γὰρ...**
Σωκράτη αὐτόν = γὰρ μὲν οὐδὲ ἠξίου παραβάλλειν τὸν Σινωπέα ἢ τὸν διδάσκαλον αὐτοῦ Ἀντισθένη αὐτῷ, ἀλλ᾽ οὐδὲ (ἠξίου παραβάλλειν) τὸν Σωκράτη αὐτόν (αὐτῷ).　　**Σινωπέα**: *the Sinopean* or *citizen of Sinope* refers to Diogenes (*c.* 412 – 323 BCE), one of the founders of the Cynic school of philosophy. Exiled from Sinope (a Greek city-state on the south coast of the Black Sea), Diogenes made his way to Athens where, according to some accounts, he hounded Antisthenes' every move until the latter finally accepted him as his first (and only) disciple.　　**Ἀντισθένη**: Athenian philosopher (*c.* 445 – *c.* 365 BCE) and friend of Socrates. Although considered by many to be the founder of Cynicism because of his rigorously ascetic lifestyle and for the lectures he gave at the Cynosarges gymnasium, he himself would probably not have recognized such an honor.　　**ἠξίου**: 3rd sing. imperf. act. indic. < ἀξιόω.　　**Σωκράτη**: Athenian philosopher (470/469 – 399 BCE) who is often depicted in Plato's dialogues employing his eponymous Socratic method of philosophical inquiry.　　**τὸν Δία**: in the oblique cases (gen., dat., acc.), the ζ of Ζεύς (pronounced during the classical period 'σδ'), loses its σ.　　**τὸν Δία τὸν Ὀλύμπιον**: the statue of Zeus at Olympia, one of the Seven Wonders of the Ancient World, was created by the sculptor Pheidias in 435 BCE. Located inside the Temple of Zeus, the *c.* 43-foot statue constructed of gold-and-ivory over a wooden core depicted Zeus enthroned holding the figure of Nike in his right hand and a scepter in his left.　　**τοῦ μὲν**: i.e., the statue of Olympian Zeus.　　**Φειδίας**: masc. nom. sing., in apposition, like ἡ φύσις, to πλάσται, καὶ τεχνῖται. **τοῦ δὲ**: i.e., Proteus.

Vocabulary

ἄνθρωπος, ὁ, *man, human being*

ἄμιλλα, ἡ, *contest, contest for superiority*

ἀξιόω, *think, deem worthy; think one has the right, expect* (+ inf.)

ἄριστος, -η, -ον, *best, finest, most excellent*

αὐτός, -ή, -ό, (intensive adj.) *-self, -selves;* (adj.) *same;* (pron. in gen., dat., acc.) *him, her, it, them*

βίος, ὁ, *life; the world, the world we live in*

δημιουργήμα, -ατος, τό, *work of art; masterpiece*

διδάσκαλος, ὁ, *teacher, master*

διεξέρχομαι, διέξειμι, διεξῆλθον, *go through in detail, recount in full*

δοκῶ, (uncontracted = δοκέω) *think, suppose, imagine;* (3rd sing.) *it seems (good)*

δύο, (indecl.) *two*

εἶτα, adv., *then, next; soon, presently; and so, therefore, accordingly*

ἐπί, prep. (+ acc.), *to, towards*

Ζεύς, Διός, Διῖ, Δία, ὁ, *Zeus*

ἤ, conj., *or;* (with comparatives) *than*

θεάομαι, (dep.) *look on, gaze at, view (as spectator)*

θεός, ὁ, *god*

ἴσος, -η, -ον, *equal, the same*

καλέω, *call, call in, summon*

κατά, prep. (+ acc.), *with regard to, concerning*

καταπαύω, *end, bring an end to, conclude*

λόγος, ὁ, *word, speech*

μέντοι, particle, *indeed, to be sure, of course; however*

νῦν, adv., *now*

Ὀλύμπιος, -ον, *Olympian*

οὐδέ, *(and/but) not;* ἀλλ' οὐδὲ, *and not even*

οὗτος, αὕτη, τοῦτο, *this;* (pl.) *these*

οὕτω, οὕτως, adv., *so, thus; as follows*

παραβάλλω, παραβαλῶ, παρέβαλον, *compare X (acc.) with Y (dat.)*

πλάστης, -ου, ὁ, *sculptor, creator*

πως, adv., *in any way, at all, by any means; somehow*

Σινωπεύς, -έως, ὁ, *an inhabitant of Sinope, a Sinopean*

τεχνίτης, -ου, ὁ, *artisan, craftsman*

φημί, φήσω, ἔφην (imperf.), ἔφησα (aor., rare), *say*

φυλάσσω, φυλάξω, ἐφύλαξα, *keep*

φύσις, -εως, ἡ, *nature*

τὸ ἄγαλμα τοῦτο οἰχήσεται, ὀχούμενον ἐπὶ τοῦ πυρός,

ὀρφανοὺς ἡμᾶς καταλιπόν." ταῦτα ξὺν πολλῷ ἱδρῶτι

διεξελθὼν ἐδάκρυε μάλα γελοίως καὶ τὰς τρίχας ἐτίλλετο,

ὑποφειδόμενος μὴ πάνυ ἕλκειν καὶ τέλος ἀπῆγον αὐτὸν

λύζοντα μεταξὺ τῶν Κυνικῶν τινες παραμυθούμενοι.

[7] μετὰ δὲ τοῦτον ἄλλος εὐθὺς ἀναβαίνει, οὐ περιμείνας

τὸ ἄγαλμα: the regular meaning of this noun is a statue dedicated to a god (that brings them delight), and so in this context would at first – if only momentarily – suggest Pheidias' statue of Olympian Zeus. Theagenes, however, has connected that word to mean the living person of Peregrinus, thus once again equating Peregrinus with Pheidias' celebrated masterpiece. ξὺν: an early Attic spelling for the prep. σύν that was still being used by Thucydides at the end of the fifth century BCE; later imitators of Attic prose style during the Second Sophistic (such as Lucian) could use either form. ἐδάκρυε, ἐτίλλετο: inchoative or inceptive imperfects; i.e., *he began to...* τῶν Κυνικῶν: can be taken with both μεταξὺ and τινες. μετὰ δὲ τοῦτον: i.e., Theagenes. ἄλλος: most scholars believe that this new speaker is none other than Lucian himself. Harmon (8-9, n. 2), for example, states that "What Lucian has previously said (§ 2), together with his failure here to say a word about the identity or personality of these remarks, puts it beyond doubt that the "other man" is Lucian himself, and that he expects his readers to draw this inference." Of course, this being Lucian, the fact that he actually delivered this speech in public at the time is up for grabs. See also LUCIAN, "LUCIAN," AND "LUCIAN'S DOUBLE" in the introductory sections of this text for Lucian's characterization of this "other man." ἀναβαίνει: sc. *speaker's platform* or *elevated area*; "perhaps," as Harmon (p. 8, n. 2) notes, "the portico of the gymnasium."

Vocabulary

ἄγαλμα, τό, glory, delight; gift (pleasing to the gods); sacred image / statue

ἀλλός, -ή, -ό, another, other

ἀναβαίνω, ἀναβήσομαι, ἀνέβην, go up, mount

ἀπάγω, ἀπάξω, ἀπήγαγον, lead away

αὐτός, -ή, -ό, (intensive adj.) -self, -selves; (adj.) same; (pron. in gen., dat., acc.) him, her, it, them

γελοίως, adv., ridiculously, laughably

δακρύω, cry, lament, weep, shed tears

ἐκ, ἐξ, prep. (+ gen.), from

διεξέρχομαι, διέξειμι, διεξῆλθον, go through in detail, recount in full

εἰς, prep. (+ acc.), to

ἕλκω, pull, tear

ἐπί, prep. (+ gen.), on, upon

εὐθύς, adv., immediately, at once; straight, directly

θρίξ, τριχός, ἡ, hair

ἱδρώς, -ῶτος, ὁ, sweat

καταλείπω, καταλείψω, κατέλιπον, leave, leave behind, desert

λύζω, sob violently

μάλα, adv., very, very much, exceedingly

μέτα, prep. (+ acc.), after

μεταξύ, prep. (+ gen.), between, among; (adv.) in the midst / middle of (+ part.).

ξύν, σύν, prep. (+ dat.), with

οἴχομαι, (dep.) go, go away, depart; be gone, have gone

ὀρφανός, -ή, -όν, orphan

ὀχέω, carry; (mid.) have oneself carried, be carried or borne

πάνυ, adv., altogether, entirely; very, exceedingly, too much

παραμυθέομαι, console, comfort

περιμένω, περιμενῶ, περέμεινα, wait for, wait around for

πολύς, πολλή, πολύ, much; (pl.) many

πῦρ, πυρός, τό, fire

τέλος, -ους, τό, end; (acc. sing. often as adv.) finally, at last

τίλλω, tear or pull out (one's hair); (mid.) tear of pull out one's hair in sorrow

τις, τι, (gen. τινος) (indefinite pron.) someone; something; anyone; anything

ὑποφείδομαι, (dep.) spare a little; be moderate or restrained

διαλυθῆναι τὸ πλῆθος ἀλλὰ ἐπ' αἰθομένοις τοῖς προτέροις

ἱερείοις ἐπέχει τῶν σπονδῶν. καὶ τὸ μὲν πρῶτον ἐπὶ πολὺ

ἐγέλα καὶ δῆλος ἦν νειόθεν αὐτὸ δρῶν· εἶτα ἤρξατο ὧδέ

πως· "ἐπεὶ ὁ κατάρατος Θεαγένης τέλος τῶν μιαρωτάτων

αὐτοῦ λόγων τὰ Ἡρακλείτου δάκρυα ἐποιήσατο, ἐγὼ κατὰ

τὸ ἐναντίον ἀπὸ τοῦ Δημοκρίτου γέλωτος ἄρξομαι."

καὶ αὖθις ἐγέλα ἐπὶ πολύ, ὥστε καὶ ἡμῶν τοὺς πολλοὺς

ἐπὶ τὸ ὅμοιον ἐπεσπάσατο. [8] εἶτα ἐπιστρέψας ἑαυτόν,

τῶν σπονδῶν: a partitive gen. with ἐπέχει; i.e., *he was pouring some of the libations on.*   **ἐπὶ πολὺ**: *for a long time.*   **δῆλος ἦν**: pred. adjs. often function as advs., i.e., *he was clearly.*   **αὐτὸ**: i.e., the laughing.   **αὐτοῦ** (later Greek) = ἑαυτοῦ (Classical Greek).   **τὰ Ἡρακλείτου δάκρυα**: Heraclitus (*c.* 535 – 475 BCE) was a pre-Socratic philosopher famous for his enigmatic statements. Casson (382, n. 8) notes that Heraclitus' "philosophical and scientific ideas were distorted by later interpreters, who came to associate his cosmogonical views (that the universe was created in a sort of big bang and would one day end that way) with his character: i.e., he was the weeping philosopher because he believed that the universe would one day be destroyed in a fiery explosion."   **κατὰ τὸ ἐναντίον**: *on the contrary.*   **τοῦ Δημοκρίτου γέλωτος**: Democritus (*c.* 460 – 370 BCE), along with his teacher Leucippus (*fl.* 5th century BCE), developed the theory of atomism, a belief that the universe was created of invisible, indivisible particles of matter. Like Heraclitus, his views too were distorted by later interpreters. In his case, Casson (382, n. 8) notes, "Since his scientific theories postulated that atoms combine in rather random ways, later peoples concluded that he must have meant that life itself is governed by chance. If this is so, they reasoned, then what is the the point of planning anything. Thus, the best attitude toward life was to simply laugh at all the absurdity around you." Lucian's *Sale of Lives* 13-14 presents a satirical sketch of Heraclitus as "the weeping philosopher" and Democritus as "the laughing philosopher."   **τὸ ὅμοιον**: i.e., a fit of laughter.   **ἐπιστρέψας ἑαυτόν**: the act. part. + reflexive pron. = mid. voice.

20

Vocabulary

αἴθω, *light, kindle*; (pass. often) *burn, blaze*

ἀπό, prep. (+ gen.), *from, away from*; *by*

ἄρχω, *begin*; *rule, govern*; (mid.) *begin*

αὖθις, adv., *again, once again*

γελάω, γελάσομαι, ἐγέλασα, *laugh*

γέλως, -ωτος, ὁ, *laughter*

δάκρυον, τό, *tear*

δῆλος, -η, -ον, *clear, obvious, evident*

διαλύω, *disband, break up*; (pass., of a gathering/assembly) *break up, disperse*

δράω, *do*

ἑαυτοῦ, ἑαυτῆς, ἑαυτοῦ, (reflex. pron. in gen., dat., acc.) *himself, herself, itself*

εἶτα, adv., *then, next*; *soon, presently*; *and so, therefore, accordingly*

ἐναντίος, -η, -ον, *opposite, over against, contrary*

ἐπεί, conj., *since, when*

ἐπί, prep. (+ dat.), *upon, on to*; (+ acc.) *to, up to*

ἐπισπάω, (act. or mid.) *draw* or *drag*; *bring on, cause*

ἐπιστρέφω, *turn about/around*; (mid.) *turn oneself around, change, recover*

ἐπιχέω, *pour (water) over*

ἱερεῖον, τό, *sacrifice, sacrificial victim*

κατά, prep. (+ acc.), *with regard to, with respect to, in accordance with*

κατάρατος, -ον, *accursed*

λόγος, ὁ, *word, speech*

μιαρός, -ή, -όν, *foul, repulsive*; *unclean, ritually impure*

νειόθεν, adv., *from the bottom (of his heart), heartily*

ὅμοιος, -η, -ον, *like, resembling*; τὸ ὅμοιον, *the same thing*

πλῆθος, τό, *throng, crowd, multitude*

ποιέω, *make, produce, create*; *do*; (mid.) *make X (acc.) (one's) Y (acc.)*.

πολύς, πολλή, πολύ, *much*; (pl.) *many*; (as substantive) *the majority*

πρότερος, -η, -ον, *former, prior, previous*

πρῶτος, -η, -ον, *first*; τὸ πρῶτον (adv.), *first, first of all, in the first place*

πως, adv., *somehow*; ὧδέ πως, *somehow so/thus/in this way*

σπονδή, ἡ, *libation, drink-offering* (poured out to the gods)

τέλος, -ους, τό, *end*

τίς, τί, (gen. τίνος) interrog. pron. and adj., *who? which? what?*

ὧδε, adv., *in this way, so, thus*; ὧδέ πως, *somehow so/thus/in this way*

ὥστε, conj., *so that, that, with the result that*

"ἢ τί γὰρ ἄλλο," ἔφη, "ὦ ἄνδρες, χρὴ ποιεῖν ἀκούοντας

μὲν οὕτω γελοίων ῥήσεων, ὁρῶντας δὲ ἄνδρας γέροντας

δοξαρίου καταπτύστου ἕνεκα μονονουχὶ κυβιστῶντας

ἐν τῷ μέσῳ; ὡς δὲ εἰδείητε οἷόν τι τὸ ἄγαλμά ἐστι τὸ

καυθησόμενον, ἀκούσατέ μου ἐξ ἀρχῆς παραφυλάξαντος

τὴν γνώμην αὐτοῦ καὶ τὸν βίον ἐπιτηρήσαντος· ἔνια δὲ παρὰ

τῶν πολιτῶν αὐτοῦ ἐπυνθανόμην καὶ οἷς ἀνάγκη ἦν ἀκριβῶς

εἰδέναι αὐτόν."

ἢ τί γὰρ ἄλλο, χρὴ ποιεῖν…: a rhetorical question; i.e., we can't help but laugh at Theagenes' ridiculous words and Peregrinus' notoriety-seeking spectacle.   **χρὴ**: sc. ἡμᾶς (modified by ἀκούοντας and ὁρῶντας) as the subj. of the impersonal verb.   **ἀκούοντας**: regularly ἀκούω + acc. of thing heard, + gen. of person from whom it is heard. Here the thing heard (γελοίων ῥήσεων) is in the gen.   **δοξαρίου**: diminutive of δόξα (*reputation, honor, glory*); diminutives can be used to express size (*little* or *small* X), as terms of endearment (*sweet* or *dear* X), or as pejoratives (*silly* or *stupid little* X). The first and the last are in operation here; cf., e.g., the translations of Harmon, *a little...notoriety*, and Casson and Costa, *a bit...of notoriety*.   **ἐν τῷ μέσῳ**: i.e., in public.   **ὡς**: + subju. or opt. = a final/purpose clause; i.e., *so that, in order that*.   **εἰδείητε**: 2nd pl. perf. act. opt. < οἶδα; opt. in final/purpose clause in primary sequence (the imper. ἀκούσατέ); this is a common irregularity in Lucian, since the opt. in final/purpose clauses is normally found in secondary sequence.   **καυθησόμενον**: neut. nom. sing. fut. pass. part. < καίω.   **οἷς**: sc. παρὰ τῶν ἀνθρώπων as the antecedent of the rel. pron.   **εἰδέναι**: perf. act. inf. < οἶδα.

Vocabulary

ἄγαλμα, τό, *glory, delight; gift (pleasing to the gods); sacred image / statue*

ἀκούω, ἀκούσομαι, ἤκουσα, *hear* (+ gen. of persons; + acc. of things)

ἀκριβῶς, adv., *accurately, thoroughly*

ἀλλός, -ή, -ό, *another, other*

ἀνάγκη, ἡ, *necessity*; ἀνάγκη ἐστί(ν), *it is necessary* (+ inf.)

ἀνήρ, ἀνδρός, ὁ, *man, gentleman*

ἀρχή, ἡ, *beginning*

βίος, ὁ, *life, manner of living; career*

γέλοιος, -α, -ον, *ridiculous, laughable*

γέρων, -οντος, ὁ, *old man*; (as adj. with masc. nouns) *old*

γνώμη, ἡ, *disposition, purpose; character*

δοξάριον, τό, (diminutive of ἡ δόξα) *a little estimation / reputation / honor / glory*

ἐκ, ἐξ, prep. (+ gen.), *from, out of*

ἐν, prep. (+ dat.), *in, by, by means of, among*; (later Greek) *into, on*

ἕνεκα, prep. (+ preceding gen.), *for the sake of, because of*

ἔνιοι, -αι, -α, *some*

ἐπιτηρέω, *keep an eye on, watch carefully*

ἤ, conj., *or*; (with comparatives) *than*

καίω, καύσω, ἔκαυσα, *set on fire, burn up*

κατάπτυστος, -ον, *be spat upon, despicable, contemptible*

κυβιστάω, *tumble head foremost, turn somersaults*

μέσος, -η, -ον, *middle, in the middle*; μέσον, adv., *in the middle*

μονονουχί, adv., *all but, practically*

οἶδα, (perf. with pres. meaning) *know*

οἶος, οἶα, οἶον, rel. pron., *such as, of what sort*; οἶόν τι, *what sort of thing*

ὁράω, ὄψομαι, εἶδον, *see*

ὅς, ἥ, ὅ, rel. pron., *who, whose, whom, which, that*

οὕτω, οὕτως, adv., *so, thus; as follows*

παρά, prep. (+ gen.), *from*

παραφυλάττω, παραφυλάξω, παρεφύλαξα, *watch* or *observe carefully*

ποιέω, *make, produce, create; do*

πολίτης, -ου, ὁ, *citizen, fellow-citizen*

πυνθάνομαι, *learn by hearsay* or *inquiry*

ῥῆσις, -εως, ἡ, *saying, speech*

τίς, τί, (gen. τίνος) interrog. pron. and adj., *who? which? what?*

φημί, φήσω, ἔφην (imperf.), ἔφησα (aor., rare), *say*

χρή, (imperf. ἐχρῆν), *it is necessary, one must* (+ inf.)

ὡς, conj., (+ subju./opt.) *so that, in order that*

[9] τὸ γὰρ τῆς φύσεως τοῦτο πλάσμα καὶ δημιούργημα,

ὁ τοῦ Πολυκλείτου κανών, ἐπεὶ εἰς ἄνδρας τελεῖν ἤρξατο,

ἐν Ἀρμενίᾳ μοιχεύων ἁλοὺς μάλα πολλὰς πληγὰς ἔλαβεν

καὶ τέλος κατὰ τοῦ τέγους ἁλόμενος διέφυγε, ῥαφανῖδι

τὴν πυγὴν βεβυσμένος. εἶτα μειράκιόν τι ὡραῖον διαφθείρας

τρισχιλίων ἐξωνήσατο παρὰ τῶν γονέων τοῦ παιδός,

πενήτων ὄντων, μὴ ἐπὶ τὸν ἁρμοστὴν ἀπαχθῆναι τῆς Ἀσίας.

φύσεως, πλάσμα, δημιούργημα: these words repeat – in reverse order – the language of the opening of Theagenes' praise of Peregrinus in 6 (δημιουργήματα, πλάσται, φύσις), in which he compared Peregrinus to Pheidias' statue of Zeus at Olympia. Here the speaker will do a similar thing (though in a heavily ironic manner), by equating Peregrinus with an equally famous statue, the "Canon" of Polycleitus.   **τοῦτο πλάσμα καὶ δημιούργημα**: in apposition to τὸ τῆς φύσεως (*that thing of nature*). **ὁ τοῦ Πολυκλείτου κανών**: Polycleitus (*fl.* 5th century BCE) was a classical sculptor famous for several works, perhaps the most important being his so-called "Canon," a sculpture of a naked young man carrying a spear (also called *Doryphorus*). Polycleitus wrote a theoretical treatise on sculpture also called "Canon" in which he laid out the rational bases for a perfect human body according to certain ideal mathematical proportions developed around the ideas of commensurability, equilibrium, and rhythm. **εἰς ἄνδρας τελεῖν**: literally, *to come to* or *belong to men*; i.e., *reach adulthood, become a man*.   **Ἀρμενίᾳ**: fought over by the Romans and the Parthians throughout the 2nd and 3rd centuries CE, Armenia was only briefly a province of the Roman Empire (from 114 – 118 CE); from 140 – 161 CE it was a Roman protectorate.   **ἁλοὺς**: masc. nom. sing. aor. act. (in form, pass. in meaning) part. < ἁλίσκομαι.   **βεβυσμένος**: masc. nom. sing. perf. mid./pass. part. < βύω. One of the forms that punishment could take for men caught committing adultery in the ancient Greek world was the insertion of a large radish into the rectum. **τρισχιλίων**: sc. *drachmas*; i.e., roughly equivalent to an average citizen's yearly income in the Roman Empire of the 2nd century CE.   **μὴ**: + inf. can introduce a negative purpose clause; i.e., *so as not, so that he not...* **τῆς Ἀσίας**: the Roman province of Asia encompassed what is today much of the western part of Asia Minor (modern Turkey). **ἀπαχθῆναι**: aor. pass. inf. < ἀπάγω.

Vocabulary

ἄγαλμα, τό, *glory, delight; gift (pleasing to the gods)*; *sacred image / statue*

ἀλίσκομαι, ἀλώσομαι, ἑάλων / ἥλων, (defective pass; + part.) *be caught* or *seized* (doing a thing); *be detected* (doing a thing).

ἅλλομαι, ἀλοῦμαι, ἡλόμην (2nd aor.), (dep.) *leap, jump*

ἀνήρ, ἀνδρός, ὁ, *man, gentleman*

ἀπάγω, ἀπάξω, ἀπήγαγον, *lead away*

ἁρμοστής, -οῦ, ὁ, *governor*

ἄρχω, *begin; rule, govern*; (mid.) *begin*

βύω, *stuff, plug*; (pass.) *be stuffed* or *plugged, have one's X* (acc.) *plugged* or *stopped* (with, + dat.)

γονεύς, γονέως, ὁ, *father*; (pl.) *parents*

δημιουργήμα, -ατος, τό, *work of art; masterpiece*

διαφθείρω, διαφθερῶ, διέφθειρα, *corrupt, ruin*

διαφεύγω, διαφεύξομαι, διέφυγον, *escape*

ἐξωνέομαι, (dep.) *buy off* (+ gen. of price paid and acc. or παρά + gen. of person paid)

ἐπεί, conj., *after, since, when*

ἐπί, prep. (+ acc.), *to; before*

κανών, -όνος, ὁ, *canon, rule, standard, model*; *Polycleitan sculpture* and *treatise*

κατά, prep. (+ gen.), *down from*

λαμβάνω, λήψομαι, ἔλαβον, *take*

μάλα, adv., *very, very much, exceedingly*

μειράκιον, τό, (diminutive of μεῖραξ) *boy, young man* (under the age of 21)

μοιχεύω, *commit adultery (with a woman)*

οὗτος, αὕτη, τοῦτο, *this*; (pl.) *these*

παῖς, παίδος, ὁ or ἡ, *boy, girl, son, daughter, child*

παρά, prep. (+ gen.), *from*

πένης, -ητος, ὁ, *poor person*

πλάσμα, -ατος, τό, *figure, image; counterfeit, forgery, fiction*

πληγή, ἡ, *blow, strike, beating*

πυγή, ἡ, *ass, buttocks*

ῥαφανίς, -ῖδος, ἡ, *radish*

τέγος, -ους, τό, *roof*

τελέω, (+ εἰς) *belong to, become, reach the state of*

τέλος, -ους, τό, *end*; (acc. sing. often as adv.) *finally, at last*

τρισχίλιοι, -αι, -α, *three thousand*

φύσις, -εως, ἡ, *nature, being, essence*

ὡραῖος, -α, -ον, *beautiful, youthful, ripe*

25

[10] "ταῦτα καὶ τὰ τοιαῦτα ἐάσειν μοι δοκῶ· πηλὸς

γὰρ ἔτι ἄπλαστος ἦν καὶ οὐδέπω ἐντελὲς ἄγαλμα ἡμῖν

δεδημιούργητο. ἃ δὲ τὸν πατέρα ἔδρασεν καὶ πάνυ ἀκοῦσαι

ἄξιον· καίτοι πάντες ἴστε, καὶ ἀκηκόατε ὡς ἀπέπνιξε τὸν

γέροντα, οὐκ ἀνασχόμενος αὐτὸν ὑπὲρ ἐξήκοντα ἔτη ἤδη

γηρῶντα. εἶτα ἐπειδὴ τὸ πρᾶγμα διεβεβόητο, φυγὴν ἑαυτοῦ

καταδικάσας ἐπλανᾶτο ἄλλοτε ἄλλην ἀμείβων.

πηλός: the usual material employed by sculptors when making the model for a statue that would later be cast in bronze.   **δεδημιούργητο**: 3rd sing. pluperf. mid./pass. indic. < δημιουργέω.   **ἡμῖν**: *for us*, i.e., *for our benefit* (a dat. of interest or advantage; in this case ironically so). **ἔδρασεν**: δράω can take a double acc. construction; i.e., *do* X (acc.) *to* Y (acc.).   **ἄξιον**: sc. ἐστί.   **ἴστε**: 2nd pl. perf. (pres. meaning) act. indic. < οἶδα.   **ἀκηκόατε**: 2nd pl. perf. act. indic. < ἀκούω. **ἀνασχόμενος**: masc. nom. sing. aor. mid. part. < ἀνέχω.   **ἤδη**: i.e., that he had already lived.   **διεβεβόητο**: 3rd sing. pluperf. mid./pass. indic. < διαβοάω.   **φυγὴν ἑαυτοῦ καταδικάσας**: euphemistic irony on the part of the speaker; instead of waiting around to be tried and convicted (and most likely sentenced to death), Peregrinus hightailed it out of his hometown.   **ἄλλην**: sc. γῆν.

26

Vocabulary

ἄγαλμα, τό, glory, delight; gift (pleasing to the gods); sacred image / statue

ἀκούω, ἀκούσομαι, ἤκουσα, hear (+ gen. of person)

ἄλλοτε, adv., (+ ἄλλος, -η, -ο) sometimes to this, sometimes to that

ἀμείβω, pass, cross, leave, exchange

ἀνέχω, ἀνέξω, ἀνέσχον, hold up; (mid.) allow, tolerate (+ part.)

ἄξιος, -α, -ον, worth, worthy of, deserving of, fitting (+ gen. or inf.)

ἄπλαστος, -ον, not moulded, unformed; in its natural state

ἀποπνίγω, strangle, choke

γέρων, -οντος, ὁ, old man

γηράω (alternative pres. of γηράσκω), grow old

δημιουργέω, fabricate, fashion, construct

διαβοάω, διαβοήσομαι, διεβόησα proclaim, publish; (pass.) be made public, be well known

δοκῶ, (uncontracted = δοκέω) seem; think; expect; δοκῶ μοι, I think; I intend; I am determined, I have resolved (+ inf.)

δράω, do

ἐάω, let alone, let be

ἐντελής, -ές, finished, completed

ἑξήκοντα, indecl., sixty

ἔτι, adv., still, yet, as yet

ἔτος, -ους, τό, year

ἤδη, adv., already, now

καίτοι, conj. + particle, and yet; and indeed, and further, furthermore, moreover

καταδικάζω, condemn person X (gen.) to punishment Y (acc.)

οἶδα, (perf. with pres. meaning) know

ὅς, ἥ, ὅ, rel. pron., who, whose, whom, which, that

οὐδέπω, adv., (and) not yet, not as yet

πάνυ, adv., altogether, entirely; very, exceedingly, too much

πᾶς, πᾶσα, πᾶν, all, every, whole

πατήρ, πατρός, ὁ, father

πηλός, ὁ, clay

πλανάω, make to wander; lead astray; (pass.) wander, roam about

πρᾶγμα, -τος, τό, matter, thing, affair

τοιοῦτος, τοιαύτη, τοιοῦτο, such; τὰ τοιαῦτα, such things as these, suchlike

ὑπέρ, prep. (+ acc.), beyond

φυγή, ἡ, banishment, exile; flight, escape

ὡς, adv., how

[11] "ὅπερ καὶ τὴν θαυμαστὴν σοφίαν τῶν Χριστιανῶν

ἐξέμαθεν, περὶ τὴν Παλαιστίνην τοῖς ἱερεῦσιν καὶ

γραμματεῦσιν αὐτῶν ξυγγενόμενος. καὶ τί γάρ; ἐν βραχεῖ

παῖδας αὐτοὺς ἀπέφηνε, προφήτης καὶ θιασάρχης καὶ

ξυναγωγεὺς καὶ πάντα μόνος αὐτὸς ὤν, καὶ τῶν βίβλων τὰς

μὲν ἐξηγεῖτο καὶ διεσάφει, πολλὰς δὲ αὐτὸς καὶ συνέγραφεν,

καὶ ὡς θεὸν αὐτὸν ἐκεῖνοι ᾐδοῦντο καὶ νομοθέτῃ ἐχρῶντο καὶ

προστάτην ἐπεγράφοντο, μετὰ γοῦν ἐκεῖνον ὃν ἔτι σέβουσι,

τὸν ἄνθρωπον τὸν ἐν τῇ Παλαιστίνῃ ἀνασκολοπισθέντα,

ὅτι καινὴν ταύτην τελετὴν εἰσῆγεν ἐς τὸν βίον.

θαυμαστὴν σοφίαν: most likely meant ironically, though Macleod (271) suggests that Lucian may simply be expressing surprise rather than contempt.　　**τὴν Παλαιστίνην**: sc. γῆν; with regard to Roman rule, Palestine (then called Judea) became a client Kingdom of Rome in 37 BCE, a Roman province in 6 CE, and was joined with the province of Syria in 135 CE (and thereafter officially called Syria Palaestina).　　**τί γάρ**: *how else (could it be)?*, i.e., *of course, naturally.*　　**ἐν βραχεῖ...τὸν βίον**: the second longest sentence in the text, detailing Proteus' instantaneous ascent to the pinnacle of power and authority over the Christians (cf. especially the phrase πάντα μόνος αὐτὸς ὤν, *he himself alone being everything*); the tone is clearly hyperbolic.　　**ἐν βραχεῖ**: since this prep. phrase means both *in a short time / in no time* and *in a few words* (after which more than fifty follow), Lucian is being both literal with respect to Peregrinus' rise to power within Christianity and (gently?) mocking his speaker's prolixity.
ξυναγωγεὺς: if the meaning of the word here is *Head of the synagogue*, then Lucian, like many ancient writers, confused Jews and Christians (see also **LUCIAN AND CHRISTIANITY** in the introductory sections of this edition).　　**τὰς μὲν**: *some* (+ partitive gen.).　　**πολλὰς**: sc. *other books*.　　**νομοθέτῃ ἐχρῶντο** = ἐχρῶντο αὐτῷ ὡς νομοθέτῃ.
προστάτην ἐπεγράφοντο: *they had him entered in the public register as their patron/protector*; a phrase that was applied to resident foreigners in Athens who had to register under a προστάτην.　　**γοῦν**: a restrictive particle γε + a connecting adv. οὖν; *at any rate, to be sure, at least.*

Vocabulary

αἰδέομαι, (dep.) *stand in awe of, fear, respect, revere*

ἀνασκολοπίζω, *fix on a pole* or *stake, impale*; *crucify*

ἄνθρωπος, ὁ, *man, human being*

ἀποφαίνω, ἀποφανῶ, ἀπέφηνα, *make clear that* X (acc.) *(is)* Y (acc.)

βίβλον, τό, *roll, scroll, book*

βίος, ὁ, *life*; *world*

βραχύς, -εῖα, -ύ, *short, brief*; ἐν βραχεῖ, *in a short time*; *in few words, briefly*

γραμματεύς, -έως, ὁ, *scribe, clerk*; *scholar*

διασαφέω, *make quite clear, explain clearly*

εἰσάγω, εἰσάξω, εἰσήγαγον, *lead* or *bring in / into, introduce*

ἐκμανθάνω, ἐκμαθήσομαι, ἐξέμαθον, *learn thoroughly, master completely*

ἐξηγέομαι, (dep.) *expound, interpret*

ἐπιγράφω, *inscribe* ; (mid.) *have one registered as*

ἔτι, adv., *still*

θαυμαστός, -ή, -όν, *wonderful, marvelous*; *extraordinary*; *strange, absurd*

θεός, ὁ, *god*

θιασάρχης, -ου, ὁ, *cult-leader* (originally, *leader of the Bacchic revel*)

ἱερεύς, -έως, ὁ, *priest*

καινός, -ή, -όν, *new*; *innovative*; *novel*; *weird* (in a pejorative sense)

μονός, -ή, -όν, *alone, only, single*

νομοθέτης, -ου, ὁ, *lawgiver*

ξ/συγγίγνομαι, ξ/συγγενήσομαι, ξ/συνεγενόμην, (dep.) *associate with*; (of disciples), *converse (with a master)*

ξ/συναγωγεύς, -έως, ὁ, *convener, uniter*; *Head of the synagogue*

ὅς, ἥ, ὅ, rel. pron., *who, whose, whom, which, that*

ὅτεπερ, (intensive form of ὅτε) *at which time, at that time*

παῖς, παίδος, ὁ or ἡ, *boy, girl, son, daughter, child*

Παλαιστίνος, -η, -ον, *of* or *from Palestine, Palestinian*

περί, prep. (+ acc.), *in, about, around*

προστάτης, -ου, ὁ, *ruler, leader, patron, president*; *champion, protector*

προφήτης, -ου, ὁ, *prophet*

σέβω, *worship*

σοφία, ἡ, *wisdom, insight, intelligence, knowledge*; *philosophy*

συγγράφω, *compose, write*

τελετή, ἡ, *mystic rite, initiation into the mystery religions, cult*

χρῶμαι (uncontracted = χράομαι), χρήσομαι, ἐχρησάμην, *make use of* (+ dat.)

Χριστιανός, ὁ, *Christian*

ὡς, adv., *as, like*

[12] "τότε δὴ καὶ συλληφθεὶς ἐπὶ τούτῳ ὁ Πρωτεὺς ἐνέπεσεν

εἰς τὸ δεσμωτήριον, ὅπερ καὶ αὐτὸ οὐ μικρὸν αὐτῷ ἀξίωμα

περιεποίησεν πρὸς τὸν ἑξῆς βίον καὶ τὴν τερατείαν καὶ

δοξοκοπίαν ὧν ἐρῶν ἐτύγχανεν. ἐπεὶ δ᾽ οὖν ἐδέδετο, οἱ

Χριστιανοὶ συμφορὰν ποιούμενοι τὸ πρᾶγμα πάντα ἐκίνουν

ἐξαρπάσαι πειρώμενοι αὐτόν. εἶτ᾽, ἐπεὶ τοῦτο ἦν ἀδύνατον,

ἥ γε ἄλλη θεραπεία πᾶσα οὐ παρέργως ἀλλὰ σὺν σπουδῇ

ἐγίγνετο· καὶ ἕωθεν μὲν εὐθὺς ἦν ὁρᾶν παρὰ τῷ δεσμωτηρίῳ

συλληφθεὶς: masc. nom. sing. aor. pass. part. < συλλαμβάνω.   **ἐπὶ τούτῳ**: *for this*, i.e., for being a Christian.   **οὐ μικρὸν**: a possible example of *litotes* ("plainness," "simplicity") a rhetorical device in which understatement is employed for rhetorical effect, often via the use of double negatives, with the intention of emphasis; i.e., *no little = quite a bit (of)*.   **τερατείαν**: a τέρας is a *sign, wonder, marvel* (especially of signs / portents in heaven); it is also a *monster* or *monstrosity*; from these definitions a more colloquial usage developed over time, encompassing anything which appeared rather marvelous, such as fairy tales and juggling tricks. From these, in turn, come the definitions of τερατεία which seem to be in play here: *charlatanism, performing hocus-pocus, the art of clap-trap*.   **ὧν**: the case of the rel. pron. is governed by ἐρῶν.   **ἐδέδετο**: 3rd sing. pluperf. mid./pass. indic. < δέω.   **ἐγίγνετο**: sc. αὐτῷ.   **ἦν ὁρᾶν**: *it was possible to see*; the 3rd sing. imperfect of εἰμί in this sense is from impersonal ἔστι (*it is possible*).

30

Vocabulary

ἀδύνατος, -ον, *impossible*

ἀλλός, -ή, -ό, *another, other*

ἀξίωμα, -ατος, τό, *reputation, honor*

βίος, ὁ, *life; career*

γε, particle, *at least, at any rate; namely, that is, indeed*

γίγνομαι, γενήσομαι, ἐγενόμην, (dep.) *become, be*

δεσμωτήριον, τό, *prison*

δέω, *bind, tie, enchain; put in prison*

δή, particle, *indeed; in fact; then, therefore, now*

δοξοκοπία, ἡ, *thirst for fame* or *popularity*

ἐμπίπτω, ἐμπεσοῦμαι, ἐνέπεσον, *fall into*; (of prison or punishment with pass. sense) *be thrown into*

ἐξαρπάζω, *rescue*

ἐξῆς, adv., *future, next*

ἐπί, prep. (+ dat.), *for*

ἐράω, *love* or *desire (passionately)* (+ gen.)

εὐθύς, adv., *immediately, at once; straight, directly*

ἔωθεν, adv., *at earliest dawn, from the break of dawn*

θεραπεία, ἡ, *attention, care, service*

κινέω, *move, set in motion*; + πάντα, *move heaven and earth, leave nothing undone*

μικρός, -ά, -ό, *little, small*

ὁράω, ὄψομαι, εἶδον, *see*

ὅς, ἥ, ὅ, rel. pron., *who, whose, whom, which, that*

ὅσπερ, ἥπερ, ὅπερ, rel. pron., emphatic forms, *who, whose, whom, which, that*

πᾶς, πᾶσα, πᾶν, *all, every, whole*

παρά, (+ dat.) *at, near, by*

παρέργως, adv., *desultorily, halfheartedly*

πειράομαι, πειράσομαι, ἐπειράθην, *attempt, endeavor, try* (often + inf.)

περιποιέω, *procure, secure, achieve*

ποιέω, *make, produce, create*; (mid.) *regard, consider, reckon X* (acc.) *(as) Y* (acc.)

πρᾶγμα, -τος, τό, *matter, thing, affair*

πρός, prep. (+ acc.), *for*

σπουδή, ἡ, *zeal, effort, passion, eagerness, assiduousness, haste*

συλλαμβάνω, συλλήψομαι, συνέλαβον, *arrest, seize*

συμφορά, ἡ, *disaster, catastrophe*

τερατεία, ἡ, *charlatanism, performing hocus-pocus, the art of clap-trap*

τότε, adv., *then, at that time*

τυγχάνω, τεύξομαι, ἔτυχον, *happen* (+ supplementary participle)

περιμένοντα γρᾴδια χήρας τινὰς καὶ παιδία ὀρφανά,

οἱ δὲ ἐν τέλει αὐτῶν καὶ συνεκάθευδον ἔνδον μετ' αὐτοῦ

διαφθείραντες τοὺς δεσμοφύλακας. εἶτα δεῖπνα ποικίλα

εἰσεκομίζετο καὶ λόγοι ἱεροὶ αὐτῶν ἐλέγοντο, καὶ

ὁ βέλτιστος Περεγρῖνος — ἔτι γὰρ τοῦτο ἐκαλεῖτο —

καινὸς Σωκράτης ὑπ' αὐτῶν ὠνομάζετο.

χήρας τινὰς: in apposition to γρᾴδια. English would combine the two nouns into an adj.-noun phrase; i.e., *certain old widows*. **δεῖπνα ποικίλα εἰσεκομίζετο**: a neut. pl. subj. normally takes a sing. verb. **εἰσεκομίζετο, ἐλέγοντο**: sc. αὐτῷ in each case. **ὁ βέλτιστος**: see 1. **καινὸς Σωκράτης**: Jones (122), notes that some Christian apologists (e.g., Athenagoras and Justin) considered Socrates' fate as prefiguring that of Jesus and his followers.

[13] "καὶ μὴν κἀκ τῶν ἐν Ἀσίᾳ πόλεων ἔστιν ὧν ἧκόν τινες,

τῶν Χριστιανῶν στελλόντων ἀπὸ τοῦ κοινοῦ, βοηθήσοντες

καὶ συναγορεύσοντες καὶ παραμυθησόμενοι τὸν ἄνδρα.

ἀμήχανον δέ τι τὸ τάχος ἐπιδείκνυνται, ἐπειδάν τι τοιοῦτον

γένηται δημόσιον· ἐν βραχεῖ γὰρ ἀφειδοῦσι πάντων.

κἀκ: crasis of καί ἐκ. **ἔστιν ὧν**: literally, *of which things there are*; an idiom meaning *some*, modifying πόλεων; such cities included Ephesus and Smyrna, which had relatively large Christian communities at this time. **τῶν Χριστιανῶν στελλόντων**. gen. abs.; στελλόντων = *sending (them) out provisioned*. **βοηθήσοντες, συναγορεύσοντες, παραμυθησόμενοι**: the fut. part., with or without ὡς, can express purpose. **ἐπειδάν**: ἐπειδή + ἄν, *when(ever)* + subju. **δημόσιον**: *common to* or *shared by* (sc. members of their group). **ἐν βραχεῖ**: either *in a short time*, i.e., *in no time*, or *in short*, i.e., *to put in succinctly*. **ἀφειδοῦσι πάντων**: cf. the English expression, *they spare nothing*, which reverses the respective meanings of the Greek verb and noun.

Vocabulary

ἀμήχανος, -ον, *extraordinary, incredible*

ἀνήρ, ἀνδρός, ὁ, *man*

Ἀσία, ἡ, *Asia* (i.e., modern-day Western Asia Minor)

ἀφειδέω, *do not spare, lavish* (+ gen.)

βέλτιστος, -η, -ον, *best, very good*; (as mode of address) *(my) good friend*

βοηθέω, *help, aid, assist*

βραχύς, -εῖα, -ύ, *short, brief*; ἐν βραχεῖ, *in a short time*; *in few words, briefly*

γίγνομαι, γενήσομαι, ἐγενόμην, (dep.) *become*

γρᾴδιον, τό, (diminutive of γραῖα) *(little) old woman*

δεῖπνον, τό, *meal, food*

δεσμοφύλαξ, -ακος, ὁ, *prison guard*

δημόσιος, -ον, *common, shared*

διαφθείρω, διαφθερῶ, διέφθειρα, *corrupt with bribes, bribe*

εἰσκομίζω, *bring in*

ἔνδον, adv., *within, inside*

ἐπιδείκνυμι, (mid. is more common, with same meaning) *exhibit, show, display*

ἥκω, (imperf.) ἧκον, (pres. = perf.; imperf. = pluperf.) *have come*

ἱερός, -ά, -όν, *holy, sacred*

καινός, -ή, -όν, *new*

καλέω, *call, call in, summon*

κοινός, -ή, -όν, *shared, common*; τὸ κοινόν, *shared or common funds*

λέγω, ἐρῶ, εἶπον, *say, speak, tell*

λόγος, ὁ, *story, narrative*

μήν, adv., *indeed, truly*

ὀνομάζω, *name, call*

ὀρφανός, -ή, -όν, *orphan*

παιδίον, τό, (diminutive of παῖς) *(little or young) child*

παραμυθέομαι, (dep.) *console, comfort*

περιμένω, περιμενῶ, περιέμεινα, *wait, wait for*

ποικίλος, -η, -ον, *various, diverse, elaborate*

πόλις, πόλεως, ἡ, *city, city-state*

στέλλω, στελῶ, ἔστειλα, *equip; send*

συγκαθεύδω, συγκαθευδήσω, (no aor. in Attic Greek), *sleep with*

συναγορεύω, *support, speak on behalf of someone*

τάχος, -ους, τό, *speed, quickness*

τέλος, -ους, τό, *end; magistracy, office*; οἱ ἐν τέλει, *magistrates, officials*

τοιοῦτος, τοιαύτη, τοιοῦτο, *such*

χήρα, ἡ, *widow*

καὶ δὴ καὶ τῷ Περεγρίνῳ πολλὰ τότε ἧκεν χρήματα παρ᾽
αὐτῶν ἐπὶ προφάσει τῶν δεσμῶν, καὶ πρόσοδον οὐ μικρὰν
ταύτην ἐποιήσατο. πεπείκασι γὰρ αὐτοὺς οἱ κακοδαίμονες
τὸ μὲν ὅλον ἀθάνατοι ἔσεσθαι καὶ βιώσεσθαι τὸν ἀεὶ χρόνον,
παρ᾽ ὃ καὶ καταφρονοῦσιν τοῦ θανάτου καὶ ἑκόντες αὐτοὺς
ἐπιδιδόασιν οἱ πολλοί. ἔπειτα δὲ ὁ νομοθέτης ὁ πρῶτος
ἔπεισεν αὐτοὺς ὡς ἀδελφοὶ πάντες εἶεν ἀλλήλων,
ἐπειδὰν ἅπαξ παραβάντες θεοὺς μὲν τοὺς Ἑλληνικοὺς
ἀπαρνήσωνται, τὸν δὲ ἀνεσκολοπισμένον ἐκεῖνον σοφιστὴν
αὐτὸν προσκυνῶσιν καὶ κατὰ τοὺς ἐκείνου νόμους βιῶσιν.

καὶ δὴ καὶ: *and what is more, and in particular.*   **οὐ μικρὰν**:
possible *litotes* (see 12).   **πεπείκασι**: 3rd pl. perf. act. indic. < πείθω.
αὐτοὺς = ἑαυτούς.   **οἱ κακοδαίμονες**: cf. 1, where the same word
was used of Peregrinus.   **ἔσεσθαι**: fut. mid. (dep.) inf. < εἰμί.   **παρ᾽
ὃ**: *on account of which.*   **ἑκόντες**: adj. as adv.   **αὐτοὺς
ἐπιδιδόασιν**: sc. *into custody* (Harmon) or *up to it* (i.e., death; Casson).
οἱ πολλοί: *the majority.*   **ὁ νομοθέτης ὁ πρῶτος**: i.e., Jesus.
(or, less likely, St. Paul).   **ἀδελφοὶ πάντες εἶεν ἀλλήλων**: cf.
Matthew 23:8, πάντες δὲ ὑμεῖς ἀδελφοί ἐστε.   **εἶεν**: 3rd pl. pres.
opt. < εἰμί; opt. in indir. statement in secondary sequence after ὡς. Jesus'
actual words in dir. discourse would have been ἀδελφοὶ πάντες ἐστε
ἀλλήλων.   **ἐπειδάν**: ἐπειδὴ + ἄν, *when(ever)* (+ subju.); note the
difference in aspect between the three subjunctives that are dependent on
this modal: ἀπαρνήσωνται (aor.) προσκυνῶσιν (pres.), and βιῶσιν
(pres.).   **σοφιστὴν**: the term in this context can possibly be interpreted
three different ways: (1) (pejorative) a *sophist*, i.e., a cheat or fraud who
peddles "wisdom" without truly possessing any; (2) and (3) (either neutral
or complimentary) a *(skilled) practioner* or *teacher of wisdom*. Macleod
prefers (2) and (3), though (1) seems more likely, especially considering
that the only other time this word is employed in this text is with reference
to Peregrinus as he is about to commit suicide (32). Also consider the
adjectives paired with each of these occurences, both of which carry rather
negative connotations: *that crucified sophist* (13) and *to the death-fixated
sophist* (32). Lastly, Lucian in general has a low opinion of sophists.

Vocabulary

ἀδελφός, ὁ, brother

ἀεί, adv., always; ὁ ἀεί χρόνος, eternity, forever

ἀθάνατος, -ον, immortal

ἀλλήλων, of one another

ἀνασκολοπίζω, fix on a pole or stake, impale; crucify

ἅπαξ, adv., once, once for all

ἀπαρνέομαι, (dep.) deny, deny utterly; reject

βιόω, βιώσομαι, ἐβίωσα / ἐβίων (2nd aor.), live

δεσμός, ὁ, bond, chain; (pl.) bonds, chains, imprisonment

ἑκών, ἑκοῦσα, ἑκόν, willingly, of free will, readily, voluntarily

Ἑλληνικός, -ή, -όν, Greek, Hellenic

ἐπιδίδωμι, ἐπιδώσω, ἐπιέδωκα, give freely; give into (another's hands), deliver

ἥκω, (imperf.) ἧκον, (pres. = perf.; imperf. = pluperf.) have come

θάνατος, ὁ, death

θεός, ὁ, god

κακοδαίμων (gen., κακοδαίμονος), possessed by an evil spirit, unlucky, wretched

καταφρονέω, despise, think lightly of (+ gen.)

μικρός, -ά, -ό, little, small

νομοθέτης, -ου, ὁ, lawgiver

νόμος, ὁ, law

ὅλος, -η, -ον, whole, entire; τὸ ὅλον, wholly, entirely

ὅς, ἥ, ὅ, rel. pron., who, whose, whom, which, that

παρά, prep. (+ gen.), from

παραβαίνω, παραβήσομαι, παρέβην, transgress, sin against

πείθω, πείσω, ἔπεισα, persuade, convince

ποιέω, make, produce, create; do; (mid.) procure for oneself, gain

προσκυνέω, worship

πρόσοδος, ἡ, revenue, income

πρόφασις, -εως, ἡ, pretext; cause; ἐπὶ προφάσει, because of, on account of

πρῶτος, -η, -ον, first

σοφιστής, -οῦ, ὁ, sophist

τότε, adv., then, at that time

χρῆμα, -ατος, τό, thing; (pl.) money, goods

χρόνος, ὁ, time

ὡς, conj., (= ὅτι) that

καταφρονοῦσιν οὖν ἁπάντων ἐξ ἴσης καὶ κοινὰ ἡγοῦνται,

ἄνευ τινὸς ἀκριβοῦς πίστεως τὰ τοιαῦτα παραδεξάμενοι.

ἢν τοίνυν παρέλθῃ τις εἰς αὐτοὺς γόης καὶ τεχνίτης

ἄνθρωπος καὶ πράγμασιν χρῆσθαι δυνάμενος, αὐτίκα μάλα

πλούσιος ἐν βραχεῖ ἐγένετο ἰδιώταις ἀνθρώποις ἐγχανών.

ἁπάντων: *all things*; i.e., all of their material possessions. κοινὰ
ἡγοῦνται = ἡγοῦνται (αὐτὰ εἶναι) κοινά. Christian views on the value
and use of material possessions in large part resonated with the
philosophical tenets of Cynicism (cf. 15); another reason, perhaps, why
Peregrinus was able so easily to switch back and forth between Christianity
and Cynicism. πίστεως: *proof*; the irony is that this word also means
faith, belief, trust – which is how the Christians would have understood it.
τὰ τοιαῦτα: i.e., doctrines or teachings. ἢν: contracted form of ἐάν,
which itself is crasis of εἰ ἄν, *if ever* (+ subju.); this is a present general
condition (παρέλθῃ: 3rd sing. aor. act. subju. < παρέρχομαι [the protasis,
or 'if' clause] + ἐγένετο: gnomic aor. [translated as pres. in apodosis;
Smyth 2338]); i.e., *if someone (ever) comes... he (always) becomes...*
ἄνθρωπος: when joined with another substantive in Attic Greek it
frequently conveys a contemptuous sense (so too ἀνθρώποις in the
following clause). πράγμασιν χρῆσθαι: literally, *to make use of
the circumstances* or *situation*, i.e., *to seize any opportunity*. ἰδιώταις:
where our word "idiot" comes from; a meaning – especially bolstered by
ἀνθρώποις – not too far from the speaker's intention here (see also 18).

---

[14] "πλὴν ἀλλ' ὁ Περεγρῖνος ἀφείθη ὑπὸ τοῦ τότε τῆς

Συρίας ἄρχοντος, ἀνδρὸς φιλοσοφίᾳ χαίροντος, ὃς συνεὶς

τὴν ἀπόνοιαν αὐτοῦ καὶ ὅτι δέξαιτ' ἂν ἀποθανεῖν ὡς δόξαν

ἀφείθη: 3rd sing. aor. pass. indic. < ἀφίημι. ὑπό: + gen. of agent
with pass. voice. ἀνδρὸς, χαίροντος: genitives in apposition to
τοῦ ἄρχοντος. συνεὶς: masc. nom. sing. aor. act. part. < συνίημι.
δέξαιτ': 3rd sing. aor. mid. opt. < δέχομαι; opt. in secondary sequence
after ὅτι. ὡς: + subju. or opt. = a final/purpose clause; i.e., *so that, in
order that*.

Vocabulary

ἀκριβής, -ές, *exact, accurate, precise*; *definite*

ἄνευ, prep. (+ gen.), *without*

ἀνήρ, ἀνδρός, ὁ, *man*

ἄνθρωπος, ὁ, *man, human being*

ἅπας, ἅπασα, ἅπαν, *all*; *every*; *whole*

ἀποθνήσκω, ἀποθανοῦμαι, ἀπέθανον, *die*

ἀπόνοια, ἡ, *madness; recklessness; rebellion; desperation*

ἄρχων, -οντος, ὁ, *governor*

αὐτίκα, adv., *at once*

ἀφίημι, ἀφήσω, ἀφῆκα, *let go, set free*

βραχύς, -εῖα, -ύ, *short, brief*; ἐν βραχεῖ, *in a short time, in no time*

γίγνομαι, γενήσομαι, ἐγενόμην, (dep.) *become*

γόης, -ητος, ὁ, *charlatan, con artist; sorcerer, wizard*

δέχομαι, (dep.) *take, accept, receive*; *prefer* (+ inf.)

δόξα, ἡ, *honor, glory, reputation*

δύναμαι, (dep.) *be able, can* (+ inf.)

ἐγχάσκω, ἐγχανοῦμαι, ἐγχανεῖν, *laugh* or *scoff at* (+ dat.)

ἡγέομαι, (dep.) *believe, consider*

ἰδιώτης, -ου, ὁ, *simple, average,* or *ignorant person/citizen*

ἴσος, -η, -ον, *equal, the same*; ἐξ ἴσης, *equally*

καταφρονέω, *despise, think lightly of* (+ gen.)

κοινός, -ή, -όν, *shared, common*

μάλα, adv., *very, very much, exceedingly*

παραδέχομαι, (dep.) *receive, accept; recognize as correct*

παρέρχομαι, πάρειμι, παρῆλθον, *come (among)*

πίστις, -εως, ἡ, *proof*

πλήν, conj., (+ ἀλλά is a Koine Greek construction) *however, but, as it happened*

πλούσιος, -α, -ον, *wealthy*

πρᾶγμα, -τος, τό, *matter, thing, affair*; (pl.) *circumstances, situation*

συνίημι, συνήσω, συνῆκα, *perceive, hear; understand*

Συρία, ἡ, *Syria*

τεχνίτης, -ου, ὁ, *trickster*

τοίνυν, particle, *therefore, accordingly; moreover*

τοιοῦτος, τοιαύτη, τοιοῦτο, *such*; τὰ τοιαῦτα, *such things as these*

τότε, adv., *then, at that time*

φιλοσοφία, ἡ, *philosophy*

χαίρω, *take pleasure in* (+ dat.)

χρῶμαι (uncontracted = χράομαι), χρήσομαι, ἐχρησάμην, *make use of* (+ dat.)

ἐπὶ τούτῳ ἀπολίποι, ἀφῆκεν αὐτὸν οὐδὲ τῆς κολάσεως

ὑπολαβὼν ἄξιον. ὁ δὲ εἰς τὴν οἰκείαν ἐπανελθὼν

καταλαμβάνει τὸ περὶ τοῦ πατρῴου φόνου ἔτι φλεγμαῖνον

καὶ πολλοὺς τοὺς ἐπανατεινομένους τὴν κατηγορίαν.

διήρπαστο δὲ τὰ πλεῖστα τῶν κτημάτων παρὰ τὴν

ἀποδημίαν αὐτοῦ καὶ μόνοι ὑπελείποντο οἱ ἀγροὶ ὅσον εἰς

πεντεκαίδεκα τάλαντα. ἦν γὰρ ἡ πᾶσα οὐσία τριάκοντά

που ταλάντων ἀξία ἦν ὁ γέρων κατέλιπεν, οὐχ ὥσπερ

ὁ παγγέλοιος Θεαγένης ἔλεγε πεντακισχιλίων· τοσούτου

γὰρ οὐδὲ ἡ πᾶσα τῶν Παριανῶν πόλις πέντε σὺν αὐτῇ

ἐπὶ τούτῳ: *for this (thing)*; i.e., *a reputation* (δόξαν) for being a martyr willing to die for his beliefs.   **ἀπολίποι**: 3rd sing. aor. act. opt. < ἀπολείπω; opt. in final/purpose clause in secondary sequence.   **οὐδέ**: *not even*.   **ὑπολαβών**: sc. αὐτὸν as dir. obj.   **κολάσεως**: the usual punishment would have been to receive a public flogging.   **τὴν οἰκείαν**: sc. γῆν.   **τὸ**: *the matter*.   **τοὺς ἐπανατεινομένους τὴν κατηγορίαν**: literally, *who were holding out over (him) the charge (of murder)*, i.e., *who were threatening to bring the charge of murder against him*.   **διήρπαστο**: 3rd sing. pluperf. mid./pass. indic. < διαρπάζω; the subj. is τὰ πλεῖστα τῶν κτημάτων.   **ὅσον εἰς**: *as much as an amount (equal to)*, i.e., *valued at*.   **πεντεκαίδεκα τάλαντα**: *c.* $400,000 in today's terms.   **τοσούτου**: gen. of value or price.   **ἡ πᾶσα τῶν Παριανῶν πόλις πέντε**: note the alliteration, emphasizing the speaker's utter astonishment at Theagenes' lie. Harmon (17, n. 2), however, notes that, "Parium was a small (but not so contemptible) Greek town on the Hellespont, site of a Roman colony since Augustus." In fact, the speaker's diminishment of Peregrinus' hometown can be seen as a rhetorically exaggerated counterpunch to Theagenes' lie.   **πέντε**: sc. πόλεις; the phrase goes with τὰς γειτνιώσας.

Vocabulary

ἀγρός, ὁ, *field, farm, land*

ἄξιος, -α, -ον, *worth, worthy of, deserving of, fitting* (+ gen. or inf.)

ἀποδημία, ἡ, *being abroad, being away*

ἀπολείπω, ἀπολείψω, ἀπέλιπον, *leave behind*

ἀφίημι, ἀφήσω, ἀφῆκα, *let go, set free*

γέρων, -οντος, ὁ, *old man*

διαρπάζω, *carry off, seize as plunder*

ἐπανέρχομαι, ἐπάνειμι, ἐπανῆλθον, *return, come back*

ἐπανατείνω, ἐπανατενῶ, ἐπανέτεινα, *stretch out and hold up, hold out*;
   (mid.) *hold over as a threat, threaten* someone (dat.) *with* something (acc.)

καταλαμβάνω, καταλήψομαι, κατέλαβον, *find, learn*

καταλείπω, καταλείψω, κατέλιπον, *leave, leave behind*

κατηγορία, ἡ, *accusation, charge*

κόλασις, -εως, ἡ, *punishment*

κτῆμα, -ατος, τό, *possession, piece of property*

λέγω, ἐρῶ, εἶπον, *say, speak, tell*

μονός, -ή, -όν, *only*

οἰκεῖος, -α, -ον, *in* or *of the house; one's own*

ὅσος, -η, -ον, *as great as, as much as*; (pl.) *as many as*

οὐσία, ἡ, *property*

παγγέλοιος, -ον, *utterly ridiculous*

παρά, prep. (+ acc.), *throughout, during*

Παριάνος, -α, -ον, *Parian*

πατρῷος, -α, -ον, *of one's father*

πεντακισχίλιοι, -αι, -α, *five thousand*

πέντε, indecl., *five*

πεντεκαίδεκα, indecl., *fifteen*

πλεῖστος, -η, -ον, *most, greatest, largest*; τὰ πλεῖστα, *the vast majority*

που, adv., *somewhere, around, perhaps*

σύν, prep. (+ dat.), *with*

τάλαντον, -ου, τό, *talent* (a weight and a sum of money = 6,000 drachmas)

τοσοῦτος, -αύτη, -οῦτον, *so much, so great*; (pl.) *so many*

τριάκοντα, indecl., *thirty*

ὑπολαμβάνω, ὑπολήψομαι, ὑπέλαβον, *consider, suppose*

ὑπολείπω, ὑπολείψω, ὑπέλιπον, *leave remaining*

φλεγμαίνω, *be heated, inflamed, fester*

φόνος, ὁ, *murder, homicide*

ὥσπερ, adv., *as, like, just as*

τὰς γειτνιώσας παραλαβοῦσα πραθείη ἂν αὐτοῖς ἀνθρώποις καὶ βοσκήμασιν καὶ τῇ λοιπῇ παρασκευῇ.

πραθείη: 3rd sing. aor. pass. opt. < πέρνημι / πιπράσκω; a potential opt. **αὐτοῖς ἀνθρώποις, βοσκήμασιν, τῇ λοιπῇ παρασκευῇ**: the datives are either of accompaniment, i.e., *together with*, or dependent on σὺν from earlier in the sentence.

[15] ἀλλ᾽ ἔτι γε ἡ κατηγορία καὶ τὸ ἔγκλημα θερμὸν ἦν, καὶ ἐῴκει οὐκ εἰς μακρὰν ἐπαναστήσεσθαί τις αὐτῷ, καὶ μάλιστα ὁ δῆμος αὐτὸς ἠγανάκτει, χρηστόν, ὡς ἔφασαν οἱ ἰδόντες, γέροντα πενθοῦντες οὕτως ἀσεβῶς ἀπολωλότα. ὁ δὲ σοφὸς οὗτος Πρωτεὺς πρὸς ἅπαντα ταῦτα σκέψασθε οἷόν τι ἐξεῦρεν καὶ ὅπως τὸν κίνδυνον διέφυγεν. παρελθὼν γὰρ εἰς τὴν ἐκκλησίαν τῶν Παριανῶν — ἐκόμα δὲ ἤδη καὶ

θερμὸν: i.e., a "hot" issue or topic.   **ἐῴκει**: 3rd sing. pluperf. (imperf. in sense) act. indic. < ἔοικα; the subj. is τις and the verb takes the fut. inf.; i.e., *and someone was likely...*   **οὐκ εἰς μακρὰν**: *shortly, before long, fairly soon.*   **ἐπαναστήσεσθαί**: fut. mid. inf. < ἐπανίστημι. **χρηστόν, γέροντα, ἀπολωλότα**: the dispersion of the modifiers of the acc. dir. obj. γέροντα intensifies the focus on Peregrinus' father as victim: *a good (man)..., an old man..., one who died so impiously...*   **οἱ ἰδόντες**: sc. *him.*   **πενθοῦντες**: modifies ὁ δῆμος; the pl. is due either to attraction to a somewhat different (but possibly related) subj., οἱ ἰδόντες, or to ὁ δῆμος being thought of (naturally) as a plurality. **ἀπολωλότα**: masc. acc. sing. perf. act. part. < ἀπόλλυμι.   **ὁ δὲ σοφὸς οὗτος Πρωτεὺς πρὸς ἅπαντα ταῦτα σκέψασθε οἷόν τι ἐξεῦρεν**: note the unusual word order (even for Greek), thus highlighting Proteus and his predicament. English word order = δὲ σκέψασθε οἷόν τι οὗτος ὁ σοφὸς Πρωτεὺς ἐξεῦρεν πρὸς ἅπαντα ταῦτα.   **πρὸς ἅπαντα ταῦτα**: *in the face of / in response to all these things.*   **σκέψασθε**: 2nd pl. aor. mid. (dep.) imper. < σκέπτομαι.

Vocabulary

ἀγανακτέω, *be angry*

ἅπας, ἅπασα, ἅπαν, *all; every; whole*

ἀπόλλυμι, ἀπολῶ, ἀπώλεσα, *destroy utterly, kill, slay*

ἀσεβῶς, adv., *impiously*

βόσκημα, -ατος, τό, *cattle*

γε, particle, *at least, at any rate; namely, that is, indeed*

γειτνιάω, *be a neighbor, be adjacent, border on*

γέρων, -οντος, ὁ, *old man*

δῆμος, ὁ, *the people, the common people*

διαφεύγω, διαφεύξομαι, διέφυγεν, *escape*

ἔγκλημα, -ατος, τό, *legal complaint; accusation, charge*

ἐκκλησία, ἡ, *assembly of the citizens, legislative assembly*

ἐξευρίσκω, ἐξευρήσω, ἐξεῦρον, *discover, invent*

ἔοικα, (perf. with pres. sense) *be like, seem; (3rd sing.) it seems, it is probable*

ἐπανίστημι, ἐπαναστήσω, ἐπανέστησα, *set up again; (mid./pass.) rise up against* (+ dat.)

ἤδη, adv., *by this time, by now*

θερμός, -ή, -όν, *hot, warm; still warm, fresh*

κατηγορία, ἡ, *accusation, charge*

κίνδυνος, ὁ, *danger*

κομάω, *wear long hair, let one's hair grow long*

λοιπός, -ή, -όν, *remaining, the rest*

μακρός, -ά, -όν, *long; large; great; (fem. acc. sing. as adv.) long time*

μάλιστα, adv., *most, most of all, very much, especially, too much*

οἷος, οἵα, οἷον, rel. pron., *such as, of what sort;* οἷόν τι, *what sort of thing*

ὅπως, adv., *how*

οὕτως, adv., *so, thus; as follows*

παραλάμβανω, παραλήψομαι, παρέλαβον, *take, receive, accept, take charge of*

παρασκευή, ἡ, *equipment, belongings*

παρέρχομαι, πάρειμι, παρῆλθον, (+εἰς) *come forward to speak to, arrive at*

πενθέω, *mourn for, lament*

πέρνημι / πιπράσκω (later form found in Lucian), *sell*

σκέπτομαι, σκέψομαι, ἐσκεψάμην, (dep.) *consider or examine (carefully)*

σοφός, -ή, -όν, *subtle, ingenious, clever; wise*

φημί, φήσω, ἔφην (imperf.), ἔφησα (aor., rare), *say*

χρηστός, -ή, -όν, *good, honest, worthy*

ὡς, adv., *as, so*

τρίβωνα πιναρὸν ἠμπείχετο καὶ πήραν παρήρτητο καὶ τὸ

ξύλον ἐν τῇ χειρὶ ἦν, καὶ ὅλως μάλα τραγικῶς ἐσκεύαστο —

τοιοῦτος οὖν ἐπιφανεὶς αὐτοῖς ἀφεῖναι ἔφη τὴν οὐσίαν ἣν

ὁ μακαρίτης πατήρ αὐτῷ κατέλιπεν δημοσίαν εἶναι πᾶσαν.

τοῦτο ὡς ἤκουσεν ὁ δῆμος, πένητες ἄνθρωποι καὶ πρὸς

διανομὰς κεχηνότες, ἀνέκραγον εὐθὺς ἕνα φιλόσοφον, ἕνα

φιλόπατριν, ἕνα Διογένους καὶ Κράτητος ζηλωτήν. οἱ δὲ

ἐχθροὶ ἐπεφίμωντο, κἂν εἴ τις ἐπιχειρήσειεν μεμνῆσθαι

παρήρτητο: 3rd sing. imperf. pass. indic. < παραρτάομαι.   **ὅλως μάλα τραγικῶς**: Peregrinus' appearance imitated that of tragic actors; i.e., it was contrived in such a way to elicit a certain response on the part of the viewer. The two intensive adverbs (ὅλως μάλα) simply take that intention – at least in the eyes of the speaker – to a much higher (practically absurd) level as Peregrinus is revealed as the consummate performer clearly affecting the guise of the Cynic philosopher in both his accoutrements (dirty cloak, leather pouch, walking stick) and his physical grooming (long hair). **ἐσκεύαστο**: 3rd sing. pluperf. mid./pass. indic. < σκευάζω. **τοιοῦτος**: *(as) such a person*; i.e., as one outfitted in such a manner. **ἐπιφανεὶς**: masc. nom. sing. aor. pass. part. < ἐπιφαίνω; ironic, since the word suggests a divine epiphany.   **ἀφεῖναι ἔφη**: indir. statement, in (for English) reverse order; i.e., ἔφη ἀφεῖναι.   **ἀφεῖναι**: aor. act. inf. < ἀφίημι.   **κεχηνότες**: masc. nom. pl. perf. act. part. < χάσκω. **ἕνα φιλόσοφον, ἕνα φιλόπατριν, ἕνα, ζηλωτήν**: accusatives in indir. statement with an understood εἶναι.   **ἕνα**: i.e., *one and only*. **Διογένους καὶ Κράτητος**: Diogenes (*c.* 412 – 323 BCE) was one of the founders of the Cynic school of philosophy (see 5 and note ad loc.); Crates of Thebes (*c.* 365 – *c.* 285 BCE) was a Cynic philosopher and, possibly, Diogenes' student. After giving away all that he had, Crates lived a life of poverty on the streets of Athens. He was the teacher of Zeno of Citium (*c.* 334 – *c.* 262 BCE), the founder of the Stoic school of philosophy. **ἐπεφίμωντο**: 3rd pl. pluperf. mid./pass. indic. < φιμόω.   **κἂν**: crasis of καί ἄν.   **ἐπιχειρήσειεν**: 3rd sing. aor. act. opt. < ἐπιχειρέω; the opt. is here used in a past general condition, i.e., *if anyone (ever) tried...* **μεμνῆσθαι**: perf. mid./pass. inf. < μιμνήσκω; the perf. of this verb is used in a pres. sense.

Vocabulary

ἀμπέχω, ἀμφέξω, ἤμπεσχον, *put on/round*; (mid.) *put round oneself, wear*

ἀνακράζω, *cry out, shout*

ἄνθρωπος, ὁ, *man, human being*

ἀφίημι, ἀφήσω, ἀφῆκα, *let go, relinquish, bequeath*

δῆμος, ὁ, *the people, the common people*

δημόσιος, -α, -ον, *belonging to the people*

διανομή, ἡ, *distribution, largess*

Διογένης, -ους, ὁ, *Diogenes*

εἷς, μία, ἕν, *one*

ἐπιφαίνω, ἐπιφανῶ, ἐπέφηνα, *display*; (pass.) *come suddenly into view, present oneself, show oneself, appear* (often of divine epiphanies)

ἐπιχειρέω, *try to, attempt to* (+ inf.)

ἐχθρός, ὁ, *enemy*

ζηλωτής, -οῦ, ὁ, *follower; rival*

καταλείπω, καταλείψω, κατέλιπον, *leave, leave behind*

Κράτης, -ητος, ὁ, *Crates*

μακαρίτης, ὁ, *one blessed, i.e., dead* (especially of one lately dead); (+ πατήρ, functions as an adj.) *recently deceased, late*

μάλα, adv., *very, very much, exceedingly*

μιμνήσκω, *remind*; (mid./pass.) *mention, make mention of* (+ gen.)

ξύλον, τό, *piece of wood, staff*

ὅλως, adv., *on the whole, generally speaking, in short*

οὐσία, ἡ, *property*

παραρτάομαι, (dep.) *have X* (acc.) *hung by one's side*

πατήρ, πατρός, ὁ, *father*

πένης, -ητος, ὁ, *poor person*; as adj. (when preceding another noun), *poor*

πήρα, ἡ, *leather pouch, wallet*

πιναρός, -ά, -όν, *dirty, squalid*

σκευάζω, *outfit, dress up*; (pass.) *be outfitted, dressed up,* or *fully accoutred*

τραγικῶς, adv., *in tragic style* or *getup*

τρίβων, -ωνος, ὁ, *threadbare cloak, worn out garment*

φημί, φήσω, ἔφην (imperf.), ἔφησα (aor., rare), *say*

φιλόπατρις, -ιδος, (acc. φιλόπατριν) ὁ or ἡ, *patriot*

φιλόσοφος, ὁ, *philosopher*

φιμόω, *muzzle, make silent*

χάσκω, χανοῦμαι, ἔχανον, *open one's mouth (in eager expectation), gape*

χείρ, χειρός, ἡ, *hand*

ὡς, conj., (+ aor. indic.) *when, after*

τοῦ φόνου, λίθοις εὐθὺς ἐβάλλετο.

[16] "ἐξῄει οὖν τὸ δεύτερον πλανησόμενος, ἱκανὰ ἐφόδια
τοὺς Χριστιανοὺς ἔχων, ὑφ' ὧν δορυφορούμενος ἐν ἅπασιν
ἀφθόνοις ἦν. καὶ χρόνον μέν τινα οὕτως ἐβόσκετο· εἶτα
παρανομήσας τι καὶ ἐς ἐκείνους — ὤφθη γάρ τι, ὡς οἶμαι,
ἐσθίων τῶν ἀπορρήτων αὐτοῖς — οὐκέτι προσιεμένων αὐτὸν
ἀπορούμενος ἐκ παλινῳδίας ἀπαιτεῖν ᾤετο δεῖν παρὰ τῆς
πόλεως τὰ κτήματα, καὶ γραμματεῖον ἐπιδοὺς ἠξίου ταῦτα
κομίσασθαι κελεύσαντος βασιλέως. εἶτα τῆς πόλεως
ἀντιπρεσβευσαμένης οὐδὲν ἐπράχθη, ἀλλ' ἐμμένειν

ἐξῄει: 3rd sing. imperf. act. indic. < ἐξέρχομαι.   πλανησόμενος:
the fut. part., with or without ὡς, can express purpose.   ἱκανὰ ἐφόδια
τοὺς Χριστιανοὺς ἔχων: literally, *having the Christians (as)
sufficient travel expenses*; i.e., *depending on the Christians for all his travel
expenses*.   χρόνον, τινα: acc. of duration of time; i.e., *for a time*.
ὤφθη: 3rd sing. aor. pass. indic. < ὁράω.   ὡς: *as*.   τῶν
ἀπορρήτων: Cynics were famously indifferent to what they ate, so
Peregrinus apparently broke some dietary taboo of the Christians (cf., e.g.,
the ones listed at Acts 15:29: *sacrifices offered to idols, blood, (animals)
that were strangled*).   προσιεμένων: masc. gen. pl. pres. mid. part. <
προσίημι; sc. αὐτῶν (i.e, the Christians) as the subj. of the gen. abs.
ἐκ παλινῳδίας: *by means of a palinode/recantation*; a παλινῳδία was
first used by the archaic writer Steischorus (*c.* 640 – *c.* 555 BCE), who
wrote a poem insulting or blaming Helen of Troy as the cause of the Trojan
War. Because of this poem, the story goes, Stesichorus became blind. He
then composed a second poem, known as his Palinode, in which he praised
Helen; consequently, his blindness was cured.   ἀπαιτεῖν ᾤετο δεῖν
= ᾤετο δεῖν ἀπαιτεῖν.   τῆς πόλεως ἀντιπρεσβευσαμένης:
gen. abs.; i.e., the city sent to the Roman emperor a delegation to file a
counter-petition/state their case.   ἐπιδοὺς: masc. nom. sing. aor. act.
part. < ἐπιδίδωμι.   κελεύσαντος βασιλέως: gen. abs.; English
prefers a prepositional phrase: *at the emperor's command* or *by order of the
emperor* (Harmon).   ἐπράχθη: 3rd sing. aor. pass. indic. < πράττω.

44

Vocabulary

ἀντιπρεσβεύομαι, (dep.) *send counter-ambassadors*

ἀξιόω, *think, deem worthy; think one has the right, expect* (+ inf.)

ἀπαιτέω, *demand back*

ἅπας, ἅπασα, ἅπαν, *all; every; whole*

ἀπορέω, (mid. often in same sense as act.) *be at a loss, be without means* or *resource*

ἀπόρρητος, -ον, *forbidden*

ἄφθονος, -ον, *without envy; plentiful;* (pl.) *wealth, prosperity, comfort*

βάλλω, βαλῶ, ἔβαλον, *hit, strike*

βασιλεύς, -έως, ὁ, *king, emperor*

βόσκω, *feed, nourish, support; maintain*

γραμματεῖον, τό, *petition*

δεύτερος, -α, -ον, *second;* τὸ δεύτερον, *a second time*

δέω, *bind;* δεῖ, *it is necessary;* δεῖν, *to be necessary*

δορυφορέω, *attend, attend as a bodyguard*

ἐμμένω, ἐμμενῶ, ἐνέμεινα, *abide by* (+ dat.)

ἐξέρχομαι, ἔξειμι, ἐξῆλθον, *go away, depart*

ἐπιδίδωμι, ἐπιδώσω, ἐπιέδωκα, *file, submit*

ἐς, εἰς, prep. (+ acc.), *against*

ἐσθίω, ἔδομαι, ἔφαγον, *eat*

εὐθύς, adv., *immediately, at once*

ἐφόδιον, τό, (usually pl.) *supplies for travelling, money and provisions*

ἔχω, ἕξω, ἔσχον, *have; hold;* (mid. + gen.) *hold onto*

ἱκανός, -ή, -όν, *sufficient, adequate*

κελεύω, *command, order*

κομίζω, *get back, recover;* (mid.) *get back for oneself, recover*

κτῆμα, -ατος, τό, *possession, piece of property*

λίθος, ὁ, *stone*

οἶμαι (uncontracted = οἴομαι), *suppose, think*

οὐδείς, οὐδεμία, οὐδέν, *no one, nothing; no*

οὐκέτι, adv., *no longer*

οὕτως, adv., *so, thus; as follows*

παλινῳδία, ἡ, *palinode, recantation*

παρανομέω, *transgress the law, commit a crime* or *outrage*

πλανάω, *make to wander; lead astray;* (pass.) *wander, roam about*

πράττω, πράξω, ἔπραξα, *do, act; achieve, accomplish*

προσίημι, *send to* or *towards;* (mid.) *admit, accept, allow to come near one*

φόνος, ὁ, *murder, homicide*

χρόνος, ὁ, *time*

45

ἐκελεύσθη οἷς ἅπαξ διέγνω μηδενὸς καταναγκάσαντος.

[17] "τρίτη ἐπὶ τούτοις ἀποδημία εἰς Αἴγυπτον παρὰ τὸν
Ἀγαθόβουλον, ἵναπερ τὴν θαυμαστὴν ἄσκησιν διησκεῖτο,
ξυρόμενος μὲν τῆς κεφαλῆς τὸ ἥμισυ, χριόμενος δὲ πηλῷ
τὸ πρόσωπον, ἐν πολλῷ δὲ τῶν περιεστώτων δήμῳ ἀναφλῶν
τὸ αἰδοῖον καὶ τὸ ἀδιάφορον δὴ τοῦτο καλούμενον
ἐπιδεικνύμενος, εἶτα παίων καὶ παιόμενος νάρθηκι εἰς
τὰς πυγὰς καὶ ἄλλα πολλὰ νεανικώτερα θαυματοποιῶν.

ἐκελεύσθη: 3rd sing. aor. pass. indic. < κελεύω.   **οἷς**: i.e., the
donation of his inheritance to his home town of Parium (15).   **διέγνω**:
3rd sing. aor. act. indic. < διαγιγνώσκω; sc. *to do.*   **μηδενὸς
καταναγκάσαντος**: gen. abs.; English prefers a prep. phrase: *under no
duress, under compulsion from nobody* (Costa).   **ἐπὶ τούτοις**: *for
these reasons, under these circumstances.*   **Ἀγαθόβουλον**: a Cynic
philosopher of the early 2nd century CE from Alexandria, "a hotbed of
Cynicism at the time" (Macleod 272); besides being the teacher of
Peregrinus, he also taught Demonax (*c.* 70 – *c.* 170 CE), a Cynic
philosopher about whom Lucian wrote a semi-fictional encomiastic mini-
biography (*Life of Demonax*).   **ἄσκησιν διησκεῖτο**: a rhetorical
trope known as *figura etymologica*, in which a verb governs its related
noun. Such cognate wordplay occurs often in Lucian (cf., e.g., 1: τροπὰς
τραπόμενος).   **ἐν πολλῷ, δήμῳ**: *in a large crowd of commoners*;
Lucian sometimes substitutes δῆμος for ὅμιλος (*assembly, crowd, throng*)
and ὄχλος (*crowd, throng*), perhaps because δῆμος conveys more
vigorously the pejorative sense of a mob of undiscriminating, unenlightened
people.   **περιεστώτων**: masc. gen. pl. perf. act. part. < περιίστημι.
τὸ ἀδιάφορον δὴ: in Stoic philosophy, this word (usually pl., τὰ
ἀδιάφορα) is an action or thing neither good nor bad. The Cynic Diogenes'
urinating and masturbating in public were considered examples of such
actions. Here the force of δὴ might best be captured in English by the use of
(mocking) scare quotes.   **νάρθηκι**: fennel stalks were used for a variety
of means: splints for broken limbs, caskets for unguents, and canes
employed by school teachers for beating recalcitrant students.

Vocabulary

Ἀγαθόβουλος, ὁ, *Agathoboulos*

ἀδιάφορον, τό, *indifference, Stoic indifference*

Αἴγυπτος, ἡ, *Egypt*

αἰδοῖον, τό, *private parts, sexual organ, penis* (literally, *the shameful thing*)

ἀλλός, -ή, -ό, *another, other*

ἀναφλάω, *masturbate* (literally, *crush* or *pound up*)

ἅπαξ, adv., *once, once for all*

ἀποδημία, ἡ, *being abroad, being away*

ἄσκησις, ἡ, *practice, training; training in asceticism; mode of life*

δή, particle, *indeed; in fact; then, therefore, now*

δῆμος, ὁ, *the people, the common people;* (Lucian) *crowd* (made up of commoners)

διαγιγνώσκω, διαγνώσομαι, διέγνων, *resolve, determine, decide*

διασκέω, *deck out;* (pass.) *train, practice*

ἐπιδείκνυμι, ἐπιδείξω, ἐπέδειξα, *exhibit, display;* (mid.) *exhibit, display, show off, give a specimen of*

ἥμισυς, -εια, -υ, *half*

θαυματοποιέω, *do hocus-pocus, perform tricks, play the miracle-mongering game*

θαυμαστός, -ή, -όν, *wonderful, marvelous; extraordinary; strange, absurd*

ἵναπερ, adv., *where*

καλέω, *call, call in, summon;* (pres. pass. part.) *being called, so-called*

καταναγκάζω, *coerce, force*

κελεύω, *command, order*

κεφαλή, ἡ, *head*

μηδείς μηδεμία, μηδέν, *not one, nobody, nothing*

νάρθηξ, -ηκος, ὁ, *stalk of fennel; cane*

νεανικός, -ή, -όν, *adolescent; vigorous, violent, excessive; insolent*

ξυρέω, *shave;* (mid./pass.) *shave oneself, have oneself shaved*

παίω, *strike, beat*

περιίστημι, περιστήσω, περιέστησα, *place around;* (2nd aor.) περιέστην, (perf.) περιέστηκα, *stand around*

πηλός, ὁ, *mud*

πρόσωπον, τό, *face*

πυγή, ἡ, *buttock*

τρίτος -η, -ον, *third*

χρίω, *rub, smear,* or *anoint with;* (mid.) *rub, smear,* or *anoint oneself with*

[18] "ἐκεῖθεν δὲ οὕτω παρεσκευασμένος ἐπὶ Ἰταλίας

ἔπλευσεν καὶ ἀποβὰς τῆς νεὼς εὐθὺς ἐλοιδορεῖτο πᾶσι,

καὶ μάλιστα τῷ βασιλεῖ, πρᾳότατον αὐτὸν καὶ ἡμερώτατον

εἰδώς, ὥστε ἀσφαλῶς ἐτόλμα· ἐκείνῳ γάρ, ὡς εἰκός, ὀλίγον

ἔμελεν τῶν βλασφημιῶν καὶ οὐκ ἠξίου τὴν φιλοσοφίαν

ὑποδυόμενόν τινα κολάζειν ἐπὶ ῥήμασι καὶ μάλιστα τέχνην

τινὰ τὸ λοιδορεῖσθαι πεποιημένον. τούτῳ δὲ καὶ ἀπὸ τούτων

τὰ τῆς δόξης ηὐξάνετο, παρὰ γοῦν τοῖς ἰδιώταις, καὶ

ἐλοιδορεῖτο: an inchoative or inceptive imperf.; i.e., *he began to...*
τῷ βασιλεῖ: the emperor at this time was Antoninus Pius (r. 138 – 161 CE).   **πρᾳότατον αὐτὸν καὶ ἡμερώτατον εἰδώς** = εἰδώς αὐτὸν (εἶναι) πρᾳότατον καὶ ἡμερώτατον.   **πρᾳότατον, ἡμερώτατον**: the reign of Antoninus was the most peaceful of any Roman emperor, and he himself participated in no single military action during all 23 years of it. Since little is known about Antoninus, perhaps the qualities of his reign came to be reflected on his person.   **εἰδώς**: masc. nom. sing. perf. act. part. < οἶδα.   **ἐκείνῳ**: i.e., Antoninus Pius.   **ὡς εἰκός**: *as (is) likely*, i.e., *as one would expect*.   **ἠξίου**: 3rd sing. imperf. act. indic. < ἀξιόω.   **τὴν φιλοσοφίαν ὑποδυόμενόν**: i.e., using philosophy as a cover or mask; ὑποδύομαι is often used to describe an actor putting on his mask to become a character in a play.   **τινὰ**: like the earlier τινα in this sentence, this one too is the dir. obj. of κολάζειν.
τὸ λοιδορεῖσθαι: an articular inf.; i.e., *the act of abusing (others)* or *name-calling*.   **πεποιημένον**: ποιέω can take a double acc. construction: *make* X (acc.) Y (acc.); here, as an acc. sing. perf. mid. part., *who had made* X (τὸ λοιδορεῖσθαι) *his* Y (acc. τέχνην).   **τούτῳ**: i.e., Peregrinus.   **τὰ τῆς δόξης**: the phrase sounds grander than the simple ἡ δόξα; also note how the two additional "t" sounds contribute to this "grandiosity" by capping off an alliterative sequence with four straight syllables beginning with "t": τούτῳ δὲ καὶ ἀπὸ τούτων τὰ τῆς. This being Lucian, however, the effect so generated through this alliteration is instantly deflated by the next phrase: παρὰ γοῦν τοῖς ἰδιώταις; the last word of this prep. phrase is where our "idiot" comes from, a meaning not too far from the speaker's intention here (cf. also 13).

48

Vocabulary

ἀξιόω, *think, deem worthy; think one has the right, expect* (+ inf.)

ἀποβαίνω, ἀποβήσομαι, ἀπέβην, *disembark, step off of / from* (+ gen.)

ἀσφαλῶς, adv., *safely, without any risk* or *danger*

αὐξάνω, αὐξήσω, ηὔξησα, *make large, increase, strengthen;* (pass.) *increase, grow*

βασιλεύς, -έως, ὁ, *king, emperor*

βλασφημία, ἡ, *slander, defamation, libel; abuse*

γοῦν, particle, *at any rate, to be sure, at least*

δόξα, ἡ, *honor, glory, reputation*

ἐκεῖθεν, adv., *from there*

εἰκός, -ότος, τό, *likely, probably, reasonable*

ἐπί, prep. (+ gen. with verbs of motion) *for, towards;* (+ dat.) *for, on account of*

εὐθύς, adv., *immediately, at once; straight, directly;* (later Greek) *then*

ἥμερος, -ον, *gentle*

ἰδιώτης, -ου, ὁ, *simple, average,* or *ignorant person / citizen*

Ἰταλία, ἡ, *Italy*

κολάζω, *punish*

λοιδοροῦμαι, (dep.) *abuse, revile* (+ dat.)

μάλιστα, adv., *most, most of all, very much, especially, too much*

μέλω, (most often impersonal 3rd sing., with the obj. in the gen. and the person in the dat.) (to whom) *there is care* or *thought for* (+ gen.), i.e, *he/she cares about* or *gives thought to* (+ gen.)

ναῦς, νεώς, ἡ, *ship*

οἶδα, (perf. with pres. meaning) *know*

ὀλίγος, -η, -ον, *little, small;* (neut. acc. sing. as adv.) *little*

οὕτω, οὕτως, adv., *so, thus; as follows*

παρασκευάζω, *get ready, prepare*

πλέω, πλεύσομαι, ἔπλευσα, *sail*

ποιέω, *make, produce, create; do*

πρᾶος, -ον, *mild, gentle*

ῥῆμα, -ατος, τό, *word*

τέχνη, ἡ, *art, craft, profession*

τολμάω, *dare, be brave* or *bold enough* (to do something terrible or difficult)

ὑποδύομαι, *creep under; put on a character* (because ancient actors wore masks)

φιλοσοφία, ἡ, *philosophy*

ὥστε, conj., *and so, therefore, consequently*

περίβλεπτος ἦν ἐπὶ τῇ ἀπονοίᾳ, μέχρι δὴ ὁ τὴν πόλιν

ἐπιτετραμμένος ἀνὴρ σοφὸς ἀπέπεμψεν αὐτὸν ἀμέτρως

ἐντρυφῶντα τῷ πράγματι, εἰπὼν μὴ δεῖσθαι τὴν πόλιν

τοιούτου φιλοσόφου. πλὴν ἀλλὰ καὶ τοῦτο κλεινὸν

αὐτοῦ καὶ διὰ στόματος ἦν ἅπασιν, ὁ φιλόσοφος διὰ

τὴν παρρησίαν καὶ τὴν ἄγαν ἐλευθερίαν ἐξελαθείς, καὶ

προσήλαυνε κατὰ τοῦτο τῷ Μουσωνίῳ καὶ Δίωνι καὶ

Ἐπικτήτῳ καὶ εἴ τις ἄλλος ἐν περιστάσει τοιαύτῃ ἐγένετο.

τῇ ἀπονοίᾳ: cf. 2, 14.   τὴν πόλιν i.e., Rome.   ἐπιτετραμμένος: masc. nom. sing. perf. mid./pass. part. < ἐπιτρέπω; this would be the Prefect of Rome (*praefectus urbi*), a man entrusted from the time of the emperor Augustus (r. 27 BCE – 14 CE) with the authority and power to maintain order within the city by means of Rome's police force and its night watchmen.   τῷ πράγματι: i.e., Peregrinus' verbal abuse of the emperor.   εἰπὼν μὴ δεῖσθαι: Attic Greek would have εἰπὼν ὅτι οὐ δεῖται.   καὶ τοῦτο κλεινὸν αὐτοῦ: literally, *even this thing* (i.e., his being banished by the city-prefect) *(is) well-known of him*; i.e., *even this contributed to his fame.*   διὰ στόματος ἦν ἅπασιν: literally, *was to all through the mouth*, i.e., *was on everybody's lips* (Allinson), *everyone was talking about him.*   ἐξελαθείς: masc. nom. sing. aor. pass. part. < ἐξελαύνω.   ἐξελαθείς, προσήλαυνε: more wordplay (cf. 1: τροπὰς τραπόμενος; 17: ἄσκησιν διησκεῖτο).   κατὰ τοῦτο: *in this way.*   Μουσωνίῳ: Gaius Musonius Rufus (*c.* 25 – *c.* 101 CE) was a Roman Stoic philosopher sent into exile in 65 CE by the emperor Nero. He was the teacher of the Greek philosopher Epictetus.   Δίωνι: known by the names of Dio Chrysostom (*Dio the Golden-Mouth*), Dion of Prusa or Dio Cocceianus (*c.* 40 – *c.* 115 CE), he was a Greek orator, writer, and philosopher. Like Peregrinus, he too criticized a Roman emperor (in his case Domitian), for which he was banished in 82 CE from Rome, Italy, and his home province of Bithynia. After his banishment, on the advice of the Delphic oracle, he put on the clothes of a beggar and lived the life of a Cynic philosopher.   Ἐπικτήτῳ: Epictetus (*c.* 55 – *c.* 135 CE), a Greek Stoic philosopher who was banished, along with all philosophers, by Domitian in 93 CE from the city of Rome. His work had a significant influence on the Roman emperor Marcus Aurelius (r. 161 – 180 CE).

Vocabulary

ἄγαν, adv., *too much, excessive*

ἀμέτρως, adv., *excessively, immoderately*

ἀνήρ, ἀνδρός, ὁ, *man*

ἅπας, ἅπασα, ἅπαν, *all; every; whole*

ἀπόνοια, ἡ, *rebellion; desperation; madness*

ἀποπέμπω, ἀποπέμψω, ἀπέπεμψα, *send off* or *away; get rid of*

γίγνομαι, γενήσομαι, ἐγενόμην, (dep.) *become*

δέομαι, (dep.) *be in need of* (+ gen.)

δή, particle, *indeed; in fact; then, therefore, now*

διά, prep. (+ gen.), *through*; (+ acc.) *because of, on account of*

Δίων, -ονος, ὁ, *Dio* or *Dion*

ἐλευθερία, ἡ, *freedom, liberty, license*

ἐντρυφάω, *revel in, delight in, indulge in; treat contemptuously* (+ dat.)

ἐξελαύνω, ἐξελῶ, ἐξήλασον, *drive out*

Ἐπίκτητος, ὁ, *Epictetus*

ἐπιτρέπω, *commit, entrust*; (pass.) *be entrusted with* (+ acc.)

κατά, prep. (+ acc.), *in relation to, according to, with respect to*

κλεινός, -ή, -όν, *well known, famous,*

μέχρι, adv., *until*

Μουσωνίος, ὁ, *Musonius*

παρρησία, ἡ, *outspokenness, frankness*

περίβλεπτος, -ον, *admired by many*

περίστασις, -εως, ἡ, *situation, circumstances, state of affairs*

πλήν, conj., (+ ἀλλά is a Koine Greek construction) *however, but, as it happened*

πρᾶγμα, -τος, τό, *matter, thing, affair*

προσελαύνω, προσελῶ, προσήλασον, *drive towards, arrive at, reach* (+ dat.)

σοφός, -ή, -όν, *wise*

στόμα, -ατος, τό, *mouth*

φιλόσοφος, ὁ, *philosopher*

[19] "οὕτω δὴ ἐπὶ τὴν Ἑλλάδα ἐλθὼν ἄρτι μὲν Ἠλείοις

ἐλοιδορεῖτο, ἄρτι δὲ τοὺς Ἕλληνας ἔπειθεν ἀντάρασθαι

ὅπλα Ῥωμαίοις, ἄρτι δὲ ἄνδρα παιδείᾳ καὶ ἀξιώματι

προὔχοντα, διότι καὶ ἐν τοῖς ἄλλοις εὖ ἐποίησεν τὴν

Ἑλλάδα καὶ ὕδωρ ἐπήγαγεν τῇ Ὀλυμπίᾳ καὶ ἔπαυσε δίψει

ἀπολλυμένους τοὺς πανηγυριστάς, κακῶς ἠγόρευεν ὡς

καταθηλύναντα τοὺς Ἕλληνας, δέον τοὺς θεατὰς τῶν

Ὀλυμπίων διακαρτερεῖν διψῶντας καὶ νὴ Δία γε καὶ

ἀποθνήσκειν πολλοὺς αὐτῶν ὑπὸ σφοδρῶν τῶν νόσων,

αἳ τέως διὰ τὸ ξηρὸν τοῦ χωρίου ἐν πολλῷ τῷ πλήθει

ἐπεπόλαζον. καὶ ταῦτα ἔλεγε πίνων τοῦ αὐτοῦ ὕδατος.

οὕτω δὴ...ἐπεπόλαζον: this sentence, the longest in the text, gives a portrait of Peregrinus in full-blown Cynic attack mode during the Olympic Games of 153 CE (Peregrinus also attended in 157, 161, and 165). **ἄρτι μὲν, ἄρτι δὲ, ἄρτι δὲ**: *at one moment..., at another moment..., and at another moment; one day..., the next day..., the third day...* **Ἠλείοις**: the Eleans were citizens of Elis (a city-state in the northwest part of the Peloponnese). The first Olympic festival was organized in Olympia, a sanctuary *c.* 16 miles south of the city of Elis, by the authorities of Elis in the 8th century BCE. **ἀντάρασθαι ὅπλα**: i.e., *rebel from, rise up against* (+ dat.). **ἄνδρα...προὔχοντα**: this would be Herodes Atticus (101 – 177 CE), an extremely wealthy Athenian aristocrat and Roman senator who was a prominent literary figure and philanthropist. **εὖ ἐποίησεν**: *he treated well*, i.e., *he was a benefactor to.* **ὕδωρ ἐπήγαγεν τῇ Ὀλυμπίᾳ**: in 153 CE, the year Herodes Atticus' aqueduct terminating in a grandiose fountain, the Nymphaeum, was completed. **δίψει**: an instrumental use of the dat. **κακῶς ἠγόρευεν**: *he was publicly abusing*; ἄνδρα is the dir. obj. **δέον... νόσων**: acc. abs., which is used with participles of impersonal verbs (in this case δεῖ) instead of the gen. abs. **νὴ Δία γε**: a histrionic outburst; i.e., *Goddamnit!* **τοῦ αὐτοῦ ὕδατος**: in the attributive position (i.e., following the article), αὐτοῦ means *the same.*

52

Vocabulary

ἀγορεύω, *speak* (in public)

ἀνταίρω, ἀνταρῶ, ἀντῆρα, (act./mid.) *raise* X (acc.) *against* Y (dat.)

ἀξίωμα, -ατος, τό, *honor, reputation; rank, position*

ἀποθνήσκω, ἀποθανοῦμαι, ἀπέθανον, *die*

ἀπόλλυμι, ἀπολῶ, ἀπώλεσα, *destroy, kill; lose;* (mid.) *die; be lost, perish*

ἄρτι, adv., *presently*

γε, particle, *at least; indeed*

δέον, (neut. part. of the impersonal δεῖ) *it being necessary*

διακαρτερέω, *endure to the end, put up with, bear patiently / steadfastly*

διότι, conj., *because*

διψάω, *be thirsty*

δίψος, -εος, τό, *thirst*

Ἑλλάς, -άδος, ἡ, *Greece, Hellas*

Ἕλλην, -ηνος, ὁ, *Greek, Hellene*

ἐπάγω, ἐπάξω, ἐπήγαγον, *bring to*

ἐπιπολάζω, *be prevalent, be rife, run riot*

ἔρχομαι, εἶμι, ἦλθον, *come, go*

Ἠλείος, ὁ, *Elean* (citizen of the town of Elis)

θεατής, -οῦ, ὁ, *spectator*

κακῶς, adv., *badly*

καταθηλύνω, *make* X (acc.) *effeminate, turn* X *into a woman / women, soften*

λοιδοροῦμαι, (dep.) *abuse, revile, rebuke* (+ dat.)

νή, (particle of strong affirmation) νὴ Δία = *by Zeus!*

νόσος, ἡ, *sickness, disease*

ξηρός, τό, *dryness*

ὅπλον, τό, *tool, implement;* (mostly in pl.) *arms, weapons*

παιδεία, ἡ, *culture, learning, education; accomplishments*

πανηγυριστής, -οῦ, ὁ, *one who attends a festival in honor of a national god*

παύω, *stop;* (mid.) *stop (oneself), cease from*

πείθω, πείσω, ἔπεισα, *persuade, convince*

πίνω, πίομαι, ἔπιον, *drink* (+ gen.)

πλῆθος, -εος, τό, *crowd, multitude*

προὔχω (uncontracted = προέχω), *be preeminent / superior / outstanding*

Ῥωμαῖος, -α, -ον, *Roman*

σφοδρός, -ή, -όν, *strong, violent*

τέως, adv., *up to then*

ὕδωρ, ὕδατος, τό, *water*

χωρίον, τό, *place*

"ὡς δὲ μικροῦ κατέλευσαν αὐτὸν ἐπιδραμόντες ἅπαντες,

τότε μὲν ἐπὶ τὸν Δία καταφυγὼν ὁ γενναῖος εὕρετο μὴ

ἀποθανεῖν, [20] ἐς δὲ τὴν ἑξῆς Ὀλυμπιάδα λόγον τινὰ διὰ

τεττάρων ἐτῶν συνθεὶς τῶν διὰ μέσου ἐξήνεγκε πρὸς τοὺς

Ἕλληνας, ἔπαινον ὑπὲρ τοῦ τὸ ὕδωρ ἐπαγαγόντος καὶ

ἀπολογίαν ὑπὲρ τῆς τότε φυγῆς.

ἤδη δὲ ἀμελούμενος ὑφ᾽ ἁπάντων καὶ μηκέθ᾽ ὁμοίως

περίβλεπτος ὤν — ἕωλα γὰρ ἦν ἅπαντα καὶ οὐδὲν ἔτι

καινουργεῖν ἐδύνατο ἐφ᾽ ὅτῳ ἐκπλήξει τοὺς ἐντυγχάνοντας

μικροῦ: adv., *almost* (an abbreviated form of the expression μικροῦ δεῖν: literally, *to lack a little*; i.e., *practically, almost*).   **ἐπὶ τὸν Δία**: i.e., the altar of Zeus (for sanctuary/protection).   **ὁ γενναῖος**: heavily ironic.   **εὕρετο**: 3rd sing. aor. mid. indic. < εὑρίσκω; εὕρετο μὴ ἀποθανεῖν: *found a way for himself not to die.*   **ἐς**: prep. + acc.; *for.* Attic prose (except for Thucydides) prefers the spelling εἰς.   **τεττάρων ἐτῶν συνθεὶς τῶν διὰ μέσου**: note the word order – Peregrinus' composing takes place in the midst of the four intervening years. Then as now the Olympic Games took place every four years.   **συνθεὶς**: nom. masc. sing. aor. act. part. < συντίθημι.   **ἐξήνεγκε**: 3rd sing. aor. act. indic. < ἐκφέρω.   **ἔπαινον, ἀπολογίαν**: in apposition to λόγον, detailing the two themes of Peregrinus' speech.   **τῆς, φυγῆς**: sc. *his own.*   **ἀμελούμενος ὑφ᾽ ἁπάντων καὶ μηκέθ᾽ ὁμοίως περίβλεπτος ὤν — ἕωλα γὰρ ἦν ἅπαντα καὶ οὐδὲν ἔτι καινουργεῖν ἐδύνατο**: two pairs of synonymous phrases each joined by καὶ, plus the repetition of similar negative adverbs/adverbial expressions (μηκέθ᾽ = οὐδὲν ἔτι) in each clause, emphasize how, in the age of novelty that was the Second Sophistic, fame was often quite fleeting and difficult for individuals to maintain over the long haul.   **ὑφ᾽** = ὑπό; + gen. of agent with pass. voice.   **μηκέθ᾽** = μηκέτι; Attic Greek would have used οὐκέτι.   **ὁμοίως**: sc. *as he had been.*   **ἅπαντα**: sc. *he said and did.*   **ἐφ᾽** = ἐπί.   **ἐφ᾽ ὅτῳ**: *with which, by means of which.*   **τοὺς ἐντυγχάνοντας**: sc. *him.*

Vocabulary

ἀμελέω, *disregard, pay no attention to*

ἀποθνήσκω, ἀποθανοῦμαι, ἀπέθανον, *die*

ἀπολογία, -ας, ἡ, *defense*

γενναῖος, -α, -ον, *noble, excellent*

δύναμαι, (dep.) *be able, can* (+ inf.)

ἐκπλήσσω, *amaze, astound* (literally, *strike out of [one's senses]*)

ἐκφέρω, ἐξοίσω, ἐξήνεγκον, *deliver; exhibit, display, publish*

Ἕλλην, -ηνος, ὁ, *Greek, Hellene*

ἐντυγχάνω, ἐντεύξομαι, ἐνέτυχον, *meet with, encounter, chance upon*

ἐξῆς, adv., *next*

ἐπάγω, ἐπάξω, ἐπήγαγον, *bring to*

ἔπαινος, ὁ, *praise, panegyric*

ἐπιτρέχω, ἐπιδραμοῦμαι, ἐπέδραμον, *rush upon/at* (to attack)

ἔτος, -ους, τό, *year*

εὑρίσκω, εὑρήσω, ηὗρον/εὗρον, *find;* (mid.) *find out* or *discover how to* (+ inf.)

ἕωλος, -ον, *stale, a day old, out of date*

Ζεύς, Διός, Διΐ, Δία, ὁ, *Zeus*

ἤδη, adv., *already, now*

καινουργέω, *make something new* or *novel*

καταλεύω, *stone to death*

καταφεύγω, καταφεύξομαι, κατέφυγον, *flee for refuge* or *protection*

λόγος, ὁ, *word, speech*

μέσος, -η, -ον, *middle, in the middle;* διὰ μέσου, *in the interim, intervening*

μηκέτι, adv., *no longer, no more*

μικρός, -ά, -ό, *little, small;* μικροῦ, adv., *almost*

Ὀλυμπιάς, -άδος, ἡ, *Olympic Games*

ὁμοίως, adv., *similarly, in the same way*

ὅστις, ἥτις, ὅ τι, rel. pron., *anyone who, who, anything that, that, which*

οὐδείς, οὐδεμία, οὐδέν, *no one, nobody, nothing;* no

περίβλεπτος, -ον, *admired by many*

πρός, prep. (+ acc.), *in the presence of, before*

συντίθημι, συνθήσω, συνέθηκα, *put together, compose*

τέσσαρες (m./f.), τέσσαρα (n.), (τεττάρων gen.), *four*

τότε, adv., *then, at that time*

ὕδωρ, ὕδατος, τό, *water*

ὑπέρ, prep. (+ gen.), *for, in defense of, on behalf of*

φυγή, ἡ, *flight, hasty departure, running away*

ὡς, conj., (+ aor. indic.) *when*

καὶ θαυμάζειν καὶ πρὸς αὐτὸν ἀποβλέπειν ποιήσει, οὗπερ ἐξ

ἀρχῆς δριμύν τινα ἔρωτα ἐρῶν ἐτύγχανεν — τὸ τελευταῖον

τοῦτο τόλμημα ἐβουλεύσατο περὶ τῆς πυρᾶς, καὶ διέδωκε

λόγον ἐς τοὺς Ἕλληνας εὐθὺς ἀπ' Ὀλυμπίων τῶν

ἔμπροσθεν ὡς ἐς τοὐπιὸν καύσων ἑαυτόν. [21] καὶ νῦν αὐτὰ

ταῦτα θαυματοποιεῖ, ὥς φασι, βόθρον ὀρύττων καὶ ξύλα

συγκομίζων καὶ δεινήν τινα τὴν καρτερίαν ὑπισχνούμενος.

"ἐχρῆν δέ, οἶμαι, μάλιστα μὲν περιμένειν τὸν θάνατον

καὶ μὴ δραπετεύειν ἐκ τοῦ βίου· εἰ δὲ καὶ πάντως

θαυμάζειν καὶ πρὸς αὐτὸν ἀποβλέπειν ποιήσει = ποιήσει
(sc. *them*; i.e., τοὺς ἐντυγχάνοντας) θαυμάζειν καὶ ἀποβλέπειν πρὸς
αὐτόν.   **οὗπερ**: the sing. rel. pron. refers to the two preceding
infinitives (θαυμάζειν and ἀποβλέπειν, which are essentially synonyms).
The gen. case is governed by ἐρῶν.   **δριμύν τινα ἔρωτα**:
accusatives of respect, i.e., *with respect to a certain fierce passion*; coupled
with ἐρῶν, the cognate wordplay conveys the meaning *having an absolutely
consuming passion for*.   **τὸ τελευταῖον τοῦτο τόλμημα**: note
the alliteration.   **ἐς**: prep. + acc.; *among, to*; *at*. Attic prose (except for
Thucydides) prefers the spelling εἰς.   **εὐθὺς ἀπ' Ὀλυμπίων τῶν
ἔμπροσθεν**: i.e., *immediately after the last Olympic Games*.   **ὡς** =
ὅτι.   **τοὐπιὸν**: crasis of τὸ ἐπιόν; article + neut. nom. sing. pres. act.
part. < ἔπειμι (this Attic fut. of ἐπέρχομαι is pres. tense in non-indic.
forms); i.e., *the following* or *next (festival)*.   **δραπετεύειν**: Lucian's
The Runaways (Δραπέται), is a narrative sequel of sorts to *On the Death of
Peregrinus*.

Δραπέται – Lucian's "Sequel" to *On the Death of Peregrinus*

The Runaways begins "in Olympus with Zeus complaining about the nasty
smell of Peregrinus' burning flesh which had forced him to to take temporary
refuge in the fragrant land of Arabia." (Macleod 270) The goddess Philosophy
interrupts Zeus, telling him and the Olympian gods how fake philosophers (i.e.,
the Cynics) have damaged her reputation. In response, Zeus sends Hermes and
Heracles to accompany her to Earth to punish the offenders, who are
represented as runaway slaves (hence the title).

Vocabulary

ἀποβλέπω, *look* or *pay attention to, gaze steadfastly at, look at with admiration*

ἀρχή, ἡ, *beginning*

βίος, ὁ, *life*

βόθρος, ὁ, *hole, pit*

βουλεύω, *plan, decide; deliberate, consider;* (mid.) *determine, resolve*

δεινός, -ή, -όν, *mighty, powerful, incredible*

διαδίδωμι, διαδώσω, διέδωκα, *spread (abroad)*

δραπετεύω, *run away*

δριμύς, -εῖα, -ύ, *fierce, sharp, keen*

ἑαυτοῦ, ἑαυτῆς, ἑαυτοῦ, (reflex. pron. in gen., dat., acc.) *himself, herself, itself*

εἰ, conj., *if*

Ἕλλην, -ηνος, ὁ, *Greek, Hellene*

ἔμπροσθεν, adv., *before, earlier, previous*

ἐπιών, -οῦσα, -όν (participles < ἔπειμι), *following, coming, approaching*

ἐράω, *love* or *desire passionately;* + ἔρωτα, *have a consuming passion for*

ἔρως, -ωτος, ὁ, *desire* or *passion (for)* (+ gen.)

θάνατος, ὁ, *death*

θαυμάζω, *marvel, be amazed, wonder at; admire, honor, worship*

θαυματοποιέω, *play the mountebank; perform tricks, do hocus-pocus*

καρτερία, ἡ, *fortitude, endurance;* (here =) *act* or *display of fortitude/endurance*

καίω, καύσω, ἔκαυσα, *set on fire, burn up*

λόγος, ὁ, *word, speech, report*

νῦν, adv., *now*

ξύλον, τό, *wood; piece of wood*

οἶμαι (uncontracted = οἴομαι), *suppose, think*

Ὀλύμπια, τά, (pl. only) *Olympic Games*

ὀρύττω, *dig*

ὅσπερ, ἥπερ, ὅπερ, rel. pron., emphatic forms, *who, whose, whom, which, that*

πάντως, adv., *at all costs, absolutely*

περιμένω, περιμενῶ, περιέμεινα, *await, wait for*

πυρά, -ᾶς, ἡ, *pyre, funeral-pyre*

συγκομίζω, *gather, collect, bring together*

τελευταῖος, -α, -ον, *last;* τὸ τελευταῖον, adv., *for the last time; finally*

τόλμημα, -ατος, τό, *venture, enterprise, daring* or *shameless act*

τυγχάνω, τεύξομαι, ἔτυχον, *happen* (+ supplementary participle)

ὑπισχνέομαι, ὑποσχήσομαι, ὑπεσχόμην, *promise (to do* or *undertake)*

χρή, (imperf. ἐχρῆν), *it is necessary, one must* (+ inf.)

διέγνωστο οἱ ἀπαλλάττεσθαι, μὴ πυρὶ μηδὲ τοῖς ἀπὸ τῆς

τραγῳδίας τούτοις χρῆσθαι, ἀλλ' ἕτερόν τινα θανάτου

τρόπον, μυρίων ὄντων, ἑλόμενον ἀπελθεῖν. εἰ δὲ καὶ τὸ πῦρ

ὡς Ἡράκλειόν τι ἀσπάζεται, τί δή ποτε οὐχὶ κατὰ σιγὴν

ἑλόμενος ὄρος εὔδενδρον ἐν ἐκείνῳ ἑαυτὸν ἐνέπρησεν μόνος,

ἕνα τινὰ οἷον Θεαγένη τοῦτον Φιλοκτήτην παραλαβών;

ὁ δὲ ἐν Ὀλυμπίᾳ τῆς πανηγύρεως πληθούσης μόνον οὐκ

ἐπὶ σκηνῆς ὀπτήσει ἑαυτόν, οὐκ ἀνάξιος ὤν, μὰ τὸν

Ἡρακλέα, εἴ γε χρὴ καὶ τοὺς πατραλοίας καὶ τοὺς ἀθέους

διέγνωστο: 3rd sing. pluperf. mid./pass. indic. < διαγιγνώσκω; *it had been decided*; + οἱ (= αὐτῷ; an Ionic form occasionally used by Lucian), *by him* (pluperf. passives take the dat. of agent). The subj. of διέγνωστο is the inf. ἀπαλλάττεσθαι.   **μὴ, χρῆσθαι**: sc. ἐχρῆν (from the previous clause) both here and with ἀπελθεῖν; the understood subj. of the first indir. statement is αὐτόν (i.e., Peregrinus), which is modified by ἑλόμενον in the next clause.   **πυρὶ, τοῖς, τούτοις**: datives governed by χρῆσθαι. **τοῖς ἀπὸ τῆς τραγῳδίας τούτοις**: i.e., these techniques employed in tragedy (e.g., hanging oneself, stabbing oneself, etc.). **μυρίων ὄντων**: gen. abs.   **ἑλόμενον**: masc. acc. sing. 2nd aor. mid. part. < αἱρέω.   **ἀπελθεῖν**: like ἀπαλλάττεσθαι, this is an euphemism for dying.   **τί δή ποτε**: *why in the world?*   **κατὰ σιγὴν**: *quietly, secretly*.   **Φιλοκτήτην**: in apposition to the phrase ἕνα τινὰ οἷον Θεαγένη τοῦτον; i.e., *as his Philoctetes*. Heracles, mistakenly poisoned by his jealous wife, had decided to build a funeral pyre on Mt. Oeta to end his suffering. No one of his friends or family would light it for him except Philoctetes, who received the bow and arrows of Heracles as his reward.   **ὁ δὲ**: the article without a substantive = pron.; *But he*. **τῆς πανηγύρεως πληθούσης**: gen. abs.; since πλήθω often is used in connection with water (e.g., of rivers being swollen), Lucian may be playing with the juxtaposition of water and fire imagery.   **οὐκ ἀνάξιος**: *litotes* (see 12); the same expression is also used in 38.   **μὰ τὸν Ἡρακλέα**: a traditional exclamation, though here there is also the (rather heavy-handed) humorous allusion already established to Heracles' self-immolation and Peregrinus' imitation of it.

Vocabulary

ἄθεος, -ον, *without god, godless*; (as substantive) *atheist, godless person*

αἰρέω, αἱρήσω, εἷλον, *take*; (mid.) *choose*

ἀνάξιος -α, -ον, *unworthy, undeserved*

ἀπαλλάττω, *set free, release*; (mid./pass.) *be set free* or *released (from life)*; *die*

ἀπέρχομαι, ἄπειμι, ἀπῆλθον, *go, go away, depart*

ἀσπάζομαι, (dep.) *embrace, cling fondly to*

γε, particle, *at least, at any rate*; *namely, that is, indeed*

διαγιγνώσκω, διαγνώσομαι, διέγνων, *resolve, determine, decide*

εἷς, μία, ἕν, *one*

ἐμπίμπρημι, ἐμπρήσω, ἐνέπρησα, *set on fire, burn*

ἕτερος, -α, -ον, *other, another*

εὔδενδρος, -ον, *well-wooded, covered in trees*

Ἡράκλειος, -α, -ον, *Heraclean, of Heracles, connected to Heracles*

θάνατος, ὁ, *death*

Θεαγένης, -ου, ὁ, *Theagenes*

μά, particle (used in protestations and oaths), *by*

μονός, -ή, -όν, *alone, only, single*; μόνον οὐκ, *all but, practically, virtually*

μυρίος, -α, -ον, *numberless, countless*

οἱ or οἷ, (3rd sing. dat. masc. pron. = αὐτῷ) *to / for him*

οἷος, οἵα, οἷον, rel. pron., *such as, like, for example*

Ὀλυμπία, ἡ, *Olympia*

ὀπτάω, *roast*

ὄρος -ους, τό, *mountain, hill*

πανήγυρις, -εως, ἡ, *assembly, festival*; *national assembly* or *festival*

παραλαμβάνω, παραλήψομαι, παρέλαβον, *take along, use as a substitue*

πατραλοίας, -α / -ου, ὁ, *parricide, one who murders his father*

πλήθω, (intransitive form of πίμπλημι, mostly in pres. part) *be full, be at its height*

ποτε, adv., *at some time, ever*

σιγή, ἡ, *silence*

σκηνή, ἡ, *stage*

τραγῳδία, ἡ, *tragedy*

τρόπος, ὁ, *manner, means*

Φιλοκτήτης, -ου, ὁ, *Philoctetes*

χρή, (imperf. ἐχρῆν), *it is necessary, one must* (+ inf.)

χρῶμαι (uncontracted = χράομαι), χρήσομαι, ἐχρησάμην, *make use of* (+ dat.)

δίκας διδόναι τῶν τολμημάτων. καὶ κατὰ τοῦτο πάνυ ὀψὲ

δρᾶν αὐτὸ ἔοικεν, ὃν ἐχρῆν πάλαι ἐς τὸν τοῦ Φαλάριδος

ταῦρον ἐμπεσόντα τὴν ἀξίαν ἀποτετικέναι, ἀλλὰ μὴ ἅπαξ

χανόντα πρὸς τὴν φλόγα ἐν ἀκαρεῖ τεθνάναι. καὶ γὰρ αὖ

καὶ τόδε οἱ πολλοί μοι λέγουσιν, ὡς οὐδεὶς ὀξύτερος ἄλλος

θανάτου τρόπος τοῦ διὰ πυρός· ἀνοῖξαι γὰρ δεῖ μόνον τὸ

στόμα καὶ αὐτίκα τεθνάναι.

δίκας διδόναι: *to suffer punishment for, pay the penalty for* (+ gen.).
κατὰ τοῦτο: *in this respect.*   **τοῦ Φαλάριδος**: Phalaris was the
ruler of Acragas, Sicily, from *c.* 575 – *c.* 550 BCE. Although Acragas
prospered under his rule, Phalaris was later remembered for his excessive
cruelty. Among the many atrocities accredited to him, the one he is
inextricably linked with involves his bronze bull, a combination of torture
device and executioner. Designed by Perilaus (aka Perillos) of Athens,
condemned criminals and enemies of Phalaris were locked in the bull, under
which a fire was kindled, heating the metal until the person inside roasted to
death. In Lucian's *Phalaris I* (one of his declamatory works), Phalaris,
defending himself, vividly narrates how Perilaus described the operation of
the device to him (11-12). Lucian's anachronistic mention of Phalaris' bull
as a fitting punishment for Peregrinus may be due either to satire's
propensity to make use of "everything-and-the-kitchen-sink" or to
undercutting the speaker's vitriolic attack – or, this being Lucian, it may be
both!   **ἀποτετικέναι**: perf. act. inf. < ἀποτίνω.   **ἀλλὰ μὴ
ἅπαξ χανόντα πρὸς τὴν φλόγα ἐν ἀκαρεῖ τεθνάναι**: a
paraphrase (substituting fire for water) of Eurylochus' (Odysseus' second-
in-command) preference for a quick death at sea by drowning than a slow
death via starvation on the island of the cattle of the Sun god (*Odyssey*
12.350): βούλομ' ἅπαξ πρὸς κῦμα χανὼν ἀπὸ θυμὸν ὀλέσσαι (*I
prefer once and for to lose my life with my mouth open to the wave...*).
τεθνάναι: perf. act. inf. < θνήσκω.   **καὶ γὰρ αὖ**: *and furthermore,
in fact.*   **ὡς** = ὅτι.   **ὡς οὐδεὶς ὀξύτερος ἄλλος θανάτου
τρόπος τοῦ διὰ πυρός** = ὡς οὐδεὶς ἄλλος τρόπος θανάτου
(ἐστὶ) ὀξύτερος τοῦ διὰ πυρός.   **τοῦ διὰ πυρός**: τοῦ (i.e., τοῦ
τροποῦ θανάτου) = gen. of comparison; διὰ πυρός = prep. phrase.

Vocabulary

ἀκαρής, -ές, *small, tiny*; ἐν ἀκαρεῖ (χρόνου), *in a moment (of time)*

ἀνοίγνυμι, ἀνοίξω, ἀνέῳξα, *open*

ἀξία, ἡ, *penalty, just desserts*

ἅπαξ, adv., *once, once for all*

ἀποτίνω, ἀποτείσω, ἀπέτεισα, *pay, repay, pay in full*

αὖ, adv., *further, moreover, besides*

αὐτίκα, adv., *immediately, at once*

δέω, *bind*; δεῖ, *it is necessary*

διά, prep. (+ gen.), *by, through*

δίδωμι, δώσω, ἔδωκα, *give*

δίκη, ἡ, *custom*; *justice*; *right*; *judgment*; *penalty*

δράω, *do, do some great thing* (good or bad)

ἐμπίπτω, ἐμπεσοῦμαι, ἐνέπεσον, *fall into*; (of prison or punishment with pass. sense) *be thrown into*

ἔοικα, (perf. with pres. sense) *be like*; *seem* (+ inf.); ἔοικε(ν), (often impersonal) *it seems* (+ inf.)

θάνατος, ὁ, *death*

θνήσκω, θανοῦμαι, ἔθανον, *die*; τέθνηκα (perf.), *have died*, i.e., *be dead*

μονός, -ή, -όν, *alone, only, single*; μόνον, adv., *only*

ὀξύς, -εῖα, -ύ, *quick, swift*

οὐδείς, οὐδεμία, οὐδέν, *no one, nothing*; *no*

ὀψέ, adv., *late, late in the day*

πάλαι, adv., *long ago*

πάνυ, adv., *altogether, very, exceedingly*

στόμα, -ατος, τό, *mouth*

ταῦρος, ὁ, *bull*

τόλμημα, -ατος, τό, *venture, enterprise, daring* or *shameless act*

τρόπος, ὁ, *manner, means*

Φάλαρις, -ιδος, ὁ, *Phalaris*

φλόξ, φλογός, ἡ, *flame*

χάσκω, χανοῦμαι, ἔχανον, *open one's mouth (in eager expectation), gape*

χρή, (imperf. ἐχρῆν), *it is necessary, one must* (+ inf.)

[22] "τὸ μέντοι θέαμα ἐπινοεῖται, οἶμαι, ὡς σεμνόν, ἐν ἱερῷ χωρίῳ καιόμενος ἄνθρωπος, ἔνθα μηδὲ θάπτειν ὅσιον τοὺς ἄλλους ἀποθνήσκοντας. ἀκούετε δέ, οἶμαι, ὡς καὶ πάλαι θέλων τις ἔνδοξος γενέσθαι, ἐπεὶ κατ' ἄλλον τρόπον οὐκ εἶχεν ἐπιτυχεῖν τούτου, ἐνέπρησε τῆς Ἐφεσίας Ἀρτέμιδος τὸν νεών. τοιοῦτόν τι καὶ αὐτὸς ἐπινοεῖ, τοσοῦτος ἔρως τῆς δόξης ἐντέτηκεν αὐτῷ.

ἐπινοεῖται: sc. *by him.*   **ὡς σεμνόν**: *as (something) awe-inspiring.*
καιόμενος ἄνθρωπος: in apposition to τὸ θέαμα and σεμνόν.
μηδὲ θάπτειν ὅσιον τοὺς ἄλλους ἀποθνήσκοντας = μηδὲ ὅσιόν (ἐστι) θάπτειν τοὺς ἄλλους ἀποθνήσκοντας.   **ἀκούετε**:
in form either a 2nd pl. pres. act. indic. or imper.; here it is the former, with
the meaning *you all have heard.*   **ὡς** = ὅτι.   **τῆς Ἐφεσίας**
Ἀρτέμιδος τὸν νεών: the Temple of Artemis at Ephesus, one of the
Seven Wonders of the Ancient World, was built *c.* 540 BCE. It was
destroyed in 356 BCE when Herostratus set fire to its wooden roof-beams in
order to achieve everlasting fame. The Ephesian authorities not only
executed him, but attempted to defeat his purpose by forbidding mention of
his name under penalty of death. With the exception of one ancient
historian, all later writers who reference the event (including Lucian) never
mention its perpetrator's name.   **αὐτὸς**: i.e., Peregrinus.

Vocabulary

ἀποθνῄσκω, ἀποθανοῦμαι, ἀπέθανον, *die*

Ἄρτεμις, -ιδος, ἡ, *Artemis*

γίγνομαι, γενήσομαι, ἐγενόμην, (dep.) *become*

δόξα, ἡ, *reputation, honor, glory; notion, expectation; opinion, judgment*

ἐμπίμπρημι, ἐμπρήσω, ἐνέπρησα, *set on fire, burn*

ἔνδοξος, -ον, *famous, well-known*

ἔνθα, adv., *where*

ἐντήκω, *pour in while molten;* (perf. act. = pass. sense) *sink deep in, be absorbed by, penetrate to the core* (+ dat.)

ἐπινοέω, *think of, plan, intend*

ἐπιτυγχάνω, ἐπιτεύξομαι, ἐπέτυχον, *attain, achieve, gain* (+ gen.)

Ἐφέσιος, -α, -ον, *Ephesian, of Ephesus*

ἔχω, ἕξω, ἔσχον, *have; hold;* (+ inf.) *can, be able*

ἔρως, -ωτος, ὁ, *love, desire, passion*

θάπτω, *bury*

θέαμα, -ατος, τό, *spectacle*

θέλω, *wish, desire, want* (+ inf.)

ἱερός, -ά, -όν, *holy, sacred*

καίω, καύσω, ἔκαυσα, *set on fire, burn up*

κατά, prep. (+ acc.), *in relation to, according to, with respect to*

μέντοι, particle, *indeed, to be sure, of course; however*

νεώς, νεώ, ὁ, *temple*

οἶμαι (uncontracted = οἴομαι), *suppose, think*

ὅσιος, -η, -ον, *hallowed, sanctioned by religious law;* ὅσιόν or ὅσιά (ἐστι), + inf., *it is sanctioned by religious law, it is lawful*

πάλαι, adv., *long ago*

σεμνός, -ή, -όν, *revered, august, awe-inspiring*

τοσοῦτος, -αύτη, -οῦτον, *so much, so great;* (pl.) *so many*

τρόπος, ὁ, *manner, means, way*

χωρίον, τό, *place*

63

[23] "καίτοι φησὶν ὅτι ὑπὲρ τῶν ἀνθρώπων αὐτὸ δρᾷ, ὡς διδάξειεν αὐτοὺς θανάτου καταφρονεῖν καὶ ἐγκαρτερεῖν τοῖς δεινοῖς. ἐγὼ δὲ ἡδέως ἂν ἐροίμην οὐκ ἐκεῖνον ἀλλ᾽ ὑμᾶς, εἰ καὶ τοὺς κακούργους βούλοισθε ἂν μαθητὰς αὐτοῦ γενέσθαι τῆς καρτερίας ταύτης καὶ καταφρονεῖν θανάτου καὶ καύσεως καὶ τῶν τοιούτων δειμάτων. ἀλλ᾽ οὐκ ἂν εὖ οἶδ᾽ ὅτι βουληθείητε. πῶς οὖν ὁ Πρωτεὺς τοῦτο διακρινεῖ καὶ τοὺς μὲν χρηστοὺς ὠφελήσει, τοὺς δὲ πονηροὺς οὐ φιλοκινδυνοτέρους καὶ τολμηροτέρους ἀποφανεῖ;

φησὶν ὅτι ὑπὲρ τῶν ἀνθρώπων αὐτὸ δρᾷ: in Attic Greek, φημί + inf. is far more common for indir. statement than φημί + ὅτι.   **τῶν ἀνθρώπων**: the pl. of ἄνθρωπος often carries a collective notion; i.e., *mankind, the human race, humanity*.   **ὡς**: + subju. or opt. = a final/purpose clause; i.e., *so that, in order that*.   **διδάξειεν**: 3rd sing. aor. act. opt. < διδάσκω; opt. in final/purpose clause in primary sequence (δρᾷ); this is a common irregularity in Lucian, since the opt. in final/purpose clauses is normally found in secondary sequence in Attic Greek.   **ἡδέως ἂν ἐροίμην**: *I would gladly ask, I should like to ask*; ἐροίμην: 1st sing. aor. mid. (dep.) opt. < ἔρομαι; a potential opt.   **εἰ καὶ...ταύτης** = εἰ καὶ βούλοισθε ἂν τοὺς κακούργους γενέσθαι μαθητὰς αὐτοῦ τῆς καρτερίας ταύτης.   **τοὺς κακούργους...δειμάτων**: note the heavy alliteration, especially of "t," "s," and "k."   **βούλοισθε**: 2nd pl. pres. mid./pass. (dep.) opt. < βούλομαι; opt. in indir. question in primary sequence.   **τῆς καρτερίας ταύτης**: *of this fortitude (of his)*.   **οὐκ ἂν εὖ οἶδ᾽ ὅτι βουληθείητε** = οἶδ᾽ εὖ ὅτι οὐκ ἂν βουληθείητε. **βουληθείητε**: 2nd pl. aor. pass. (dep.) opt. < βούλομαι; a potential opt. **διακρινεῖ**: note the accent.   **οὐ**: taken with ἀποφανεῖ.

64

Vocabulary

ἀποφαίνω, ἀποφανῶ, ἀπέφηνε, *render* or *make* X (acc.) *so and so* (acc) *by example*

βούλομαι, (dep.) *wish, be willing* (+ inf.)

δεῖμα, -ατος, τό, *fear, terror, horror*

δεινός, -ή, -όν, *terrible, fearful*

διακρίνω, διακρινῶ, διέκρινα, *separate* or *distinguish one from the other, draw a distinction, decide*

διδάσκω, *teach*

δράω, *do*

ἐγκαρτερέω, *endure, be strong in, remain steadfast in the face of* (+ dat.)

ἔρομαι (not found in pres. indic.), ἐρήσομαι, ἠρόμην, (dep.) *ask, inquire*

εὖ, adv., *well*

ἡδέως, adv., *gladly, sweetly, pleasantly*

θάνατος, ὁ, *death*

καίτοι, conj. + particle, *and yet*

κακοῦργος, ὁ, *criminal*

καρτερία, ἡ, *fortitude*

καταφρονέω, *despise, think lightly of* (+ gen.)

καῦσις, -εως, ἡ, *burning*

μαθητής, -οῦ, ὁ, *student, disciple*

οἶδα, (perf. with pres. meaning) *know*

πονηρός, -ή, -όν, *bad, worthless, wicked*

πῶς, adv., *how? in what manner* or *way?*

τοιοῦτος, τοιαύτη, τοιοῦτο, *such*; τὰ τοιαῦτα, *such things as these, suchlike*

τολμηρός, -ή, -όν, *daring, bold*

ὑπέρ, prep. (+ gen.), *on behalf of, for the sake of*

φιλοκίνδυνος, -ον, *adventurous, reckless, fond of danger* or *risk*

χρηστός, -ή, -όν, *good, honest, worthy*

ὠφελέω, *be of benefit, help, assist*

[24] "καίτοι δυνατὸν ἔστω ἐς τοῦτο μόνους ἀπαντήσεσθαι τοὺς πρὸς τὸ ὠφέλιμον ὀψομένους τὸ πρᾶγμα. ὑμᾶς δ' οὖν αὖθις ἐρήσομαι, δέξαισθ' ἂν ὑμῶν τοὺς παῖδας ζηλωτὰς τοῦ τοιούτου γενέσθαι; οὐκ ἂν εἴποιτε. καὶ τί τοῦτο ἠρόμην, ὅπου μηδ' αὐτῶν τις τῶν μαθητῶν αὐτοῦ ζηλώσειεν ἄν; τὸν γοῦν Θεαγένη τοῦτο μάλιστα αἰτιάσαιτο ἄν τις, ὅτι τἄλλα ζηλῶν τἀνδρὸς οὐχ ἕπεται τῷ διδασκάλῳ καὶ συνοδεύει παρὰ τὸν Ἡρακλέα, ὥς φησιν, ἀπιόντι, δυνάμενος ἐν βραχεῖ πανευδαίμων γενέσθαι συνεμπεσὼν ἐπὶ κεφαλὴν ἐς τὸ πῦρ.

"οὐ γὰρ ἐν πήρᾳ καὶ βάκτρῳ καὶ τρίβωνι ὁ ζῆλος, ἀλλὰ

καίτοι δυνατὸν...τὸ πρᾶγμα = καίτοι δυνατὸν ἔστω μόνους ἀπαντήσεσθαι ἐς τοῦτο τοὺς ὀψομένους τὸ πρᾶγμα πρὸς τὸ ὠφέλιμον. **ἔστω**: 3rd sing. pres. act. impera. < εἰμί; in argument, ἔστω = *let it be granted*; + δυνατὸν, *let the possible thing be granted*, i.e., *let's grant the possibility* (*that...* + acc. and inf. in indir. statement). **ἐς τοῦτο**: i.e., Peregrinus' self-immolation. **πρὸς τὸ ὠφέλιμον**: *for the purpose of that which is beneficial*. **δέξαισθ'**: 2nd pl. aor. mid. (dep.) opt. < δέχομαι; a potential opt. **οὐκ ἂν εἴποιτε**: *you would say that you don't (wish this)*, i.e., *you would say "no."*; a potential opt. **ζηλώσειεν**: 3rd sing. aor. act. opt. < ζηλόω; sc. *him*. An opt. in a relative clause that is causal (ὅπου μηδ') in secondary sequence. **αἰτιάσαιτο**: 3rd sing. aor. mid. (dep.) opt. < αἰτιάομαι; here, somewhat unusually, the verb takes a double acc. construction, i.e., *blame* person X (acc.) *for* thing Y (acc.); a potential opt. **τἄλλα**: crasis of τὰ ἄλλα. **τἀνδρὸς**: crasis of τοῦ ἀνδρὸς. **παρὰ τὸν Ἡρακλέα**: *to Heracles, to Heracles' abode*, i.e., *to be with Heracles (on Mt. Olympus as a god)*. **ἀπιόντι**: masc. dat. sing. pres. act. part. < ἄπειμι (this Attic fut. of ἀπέρχομαι is pres. tense in non-indic. forms); modifies τῷ διδασκάλῳ. **ὁ ζῆλος**: sc. ἐστί.

Vocabulary

αἰτιάομαι, (dep.) *blame, accuse, censure*

ἀπαντάω, ἀπαντήσομαι, ἀπήντησα, *go to meet, present oneself, turn out.*

ἀπέρχομαι, ἄπειμι, ἀπῆλθον, *go, go away, depart*

αὖθις, adv., *again, once more*

βάκτρον, τό, *staff, walking stick*

βραχύς, -εῖα, -ύ, *short, brief*; ἐν βραχεῖ, *in a short time, in no time*

γοῦν, particle, *at any rate, to be sure, at least*

δέχομαι, (dep.) *prefer* (+ inf.)

διδάσκαλος, ὁ, *teacher*

δύναμαι, (dep.) *be able, can* (+ inf.)

δυνατός, -ή, -όν, *possible*

ἕπομαι, (dep.) *follow* (+ dat.)

ἔρομαι (not found in pres. indic.), ἐρήσομαι, ἠρόμην, (dep.) *ask, inquire*

ζῆλος, ὁ, *imitation, emulation, following (a leader)*

ζηλόω, *zealously follow, imitate, emulate*

ζηλωτής, -οῦ, ὁ, *zealous follower, imitator*

Ἡρακλῆς, -έους, ὁ, *Heracles*

Θεαγένης, -ου, ὁ, *Theagenes*

καίτοι, conj. + particle, *and yet*

κεφαλή, ἡ, *head*; ἐπὶ κεφαλήν, *headlong, head first*

μαθητής, -οῦ, ὁ, *student, disciple*

μονός, -ή, -όν, *only*

ὅπου, adv., *when, since*

πανευδαίμων, -ον, *absolutely happy, eternally blissful*

πήρα, ἡ, *leather pouch, wallet*

πρᾶγμα, -τος, τό, *matter, thing, affair*

συνεμπίπτω, συνεμπεσοῦμαι, συνενέπεσον, *fall in together* or *also*

συνοδεύω, *travel together with, accompany* (+ dat.)

τίς, τί, (gen. τίνος) interrog. pron. and adj., *who? which? what? why?*

τρίβων, -ωνος, ὁ, *threadbare cloak, worn out garment*

ὠφέλιμος, -ον, *helpful, useful, beneficial, profitable, advantageous*

ταῦτα μὲν ἀσφαλῆ καὶ ῥᾴδια καὶ παντὸς ἂν εἴη, τὸ τέλος δὲ

καὶ τὸ κεφάλαιον χρὴ ζηλοῦν καὶ πυρὰν συνθέντα κορμῶν

συκίνων ὡς ἔνι μάλιστα χλωρῶν ἐναποπνιγῆναι τῷ καπνῷ·

τὸ πῦρ γάρ αὐτὸ οὐ μόνον Ἡρακλέους καὶ Ἀσκληπιοῦ, ἀλλὰ

καὶ τῶν ἱεροσύλων καὶ ἀνδροφόνων, οὓς ὁρᾶν ἔστιν ἐκ

καταδίκης αὐτὸ πάσχοντας. ὥστε ἄμεινον τὸ διὰ τοῦ καπνοῦ·

ἴδιον γὰρ καὶ ὑμῶν ἂν μόνων γένοιτο.

παντὸς ἂν εἴη: literally, *would be possible of anyone*, i.e., *anyone could do it*; **εἴη**: 3rd sing. pres. act. opt. < **εἰμί**; a potential opt. **συνθέντα**: masc. acc. sing. aor. act. part. < **συντίθημι**; modifies the understood subj. (*he*, i.e., Theagenes) of the indir. statement generated by **χρή**. **συκίνων...τῷ καπνῷ**: figtree wood is soft and spongy; when burned it generates much smoke and little fire. **ὡς ἔνι μάλιστα χλωρῶν**: *as green as possible, the greenest one can possibly (find)*; **ὡς** + superlative = a "super-superlative"; here the "superlative" is **μάλιστα χλωρῶν**. **ἔνι**: syncopated form of **ἔνεστι**. **ἐναποπνιγῆναι**: 2nd aor. pass. inf. < **ἐναποπνίγομαι**. **ἔστιν**: (thus accented + inf.) *it is possible*. **Ἡρακλέους καὶ Ἀσκληπιοῦ**: *(is) of Heracles and Asclepius*; i.e., *belongs to Heracles and Asclepius*. **ὥστε ἄμεινον**: sc. ἐστί. **τὸ διὰ τοῦ καπνοῦ** = τὸ (τέλος) διὰ τοῦ καπνοῦ. **ὑμῶν, μόνων**: i.e., Peregrinus, Theagenes (and like-minded individuals?).

[25] "ἄλλως τε ὁ μὲν Ἡρακλῆς, εἴπερ ἄρα καὶ ἐτόλμησέν

τι τοιοῦτο, ὑπὸ νόσου αὐτὸ ἔδρασεν, ὑπὸ τοῦ Κενταυρείου

αἵματος, ὥς φησιν ἡ τραγῳδία, κατεσθιόμενος· οὗτος δὲ

ὑπὸ νόσου, ὑπὸ τοῦ Κενταυρείου αἵματος: Heracles was forced to kill himself on account of the agony caused by wearing a cloak soaked in the poisonous blood of the centaur Nessus, which was sent to him by his wife Deianira who believed that it would act as a love-charm. **ὥς φησιν ἡ τραγῳδία**: i.e., Sophocles' *Trachiniae* ("The Women of Trachis"). **κατεσθιόμενος**: the part. is causal; i.e., *because he was...*

Vocabulary

αἷμα, -ατος, τό, *blood*

ἄλλως, adv., *in another way* or *manner, otherwise*; ἄλλως τε, *and besides*

ἀμείνων, -ον, *better*; ἄμεινόν (ἐστι), *it is better*

ἀνδροφόνος, ὁ, *murderer*

ἄρα, particle, *then, as it seems*

Ἀσκληπιός, ὁ, *Asclepius*

ἀσφαλής, -ές, *safe, secure*

δράω, *do*

εἴπερ, conj., *if really, if indeed*

ἐναποπνίγομαι, (mid./pass.; a Lucianic coinage) *be suffocated in, asphyxiate oneself*

ἔνειμι, *be in a place, be among*; ἔνεστι, *it is possible, one can*

ζηλόω, *zealously follow, imitate*

Ἡρακλῆς, -έους, ὁ, *Heracles*

ἴδιος, -η, -ον, *one's own, personal, peculiar*

ἱερόσυλος, ὁ, *sacrilegious person, temple robber*

καπνός, ὁ, *smoke*

καταδίκη, ἡ, *judgment given against one, judicial sentence*

κατεσθίω, κατέδομαι, κατέφαγον, *eat up, devour*

Κενταύρειος, -α, -ον, *of the Centaur, Centaur's*

κεφάλαιον, τό, *culmination, crowning act, completion (of a thing)*

κορμός, ὁ, *log*

μονός, -ή, -όν, *alone, only*

νόσος, ἡ, *sickness, disease, affliction*

πάσχω, πείσομαι, ἔπαθον, *experience; suffer, undergo*

πυρά, ἡ, *pyre, funeral-pyre*

ῥάδιος, -α, -ον, *easy*

σύκινος, -η, -ον, *of the figtree, fig wood*

συντίθημι, συνθήσω, συνέθηκα, *put together, build, make*

τέλος, -ους, τό, *end, consummation; end of life, death*

τολμάω, *dare, be brave* or *bold enough* (to do something terrible or difficult)

τραγῳδία, ἡ, *tragedy*

χλωρός, -ά, -όν, *pale-green, green*

χρή, (imperf. ἐχρῆν), *it is necessary, one must* (+ inf.)

ὥστε, conj., *so that, that, with the result that*

τίνος αἰτίας ἕνεκεν ἐμβάλλει φέρων ἑαυτὸν εἰς τὸ πῦρ; νὴ

Δί᾽, ὅπως τὴν καρτερίαν ἐπιδείξηται καθάπερ οἱ Βραχμᾶνες·

ἐκείνοις γὰρ αὐτὸν ἠξίου Θεαγένης εἰκάζειν, ὥσπερ οὐκ ἐνὸν

καὶ ἐν Ἰνδοῖς εἶναί τινας μωροὺς καὶ κενοδόξους ἀνθρώπους.

ὅμως δ᾽ οὖν κἂν ἐκείνους μιμείσθω – ἐκεῖνοι γὰρ οὐκ

ἐμπηδῶσιν ἐς τὸ πῦρ, ὡς Ὀνησίκριτος ὁ Ἀλεξάνδρου

κυβερνήτης ἰδὼν Κάλανον καόμενόν φησιν, ἀλλ᾽ ἐπειδὰν

φέρων: this part. (in all genders), is frequently joined with a verb (often of throwing + reflexive pron.); it is intransitive, with a pass. sense, and denotes unrestrained action: *full tilt, wholeheartedly.*   **οἱ Βραχμᾶνες**: this word can refer to Brachmanes, Bragmanni, Brahmans, or Gymnosophists (the first three are of Indian origin; the last is Greek: γυμνοσοφισταί, *naked philosophers/sages*), all of which are names used (mostly interchangeably) by ancient Greek writers to describe various types of Indian sages who were first encountered by Alexander the Great in Taxila, Ancient India (today Taxila is located 20 miles northwest of Islamabad, Pakistan). In Greek texts the Brahmans/Gymnosophists were often paired with the Cynics, since both subscribed to an ascetic lifestyle.   **ὅπως**: + subju. or opt. = a final/purpose clause; i.e., *so that, in order that.* **ἐπιδείξηται**: 3rd sing. aor. mid. subju. < ἐπιδείκνυμι.   **ἠξίου**: 3rd sing. imperf. act. indic. < ἀξιόω.   **ἐνὸν**: neut. acc. sing. pres. act. part. < ἔνειμι; *it being possible* (+ inf.). This is an acc. abs., which is used with participles of impersonal verbs (in this case ἔνεστι) instead of the gen. abs.   **κἂν**: crasis of καί ἄν; here, as a strengthened καί, intensifies ἐκείνους; i.e., *even them.*   **μιμείσθω**: 3rd sing. pres. mid./pass. (dep.) impera. < μιμέομαι.   **Ὀνησίκριτος**: a student of the Cynic philosopher Diogenes, Onescritus (*c.* 360 – *c.* 290 BCE) accompanied Alexander the Great on his campaigns in Asia. In India, Alexander sent him as the king's envoy to meet with the Gymnosophists. Later he served as the pilot of the king's ship. He wrote an account of Alexander's campaigns, including his and Alexander's meetings with the Gymnosophists. **Κάλανον**: an Indian gymnosophist encountered by Alexander the Great in Taxila, Calanus (*c.* 397 – 323 BCE) accompanied Alexander on his eastern campaign. In order to escape the suffering caused by old age and disease, Calanus committed self-immolation in 323 BCE.   **ἐπειδάν**: ἐπειδὴ + ἄν, *when(ever)* + subju.

Vocabulary

αἰτία, ἡ, *reason, cause*

Ἀλέξανδρος, ὁ, *Alexander*

ἀξιόω, *think, deem worthy; think one has the right, think it right* (+ inf.)

Βραχμᾶνες, οἱ, *Brachmanes, Bragmanni, Brahmans, Gymnosophists*

εἰκάζω, *compare, liken* X (acc.) *to* Y (dat.)

ἐμβάλλω, ἐμβαλῶ, ἐνέβαλον, *throw in*

ἐμπηδάω, ἐμπηδήσομαι, ἐνεπήδησα, *leap in* or *into*

ἔνειμι, *be in a place, be among;* ἔνεστι, *it is possible, one can*

ἕνεκα, prep. (+ preceding gen.), *for the sake of, because of*

ἐπιδείκνυμι, ἐπιδείξω, ἐπέδειξα, *exhibit (as a specimen), display*; (mid.) *exhibit one's powers of* (+ acc.)

Ἰνδός, ὁ, *Indian*

καθάπερ, adv., *just as, just like*

καίω, καύσω, ἔκαυσα, *set on fire, burn up*

Κάλανος, ὁ, *Calanus*

καρτερία, ἡ, *fortitude*

κενόδοξος, -ον, *vainglorious, conceited*

κυβερνήτης, -ου, ὁ, *pilot, navigator*

μιμέομαι, (dep.) *imitate*

μωρός, -ά, -όν, *dull, stupid, foolish;* (as substantive) *fool, moron*

νή, particle (of strong affirmation), νὴ Δία = *by Zeus!*

ὅμως, conj., *nevertheless*

Ὀνησίκριτος, ὁ, *Onesicritus*

ὥσπερ, adv., *just as (if)*

νήσωσι, πλησίον παραστάντες ἀκίνητοι ἀνέχονται

παροπτώμενοι, εἶτ᾽ ἐπιβάντες κατὰ σχῆμα καίονται,

οὐδ᾽ ὅσον ὀλίγον ἐντρέψαντες τῆς κατακλίσεως.

"οὗτος δὲ τί μέγα εἰ ἐμπεσὼν τεθνήξεται συναρπασθεὶς

ὑπὸ τοῦ πυρός; οὐκ ἀπ᾽ ἐλπίδος μὴ ἀναπηδήσασθαι αὐτὸν

καὶ ἡμίφλεκτον, εἰ μή, ὅπερ φασί, μηχανήσεται βαθεῖαν

γενέσθαι καὶ ἐν βόθρῳ τὴν πυράν.

νήσωσι: sc. τὴν πυράν.　　**κατὰ σχῆμα**: *in a dignified manner.*
οὐδ᾽ ὅσον: *not even, not even as much as.*　　**τῆς κατακλίσεως**:
gen. of separation.　　**οὗτος δὲ τί μέγα εἰ ἐμπεσὼν τεθνήξεται**
= δὲ τί μέγα (ἐστί) εἰ οὗτος ἐμπεσὼν τεθνήξεται.　　**τεθνήξεται**:
3rd sing. fut. perf. mid./pass. (act. in sense) indic. < θνήσκω; Lucian
idiosyncratically in his writings uses the mid. perf. of θνήσκω for the act.
συναρπασθείς: masc. nom. sing. aor. pass. part. < συναρπάζω.
οὐκ ἀπ᾽ ἐλπίδος: sc. ἐστί; *it is not beyond expectation* (Harmon), i.e.,
it is quite possible; + acc. and inf. in indir. statement.　　**μὴ**: not
translated, since μή + inf. after verbs of fearing or expressions that connote
some kind of fear (as here, since ἀπ᾽ ἐλπίδος can also mean *out of
apprehension*).　　**εἰ μή**: *unless.*　　**μηχανήσεται βαθεῖαν
γενέσθαι καὶ ἐν βόθρῳ τὴν πυράν**: literally, this says that the
pyre will be deep *and* in a pit; translate either as *he will devise the pyre to be
deep (down) in a pit* or, transferring βαθεῖαν, which grammatically goes
with πυράν, to βόθρῳ, as *he will devise the pyre to be in a deep pit.*

Vocabulary

ἀκίνητος, -ον, *motionless*

ἀναπηδάω, ἀναπηδήσομαι, ἀνεπήδησα, *jump out (in haste or fear)*

ἀνέχω, ἀνέξω, ἀνέσχον, *hold up*; (mid.) *endure, hold out*

βαθύς, βαθεῖα, βαθύ, *deep*

βόθρος, ὁ, *hole, pit*

ἐλπίς, -ίδος, ἡ, *hope, expectation*

ἐμπίπτω, ἐμπεσοῦμαι, ἐνέπεσον, *fall into*

ἐντρέπω, *turn about; change, alter*

ἐπιβαίνω, ἐπιβήσομαι, ἐπέβην, *get upon, mount on*

ἡμίφλεκτος, -ον, *half-burnt*

θνήσκω, θανοῦμαι, ἔθανον, *die*; τέθνηκα (perf.), *have died*, i.e., *be dead*

καίω, καύσω, ἔκαυσα, *set on fire, burn up*

κατάκλισις, -εως, ἡ, *lying down, way* or *position of lying down*

μέγας, μεγάλη, μέγα, *large, great*

μηχανάομαι, μηχανήσομαι, ἐμηχανησάμην, (dep.) *construct, build; contrive, devise*

νέω, *heap, pile up*

ὀλίγος, -η, -ον, *little, small*; (pl.) *few*

ὅσος, -η, -ον, *as great as, as much as*; (pl.) *as many as*

ὅσπερ, ἥπερ, ὅπερ, rel. pron., emphatic forms, *who, whose, whom, which, that*

παρίστημι, παραστήσω, (1st aor.) παρέστησα, *present, show*; (2nd aor.) παρέστην, (perf.) παρέστηκα, *stand by, be present*

παροπτάω, *roast slightly, toast, singe*

πλησίον, adv., *near, close*

πυρά, -ᾶς, ἡ, *pyre, funeral-pyre*

συναρπάζω, *seize and carry off*

σχῆμα, -ατος, τό, *form, shape, figure, appearance; bearing, comportment*

[26] εἰσὶ δ' οἳ καὶ μεταβαλέσθαι φασιν αὐτὸν καί τινα ὀνείρατα διηγεῖσθαι, ὡς τοῦ Διὸς οὐκ ἐῶντος μιαίνειν ἱερὸν χωρίον. ἀλλὰ θαρρείτω τούτου γε ἕνεκα· ἐγὼ γὰρ διομοσαίμην ἂν ἦ μὴν μηδένα τῶν θεῶν ἀγανακτήσειν, εἰ Περεγρῖνος κακῶς ἀποθάνοι. οὐ μὴν οὐδὲ ῥᾴδιον αὐτῷ ἔτ' ἀναδῦναι· οἱ γὰρ συνόντες κύνες παρορμῶσιν καὶ συνωθοῦσιν ἐς τὸ πῦρ καὶ ὑπεκκάουσι τὴν γνώμην, οὐκ ἐῶντες ἀποδειλιᾶν· ὧν εἰ δύο συγκατασπάσας ἐμπέσοι εἰς τὴν πυράν, τοῦτο μόνον χάριεν ἂν ἐργάσαιτο.

εἰσὶ δ' οἳ: *and there are those who.*   **ὡς**: + participles of cause or purpose, sometimes gen. abs., sets forth the grounds of belief on which the agent acts; i.e., *in the belief that, on the ground that.*   **τοῦ Διὸς οὐκ ἐῶντος**: gen. abs.; sc. αὐτόν as the dir. obj. of the part.   **μιαίνειν ἱερὸν χωρίον**: Harmon (25, n. 3) notes that, "As the cremation actually took place at Harpina, two miles away from Olympia, and on the day after the festival closed, it may be that religious scruples caused Peregrinus to modify an original plan which involved its taking place at Olympia itself while the festival was in progress."   **θαρρείτω**: 3rd sing. pres. act. impera. < θαρσέω.   **διομοσαίμην**: 1st sing. aor. mid. opt. < διόμνυμι; with ἀποθάνοι, a fut. less vivid condition (i.e., *should...would...*, here with the clauses syntactically reversed; i.e., *would...should...*).   **ἦ μὴν**: *truly indeed, absolutely*; this adv. + particle combination often introduces an oath or a threat; after verbs of swearing it usually precedes the acc. and inf. construction of an indir. statement.   **ἀποθάνοι**: 3rd sing. aor. act. opt. < ἀποθνήσκω.   **οὐ μὴν**: *nor indeed.*   **οὐδὲ, ἔτ'** = οὐκέτι.   **ῥᾴδιον αὐτῷ**: sc. ἐστί.   **παρορμῶσιν καὶ συνωθοῦσιν**: sc. αὐτόν.   **ὑπεκκάουσι**: literally, *light a strong fire underneath.*   **οὐκ ἐῶντες**: as with οὐκ ἐῶντος above, sc. αὐτόν.   **ὧν** = αὐτῶν: at the beginning of a sentence or clause, rel. pronouns substitute for personal pronouns in Greek.   **εἰ, ἐμπέσοι, ἐργάσαιτο**: a fut. less vivid condition (i.e., *should...would...*).   **ἐμπέσοι**: 3rd sing. aor. act. opt. < ἐμπίπτω.   **ἐργάσαιτο**: 3rd sing. aor. mid. (dep.) opt. < ἐργάζομαι.

Vocabulary

ἀγανακτέω, *be angry*

ἀναδύομαι, ἀναδύσομαι, ἀνέδυν (2nd aor.), (dep.) *draw back, withdraw, back out*

ἀποδειλιάω, *play the coward, be terrified*

ἀποθνήσκω, ἀποθανοῦμαι, ἀπέθανον, *die*

γνώμη, ἡ, *mind, will, purpose, resolve, intent*

διηγέομαι, (dep.), *describe (in detail)*

διόμνυμι, διομόσω, διώμοσα, (mid. διόμνυμαι is more common, with same meaning as act.) *swear solemnly, declare on oath that*

δύο, indecl., *two*

ἐάω, *permit, allow* (+ acc. of person and inf.)

ἐμπίπτω, ἐμπεσοῦμαι, ἐνέπεσον, *fall into*

ἕνεκα, prep. (+ preceding gen.), *for the sake of, because of*

ἐργάζομαι, (dep.) *do, accomplish*

ἔτι, adv., *still*; + οὐ or οὐδὲ, *no longer*

Ζεύς, Διός, Διΐ, Δία, ὁ, *Zeus*

ἦ, adv., *in truth*

θαρσέω, *be confident, have no fear*

ἱερός, -ά, -όν, *holy, sacred*

κακῶς, adv., *badly, wretchedly*

κύων, κυνός, ὁ or ἡ, *dog*; *Cynic philosopher*

μεταβάλλω, μεταβαλῶ, μετέβαλον, *turn about, change, alter*; (mid.) *change one's mind*

μηδείς, μηδεμία, μηδέν, *not one, not even one, nobody, nothing*

μήν, adv., *indeed, truly*

μιαίνω, *defile, pollute (morally)*

ὄνειρον, τό, *dream*; (ὀνείρατα is the common neut. nom./acc. pl. form)

παρορμάω, *urge on, incite*

ῥᾴδιος, -α, -ον, *easy*

συγκατασπάω, *pull down with himself*

σύνειμι, *attend, be with*; οἱ συνόντες, *associates, disciples*

συνωθέω, *push* or *shove together / as one*

ὑπεκκάω, ὑπεκκαύσω, ὑπεξέκαυσα, *inflame, excite, provoke*

χαρίεις, χαρίεσσα, χάριεν, (masc./neut. gen. χαρίεντος), *beautiful, nice, fine*

χωρίον, τό, *place*

[27] "ἤκουον δὲ ὡς οὐδὲ Πρωτεὺς ἔτι καλεῖσθαι ἀξιοῖ,

ἀλλὰ Φοίνικα μετωνόμασεν ἑαυτόν, ὅτι καὶ φοῖνιξ,

τὸ Ἰνδικὸν ὄρνεον, ἐπιβαίνειν πυρᾶς λέγεται πορρωτάτω

γήρως προβεβηκώς. ἀλλὰ καὶ λογοποιεῖ καὶ χρησμούς τινας

διέξεισιν παλαιοὺς δή, ὡς χρεὼν εἴη δαίμονα νυκτοφύλακα

γενέσθαι αὐτόν, καὶ δῆλός ἐστι βωμῶν ἤδη ἐπιθυμῶν καὶ

χρυσοῦς ἀναστήσεσθαι ἐλπίζων.

ὡς = ὅτι.　　 οὐδὲ...ἀξιοῖ = οὐδὲ ἔτι ἀξιοῖ καλεῖσθαι Πρωτεὺς.
οὐδὲ ἔτι = οὐκέτι.　　ἀξιοῖ: 3rd sing. pres. act. subju./opt. < ἀξιόω;
opt. in indir. statement, secondary sequence.　　φοῖνιξ: a long-lived
mythological bird reborn after a several centuries long life-cycle, near the
end of which it builds itself a nest of twigs that then ignites; both nest and
bird burn until they are reduced to ashes, from which a new, young phoenix
or egg arises. The phoenix is normally associated with Egypt (where it
symbolized resurrection) not India; Jones (127) suggests that this Indian
association may be a "new mythology" created by Peregrinus and his
followers.　　πορρωτάτω γήρως προβεβηκώς: *having gone very
far in old age*, i.e., *when it has become very old.*　　γήρως: gen. of
measure (or partitive gen.).　　προβεβηκώς: masc. nom. sing. perf. act.
part. < προβαίνω.　　παλαιοὺς δή: the adj.'s placement at the end of
the clause with the particle imparts a sarcastic inflection; to capture the tone
one might employ scare quotes: *"ancient," of course.*　　ὡς χρεὼν εἴη
αὐτόν = ὡς εἴη χρεὼν αὐτόν γενέσθαι δαίμονα νυκτοφύλακα.
ὡς: here expresses a fact (in Peregrinus' mind, at least); *that* (sometimes +
the opt. after a primary tense in Lucian).　　εἴη: 3rd sing. pres. act. opt. <
εἰμί.　　δαίμονα νυκτοφύλακα: the second noun is in apposition to
the first; *a spirit, a guardian of the night*; or, as Harmon, Macleod, and
Costa translate: *a guardian spirit of the night.*　　δῆλός ἐστι,
ἐπιθυμῶν, ἐλπίζων: literally, *he is clear desiring...(and) hoping...*;
English prefers an adv. where Greek uses a predicate adj., and an indic. verb
in place of a part.; i.e., *he clearly desires...(and) hopes...*　　χρυσοῦς:
sc. *statues (of himself)*; at Olympia, gold statues included those of Philip of
Macedon and his family, though the most famous statue at Olympia made
with gold was the enormous gold-and-ivory one of Zeus by Pheidias, to
which Peregrinus had been compared earlier by Theagenes (see 5).
ἀναστήσεσθαι: fut. mid. (here with pass. sense) inf. < ἀνίστημι.

76

Vocabulary

ἀνίστημι, ἀναστήσω, ἀνέστησα, *make* X *stand up, raise* X; (pres., imperf., and fut. mid.; 2nd aor, perf., and pluperf. act.; aor. pass.; of statues) *be set up*

ἀξιόω, *think, deem worthy; think it right* or *fit, consent* (+ inf.)

βωμός, ὁ, *altar*

γῆρας, γήρως, τό, *old age*

δαίμων, -ονος, ὁ or ἡ, *god, goddess, divine power, spirit*

δή, particle, *indeed; in fact; of course*

δῆλος, -η, -ον, *clear*

διέξειμι, *expound, set forth, relate in detail*

ἐλπίζω, *expect, hope* (frequently with a dependent clause + inf. [usually fut.])

ἐπιβαίνω, ἐπιβήσομαι, ἐπέβην, *get upon, mount on*

ἐπιθυμέω, *lust after, long for, desire* (+ gen.)

ἔτι, adv., *still;* + οὐ or οὐδὲ, *no longer*

ἤδη, adv., *already*

Ἰνδικός, -ή, -όν, *Indian*

καλέω, *call*

λογοποιέω, *invent stories, fabricate tales*

μετονομάζω, *call by a new name;* (+ reflexive pron. + acc.) *change one's name to*

νυκτοφύλαξ, -ακος, ὁ, *guardian of the night*

ὄρνεον, τό, *bird*

ὅτι: conj., *because.*

παλαιός, -ά, -όν, *ancient*

πορρωτάτω, adv., *furthest, very far*

προβαίνω, προβήσομαι, προὔβην, *go forward, advance*

φοῖνιξ, -ικος, ὁ, *phoenix (mythological bird of India-Arabia-Egypt)*

Φοῖνιξ, -ικος, ὁ, *Phoenix*

χρεών, (indecl.) *necessity, fate;* mostly in the phrase χρεών (sc. ἐστι), *it is necessary*

χρησμός, ὁ, *oracle*

χρυσοῦς, -ῆ, -οῦν, *golden, of gold*

Peregrinus' Oracular Statue

Athenagoras, a Christian apologist and contemporary of Lucian, mentions in 130-131 of his *Embassy for the Christians* (written in 176-177 CE, a little more than a decade after Peregrinus' suicide), that in Parium a statue of their hometown hero (see 14) had already been set up in his honor. Athenagoras then adds that the statue καὶ αὐτὸς λέγεται χρηματίζειν (*itself is also said to utter prophecies*); cf. 28 on the next page concerning Lucian's prediction that after Peregrinus' suicide, μαθηταὶ αὐτοῦ, χρηστήριον, μηχανήσονται (*his disciples will build an oracular shrine [to him]*).

[28] "καὶ μὰ Δία οὐδὲν ἀπεικὸς ἐν πολλοῖς τοῖς ἀνοήτοις εὑρεθήσεσθαί τινας τοὺς καὶ τεταρταίων ἀπηλλάχθαι δι' αὐτοῦ φήσοντας καὶ νύκτωρ ἐντετυχηκέναι τῷ δαίμονι τῷ νυκτοφύλακι. οἱ κατάρατοι δὲ οὗτοι μαθηταὶ αὐτοῦ καὶ χρηστήριον, οἶμαι, καὶ ἄδυτον ἐπὶ τῇ πυρᾷ μηχανήσονται, διότι καὶ Πρωτεὺς ἐκεῖνος ὁ Διός, ὁ προπάτωρ τοῦ ὀνόματος, μαντικὸς ἦν. μαρτύρομαι δὲ ἦ μὴν καὶ ἱερέας αὐτοῦ ἀποδειχθήσεσθαι μαστίγων ἢ καυτηρίων ἤ τινος τοιαύτης τερατουργίας, ἢ καὶ νὴ Δία τελετήν τινα ἐπ' αὐτῷ συστήσεσθαι νυκτέριον καὶ δαδουχίαν ἐπὶ τῇ πυρᾷ.

οὐδὲν ἀπεικὸς: sc. ἐστι; *litotes* (see 12); + acc. and inf. in indir. statement.   **εὑρεθήσεσθαί**: fut. pass. inf. < εὑρίσκω.   **καὶ, καὶ**: *even...and...* or *both...and...*   **τεταρταίων**: a malarial fever occurring every fourth day, counting inclusively (i.e., every 72 hours).   **τοὺς, φήσοντας**: *who will say* (in apposition to τινας); + infinitives in indir. statement (i.e, *that they [themselves]...*).   **ἀπηλλάχθαι**: perf. mid./pass. inf. < ἀπαλλάττω.   **ἐντετυχηκέναι**: perf. act. inf. < ἐντυγχάνω. **ἐκεῖνος ὁ Διός**: *that (son) of Zeus*; every account from the ancient world has Proteus as the son of Poseidon, so perhaps Lucian is "unconsciously following the propaganda of Peregrinus' followers" (Jones 197).   **μαντικὸς**: Menelaus seeks out Proteus in *Odyssey* 4.384 ff. because of his ability to tell the future, though he will change his shape to avoid having to do so, and will answer only to someone who is capable of capturing him (see 1).   **ἦ μὴν**: *truly indeed, absolutely*; this adv. + particle combination often introduces an oath or a threat; after verbs of swearing or testifying it often precedes the acc. and inf. construction of an indir. statement.   **ἀποδειχθήσεσθαι**: fut. pass. inf. < ἀποδείκνυμι. **μαστίγων ἢ καυτηρίων ἤ τινος τοιαύτης τερατουργίας**: genitives of explanation (aka, appositive genitives), in which the gen. of an explicit word may explain the meaning of a more general word; i.e., *(priests) with whips, or with...*   **τελετήν, νυκτέριον, δαδουχίαν**: these elements suggest that it will be modeled after the celebrated Eleusinian Mysteries.   **ἐπ' αὐτῷ**: *for him*, i.e., *in his honor*. **συστήσεσθαι**: fut. mid. (here with pass. sense) inf. < συνίστημι.

78

Vocabulary

ἄδυτον, τό, *innermost sanctuary, "holy of holies"*

ἀνόητος, -ον, *unintelligent, senseless, silly*; ὁ ἀνόητος, *fool*

ἀπαλλάττω, *set free*; (mid./pass.) *be set free* or *released from, recover from* (+ gen.)

ἀπεικώς, -υῖα, -ός, *unlikely, unreasonable*

ἀποδείκνυμι, ἀποδείξω, ἀπέδειξα, *appoint, name, create*

δᾳδουχία, ἡ, *torchlight parade, torch-bearing festival/ceremony*

δαίμων, -ονος, ὁ or ἡ, *god, goddess, divine power, spirit*

Ζεύς, Διός, Διΐ, Δία, ὁ, *Zeus*

διότι, conj., *because*

ἐντυγχάνω, ἐντεύξομαι, ἐνέτυχον, *meet with, encounter* (+ dat.)

εὑρίσκω, εὑρήσω, ηὗρον/εὗρον, *find*

ἦ, adv., *in truth*; ἦ μὴν, *absolutely in fact*

ἱερεύς, -έως, ὁ, *priest*

κατάρατος, -ον, *accursed, abominable*

καυτήριον, τό, *branding iron*

μά, particle (used in protestations and oaths), *by*

μαθητής, -οῦ, ὁ, *student, disciple*

μαντικός, -ή, -όν, *prophetic, oracular, like a prophet*

μαρτύρομαι, μαρτυροῦμαι, ἐμαρτυράμην, (dep.) *testify, solemnly declare*

μάστιξ, -ιγος, ἡ, *whip*

μήν, adv., *indeed, truly*

μηχανάομαι, μηχανήσομαι, ἐμηχανησάμην, (dep.) *construct, build*

νή, particle (of strong affirmation), νὴ Δία = *by Zeus!*

νυκτέριος, -η, -ον, *nocturnal, by night*

νυκτοφύλαξ, -ακος, ὁ, *guardian of the night*

νύκτωρ, adv., *at night*

οἶμαι (uncontracted = οἴομαι), *suppose, think*

ὄνομα, -ατος, τό, *name*

οὐδείς, οὐδεμία, οὐδέν, *no one, nothing*; *no*

προπάτωρ, -ορος, ὁ, *ancestor, progenitor*

συνίστημι, συστήσω, συνέστησα, *combine, associate*; (pass.) *form, be organized* or *put together*; *arise, take shape, come into existence*

τελετή, ἡ, *mystic rite, initiation ceremony*

τερατουργία, ἡ, *hocus-pocus, flimflammery*

τεταρταῖος, -η, -ον, *on the fourth day*; τεταρταῖος [πυρετός], *quartan fever*

φημί, φήσω, ἔφην (imperf.), ἔφησα (aor., rare), *say*

χρηστήριον, τό, *oracular shrine*

[29] "Θεαγένης δὲ ἔναγχος, ὥς μοί τις τῶν ἑταίρων ἀπήγγειλεν, καὶ Σίβυλλαν ἔφη προειρηκέναι περὶ τούτων· καὶ τὰ ἔπη γὰρ ἀπεμνημόνευεν·

ἀλλ' ὁπόταν Πρωτεὺς Κυνικῶν ὄχ' ἄριστος ἁπάντων
Ζηνὸς ἐριγδούπου τέμενος κάτα πῦρ ἀνακαύσας
ἐς φλόγα πηδήσας ἔλθῃ ἐς μακρὸν Ὄλυμπον,
δὴ τότε πάντας ὁμῶς, οἳ ἀρούρης καρπὸν ἔδουσιν,
νυκτιπόλον τιμᾶν κέλομαι ἥρωα μέγιστον
σύνθρονον Ἡφαίστῳ καὶ Ἡρακλῆϊ ἄνακτι.

Θεαγένης δὲ ἔναγχος, καὶ Σίβυλλαν ἔφη προειρηκέναι = δὲ Θεαγένης καὶ ἔναγχος ἔφη Σίβυλλαν προειρηκέναι. **Σίβυλλαν**: a Sybil was a woman who possessed prophetic powers. At first there was only one Sibyl, located at Erythrae or Cumae; later, nine or ten Sibyls are mentioned. **προειρηκέναι**: perf. act. inf. < προερῶ. **ἀλλ' ὁπόταν...**: the six lines of verse that follow are dactylic hexameter, a meter used in epic poetry, oracular responses, and riddles. Both these verses and the ones that follow in 30 are partly made up of lines recycled from Homer and Aristophanes' *Knights*. **ὁπόταν**: ὁπότε + ἄν; *when(ever)* (+ subju.). **ὄχ' ἄριστος**: the phrase gives the oracle an epic inflection, since this adv. + superlative combination is used only by Homer. **κάτα**: in verse, disyllabic prepositions can follow their cases as well as precede them (in prose, only περί can do this). When such prepositions follow their cases, the accent shifts from the last syllable to the first (this is called anastrophe). **ἔλθῃ**: 3rd sing. aor. act. subju. < ἔρχομαι. **νυκτιπόλον**: an adj. usually associated with the Bacchae, Persephone, and Artemis. **κέλομαι**: epic vocabulary, equivalent to κελεύω. **σύνθρονον**: a rare word. **Ἡφαίστῳ**: Hephaestus does not, at least initially, seem a particularly apt choice in terms of being paired with Heracles: except for the intitial alliteration of their names (perhaps the main reason Lucian's Theagenes selected his name!), there is little thematic connection between the two gods. Hephaestus, however, is the god associated with fire (cf. the counter-oracle delivered by the speaker on the following page, where his name is a metonym for fire: μένος Ἡφαίστοιο), and Peregrinus is attempting to follow Heracles to Olympus via this route.

Vocabulary

ἀνακαίω, ἀνακαύσω, ἀνέκαυσα, kindle, light (a fire)

ἄναξ, ἄνακτος, ὁ, lord

ἀπαγγέλλω, ἀπαγγελῶ, ἀπήγγειλα, report, announce, relate

ἀπομνημονεύω, quote from memory

ἄριστος, -η, -ον, best

ἄρουρα, ἡ, tilled land, ploughland, fields

δή, particle, indeed, in fact; then, therefore, now

ἔδω, (Epic pres. for which Attic uses ἐσθίω) eat

ἔναγχος, adv., just now, lately, recently

ἔπος, -ους, τό, word; (pl.) words, verses

ἐρίγδουπος, -ον, (Homeric epithet of Zeus) loud-sounding, thundering

ἔρχομαι, εἶμι, ἦλθον, come, go

ἑταῖρος, ὁ, comrade, companion, friend

Ζῆν, Ζηνός, Ζηνί, Ζῆνα, ὁ, (Epic and tragic alternative spelling of) Zeus

Ἡρακλῆς, -έους, ὁ, Heracles

ἥρως, ἥρωος, ὁ, hero

Ἥφαιστος, ὁ, Hephaestus

καρπός, ὁ, crops, produce, fruit

κατά, prep. (+ acc.), in, in the region of

κέλομαι, (dep.) urge, exhort, command

Κυνικός, ὁ, Cynic, i.e., a follower of the philosopher Antisthenes.

μακρός, -ά, -όν, great

μέγιστος, -η, -ον, greatest

νυκτιπόλος, -ον, night-roaming

Ὄλυμπος, ὁ, Olympus

ὅμως, conj., together, alike, equally

ὄχα, adv., far; ὄχ' ἄριστος, far the best

πηδάω, πηδήσομαι, ἐπήδησα, leap

προερῶ (fut. in Attic; present is from different stems: προλέγω and προαγορεύω), προεῖπον (aor.), foretell, make a prediction

Σίβυλλα, ἡ, Sibyl

σύνθρονος, -ον, enthroned with

τέμενος, -ους, τό, sacred precinct

τιμάω, honor, revere, show reverence to

τότε, adv., then, at that time

φλόξ, φλογός, ἡ, flame

ὥς, adv., as

[30] "ταῦτα μὲν Θεαγένης Σιβύλλης ἀκηκοέναι φησίν,

ἐγὼ δὲ Βάκιδος αὐτῷ χρησμὸν ὑπὲρ τούτων ἐρῶ· φησὶν δὲ

ὁ Βάκις οὕτω, σφόδρα εὖ ἐπειπών,

Ἀλλ᾽ ὁπόταν Κυνικὸς πολυώνυμος ἐς φλόγα πολλὴν

πηδήσῃ δόξης ὑπ᾽ ἐρινύι θυμὸν ὀρινθείς,

δὴ τότε τοὺς ἄλλους κυναλώπεκας, οἳ οἱ ἕπονται,

μιμεῖσθαι χρὴ πότμον ἀποιχομένοιο λύκοιο.

ὃς δέ κε δειλὸς ἐὼν φεύγῃ μένος Ἡφαίστοιο,

λάεσσιν βαλέειν τοῦτον τάχα πάντας Ἀχαιούς,

ὡς μὴ ψυχρὸς ἐὼν θερμηγορέειν ἐπιχειρῇ

χρυσῷ σαξάμενος πήρην μάλα πολλὰ δανείζων,

ἀκηκοέναι: perf. act. inf. < ἀκούω.   **Βάκιδος**: Bacis, originally the name of an old Boeotian prophet, later a generic title for any prophet. **ὁπόταν**: ὁπότε + ἄν; *when(ever)* (+ subju.).   **πολυώνυμος**: both *famous* and *of many aliases*.   **δόξης ὑπ᾽ ἐρινύι θυμὸν ὀρινθείς**: *stirred in his heart by a frenzied passion for glory*; ὑπ᾽ + dat. of agent (in verse); ἐρινύι + gen.; θυμὸν = acc. of respect; ὀρινθείς = masc. nom. sing. aor. act. part. < ὀρίνω.   **κυναλώπεκας**: a term of insult that combines a shameless creature (*dog* – with pun on Cynics) and a mischievous, cunning one (*fox*); it is the name of a πορνοβοσκός (*brothel-keeper*) in Aristophanes' *Lysistrata* (957) and of the scheming, corrupt Athenian demagogue Cleon in Aristophanes' *Knights* (1067).   **οἱ**: (Ionic) = αὐτῷ.   **ἀποιχομένοιο λύκοιο, Ἡφαίστοιο**: Epic gen. singulars. **ὃς δέ κε**: *And whoever* (+ subju.).   **ἐών**: (Ionic) = ὤν.   **λάεσσιν**: Epic masc. dat. pl.   **βαλέειν**: Epic/Ionic aor. act. inf. < βάλλω; the inf. (with subj. acc.) for the 3rd-person impera. occurs mostly in verse; this construction conveys a solemn or formal tone (i.e., *I authorize all Achaians to...*).   **ὡς...ἐπιχειρῇ** = ὡς ψυχρὸς ἐὼν μὴ ἐπιχειρῇ θερμηγορέειν. **ὡς**: + subju. or opt. = a final/purpose clause; *so that, in order that*. **θερμηγορέειν**: Epic/Ionic pres. act. inf.; apparently a Lucianic coinage. **σαξάμενος**: the mid. voice, as regularly in Greek, expresses the idea that the agent is doing an action for his/her own interest.   **πολλά**: sc. *money*.

Vocabulary

ἀποίχομαι, (dep.) *have departed, be absent; be dead and gone*

Ἀχαιοί, οἱ, *Achaeans* (in Homer the name most commonly used for the Greeks)

Βάκις, -ιδος, ὁ, *Bacis*

βάλλω, βαλῶ, ἔβαλον, *throw, hit;* (mid.) *put about oneself, wear*

δανείζω, *lending money out at interest*

δειλός, -ή, -όν, *cowardly, vile, worthless*

ἐπιλέγω, ἐπιλέξω, ἐπεῖπον, *say in connection with, say besides or afterwards, utter, pronounce, say in apposition*

ἐπιχειρέω, *try to, attempt to* (+ inf.)

ἕπομαι, (dep.) *follow* (+ dat.)

ἐρινύς, -ύος, ἡ, *frenzy, fury* ; ἡ Ἐρινύς, *Fury*

ἐρῶ, (fut., along with λέξω, of λέγω) *will say, tell, speak*

εὖ, adv., *well*

θερμηγορέω, *make a fiery speech in public*

θυμός, ὁ, *soul, spirit, heart, mind*

κε, Homeric equivalent of the modal particle ἄν

κυναλώπηξ, -εκος, ἡ, *mongrel between dog and fox, dog-fox*

Κυνικός, ὁ, *Cynic,* i.e., a follower of the philosopher Antisthenes.

λᾶας, ου, ὁ, *stone*

λύκος, ὁ, *wolf*

μένος, -ους, τό, *might, force*

μιμέομαι, (dep.) *imitate*

ὀρίνω, *stir, move, excite, rouse*

πηδάω, πηδήσομαι, ἐπήδησα, *leap*

πήρα, ἡ, *leather pouch, wallet*

πολυώνυμος, -ον, *having many names; of great name, famous*

πότμος, ὁ, *doom, fate, destiny; death*

σάττω, *fill quite full, pack, stuff* X (acc.) *with* Y (gen. or dat.)

Σίβυλλα, ἡ, *Sibyl*

σφόδρα, adv., *very, very much, greatly; strongly, violently*

τάχα, adv., *quickly, at once, without delay*

τότε, adv., *then, at that time*

ὑπέρ, prep. (+ gen.), *concerning*

φεύγω, φεύξομαι, ἔφυγον, *flee, run away*

φλόξ, φλογός, ἡ, *flame*

χρησμός, ὁ, *oracular response, oracle*

χρυσός, ὁ, *gold*

ψυχρός, -ά, -όν, *cold, frigid; vain; heartless; silly*

ἐν καλαῖς Πάτραισιν ἔχων τρὶς πέντε τάλαντα.

τί ὑμῖν δοκεῖ, ἄνδρες; ἆρα φαυλότερος χρησμολόγος
ὁ Βάκις τῆς Σιβύλλης εἶναι; ὥστε ὥρα τοῖς θαυμαστοῖς
τούτοις ὁμιληταῖς τοῦ Πρωτέως περισκοπεῖν ἔνθα ἑαυτοὺς
ἐξαερώσουσιν· τοῦτο γὰρ τὴν καῦσιν καλοῦσιν."

Πάτραισιν: located *c.* 60 miles north of Olympia on the Corinthian Gulf, Patras was a prosperous town in the 2nd century CE. It was the birthplace of Theagenes. **τρὶς πέντε τάλαντα**: approximately $400,000; see 14 where, according to Lucian, this was also the value of the land inherited by Peregrinus. **τί ὑμῖν δοκεῖ**: literally, *What does it seem to you?*, i.e., *What do you think?* **ἆρα...Σιβύλλης εἶναι** = ἆρα ὁ Βάκις (δοκεῖ ὑμῖν) εἶναι φαυλότερος χρησμολόγος τῆς Σιβύλλης. **τῆς Σιβύλλης**: gen. of comparison. **ὥστε...καλοῦσιν**: note the strong alliteration, especially of "s," "t," and "n." **ὥρα**: [ἐστίν] + inf., *it is (the right) time.* **τοῦτο**: i.e., Peregrinus' disciples are calling his cremation "aerification"; cf. Peregrinus' words at 33, where he states that he wanted ἀναμιχθῆναι τῷ αἰθέρι (*to be commingled with the aether*).

[31] ταῦτ' εἰπόντος ἀνεβόησαν οἱ περιεστῶτες ἅπαντες,
"ἤδη καιέσθωσαν ἄξιοι τοῦ πυρός." καὶ ὁ μὲν κατέβη γελῶν,
"Νέστορα δ' οὐκ ἔλαθεν ἰαχή," τὸν Θεαγένη, ἀλλ' ὡς
ἤκουσεν τῆς βοῆς, ἧκεν εὐθὺς καὶ ἀναβὰς ἐκεκράγει καὶ
μυρία κακὰ διεξήει περὶ τοῦ καταβεβηκότος· οὐ γάρ οἶδα

ταῦτ' εἰπόντος: gen. abs.; sc. αὐτοῦ. **καιέσθωσαν**: 3rd pl. pres. mid./pass. impera. < καίω. **"Νέστορα...ἰαχή"**: from *Iliad* 14.1. **τὸν Θεαγένη**: in apposition to Νέστορα; translate as either *i.e., Theagenes* or *I mean Theagenes*. **κατέβη, ἀναβὰς**: sc. *speaker's platform.* **ἐκεκράγει**: 3rd sing. pluperf. (with imperf. sense) act. indic. < κράζω; inchoative or inceptive "imperfect"; i.e., *he began to...* **καταβεβηκότος**: masc. gen. sing. perf. act. part. < καταβαίνω.

Vocabulary

ἀναβαίνω, ἀναβήσομαι, ἀνέβην, *go up, mount (the speaker's platform)*

ἀναβοάω, ἀναβοήσομαι, ἀνεβόησα, *shout, cry out*

ἄξιος, -α, -ον, *worthy of, deserving* (+ gen.)

ἆρα, particle introducing a question

βοή, ἡ, *loud cry, shout*

γελάω, γελάσομαι, ἐγέλασα, *laugh*

διέξειμι, *go through in detail, relate in detail*

δοκῶ, (uncontracted = δοκέω) *think, suppose, imagine*; (3rd sing.) *it seems*

ἔνθα, adv., *where, a place where*

ἐξαερόω, *make into air, aerify*

εὐθύς, adv., *immediately, at once; straight, directly*

ἥκω, (imperf.) ἧκον, (pres. = perf.; imperf. = pluperf.) *have come*

θαυμαστός, -ή, -όν, *wonderful, marvelous*

ἰαχή, ἡ, *cry, shout, wail, shriek* (usually of men in battle, both victors and vanquished)

καίω, καύσω, ἔκαυσα, *set on fire, burn up*

κακός, -ή, -όν, *bad, evil, malicious*

καλός, -ή, -όν, *beautiful, fine*

καταβαίνω, καταβήσομαι, κατέβην, *go* or *come down, descend*

καῦσις, -εως, ἡ, *burning, cremation*

κράζω, *croak, scream, shriek*

λανθάνω, λήσω, ἔλαθον, *escape notice*

μυρίος, -α, -ον, *numberless, countless*

Νέστωρ, -ορος, ὁ, *Nestor*

οἶδα, (perf. with pres. meaning) *know*

ὁμιλητής, -οῦ, ὁ, *disciple, follower*

παρίστημι, παραστήσω, (1st aor.) παρέστησα, *present, show*; (2nd aor.)
  παρέστην, (perf.) παρέστηκα, *stand by, be present*

Πάτραι, -ῶν, αἱ, *Patras*

πέντε, indecl., *five*

περισκοπέω, *look around* or *about, consider carefully*

τάλαντον, -ου, τό, *talent* (a weight and a sum of money = 6,000 drachmas)

τρίς, indecl., *three times, thrice*

φαῦλος, -η, -ον, *low (in rank), mean, common*; (comparative) *inferior*

χρησμολόγος, -ον, *uttering oracles, expounder of oracles; soothsayer*

ὥρα, ἡ, *time, right time*

ὡς, conj., (+ aor. indic.) *when*

ὥστε, conj., *and so, therefore*

ὅστις ἐκεῖνος ὁ βέλτιστος ἐκαλεῖτο. ἐγὼ δὲ ἀφεὶς αὐτὸν

διαρρηγνύμενον ἀπῄειν ὀψόμενος τοὺς ἀθλητάς· ἤδη γὰρ

οἱ Ἑλλανοδίκαι ἐλέγοντο εἶναι ἐν τῷ Πλεθρίῳ.

ὁ βέλτιστος: this word was used twice earlier (1, 12) to describe Peregrinus. Here it is used to describe the speaker ("Lucian's Double"; see 7 and note ad loc.) opposed to Peregrinus and Theagenes.   **ἀφεὶς**: masc. nom. sing. aor. act. part. < ἀφίημι.   **ἀπῄειν**: 1st sing. imperf. act. indic. < ἀπέρχομαι.   **ὀψόμενος**: the fut. part., with or without ὡς, can express purpose.   **οἱ Ἑλλανοδίκαι**: these were ten citizens of Elis entrusted with administering and enforcing all aspects of the Olympic Games and its rules.   **Πλεθρίῳ**: according to Pausanias (6.23.2), this was a place in the Gymnasium of Elis where the Hellanodicae matched the competitors in the wrestling events according to age and skill.

[32] ταῦτα μέν σοι τὰ ἐν Ἤλιδι. ἐπεὶ δὲ ἐς τὴν Ὀλυμπίαν

ἀφικόμεθα, μεστὸς ἦν ὁ ὀπισθόδομος τῶν κατηγορούντων

Πρωτέως ἢ ἐπαινούντων τὴν προαίρεσιν αὐτοῦ, ὥστε καὶ εἰς

χεῖρας αὐτῶν ἦλθον οἱ πολλοί, ἄχρι δὴ παρελθὼν αὐτὸς ὁ

Πρωτεὺς μυρίῳ τῷ πλήθει παραπεμπόμενος κατόπιν τοῦ τῶν

κηρύκων ἀγῶνος λόγους τινὰς διεξῆλθεν περὶ ἑαυτοῦ, τὸν

βίον τε ὡς ἐβίω καὶ τοὺς κινδύνους οὓς ἐκινδύνευσεν

διηγούμενος καὶ ὅσα πράγματα φιλοσοφίας ἕνεκα ὑπέμεινεν.

ταῦτα μέν σοι τὰ ἐν Ἤλιδι: literally, *These things (are) the things in Elis for you*; i.e., *So now you know what happened at Elis* (Costa); σοι is a dat. of interest (*for the benefit of you [knowing]*).   **ὁ ὀπισθόδομος**: of the Temple of Zeus.   **εἰς χεῖρας αὐτῶν ἦλθον**: i.e., they settled the matter with their fists.   **μυρίῳ τῷ πλήθει**: dat. of agent with pass. voice.   **τοῦ τῶν κηρύκων ἀγῶνος**: note the syntactical "nesting"; this became an official Oympic event in 396 BCE.   **βίον, ἐβίω, κινδύνους, ἐκινδύνευσεν**: *figura etymologica* x2 (see also 1, 17, 18).

Vocabulary

ἀγών, -ῶνος, ὁ, *contest*

ἀθλητής, -οῦ, ὁ, *athlete*

ἀπέρχομαι, ἄπειμι, ἀπῆλθον, *go, go away, depart*

ἀφίημι, ἀφήσω, ἀφῆκα, *leave alone*

ἀφικνέομαι, ἀφίξομαι, ἀφικόμην, (dep.) *arrive at, come to, reach*

ἄχρι, conj., *until*

βέλτιστος, -η, -ον, *best, very good*; ὁ βέλτιστος, *very fine/excellent gentleman*

βίος, ὁ, *life*

βιόω, βιώσομαι, ἐβίωσα /ἐβίων (2nd aor.), *live*

διαρρήγνυμι, *break through, cleave asunder*; (pass.) *burst* (with passion)

διεξέρχομαι, διέξειμι, διεξῆλθον, *go through in detail, relate in detail*

διηγέομαι, (dep.) *set out in detail, describe in full*

Ἑλλανοδίκαι, -ῶν, οἱ, the chief judges/officials at the Olympic Games

ἕνεκα, prep. (+ preceding gen.), *for the sake of, because of*

ἐπαινέω, *praise*

ἔρχομαι, εἶμι, ἦλθον, *come, go*

Ἦλις, -ιδος, ἡ, *Elis*

κατηγορέω, *speak against, denounce* (+ gen.)

κατόπιν, adv. (+ gen.), *after*

κῆρυξ, -υκος, ὁ, *herald*

κινδυνεύω, *venture, hazard*; *run* or *take a/the risk*

κίνδυνος, ὁ, *danger, risk*

μεστός, -ή, -όν, *full, full of, filled with* (+ gen.)

μυρίος, -α, -ον, *numberless, countless*

ὀπισθόδομος, ὁ, *rear porch* or *chamber (of a temple)*

ὅσος, -η, -ον, *as great as, as much as*; (pl.) *as many as*

παραπέμπω, *escort, attend*

παρέρχομαι, πάρειμι, παρῆλθον, *arrive, come forward (to speak)*

Πλέθριον, τό, *Plethrium*

πλῆθος, -ους, τό, *multitude*

πρᾶγμα, -τος, τό, *matter, thing, affair*; (pl.) *troubles, annoyances*

προαίρεσις, -εως, ἡ, *choice, purpose; character, reputation*

ὑπομένω, ὑπομενῶ, ὑπέμεινα, *endure, submit to*

φιλοσοφία, ἡ, *philosophy*

χείρ, χειρός, ἡ, *hand*

ὡς, adv., *how*

ὥστε, conj., *so that, that, with the result that*

τὰ μὲν οὖν εἰρημένα πολλὰ ἦν, ἐγὼ δὲ ὀλίγων ἤκουσα ὑπὸ πλήθους τῶν περιεστώτων. εἶτα φοβηθεὶς μὴ συντριβείην ἐν τοσαύτῃ τύρβῃ, ἐπεὶ καὶ πολλοὺς τοῦτο πάσχοντας ἑώρων, ἀπῆλθον μακρὰ χαίρειν φράσας θανατιῶντι σοφιστῇ τὸν ἐπιτάφιον ἑαυτοῦ πρὸ τελευτῆς διεξιόντι.

τὰ, εἰρημένα: sc. *by him*; εἰρημένα: neut. acc. pl. perf. mid./pass. part. < εἴρημαι (the perf. mid./pass. of λέγω). **περιεστώτων**: masc. gen. pl. perf. act. part. < περιίστημι. **ἦν**: neut. pl. subjects take sing. verbs. **ὀλίγων**: i.e., *only a little*. **ὑπὸ**: + gen.; *on account of*. **μὴ**: in fear clauses μὴ is not translated. **συντριβείην**: 1st sing. aor. pass. opt. < συντρίβω; opt. in a fear clause in secondary sequence. **ἑώρων**: 1st sing. imperf. act. indic. < ὁράω. **πρό**: + gen.; *before*.

---

[33] πλὴν τό γε τοσοῦτον ἐπήκουσα· ἔφη γὰρ βούλεσθαι χρυσῷ βίῳ χρυσῆν κορώνην ἐπιθεῖναι· χρῆναι γὰρ τὸν Ἡρακλείως βεβιωκότα Ἡρακλείως ἀποθανεῖν καὶ ἀναμιχθῆναι τῷ αἰθέρι. " καὶ ὠφελῆσαι," ἔφη "βούλομαι τοὺς ἀνθρώπους δείξας αὐτοῖς ὃν χρὴ τρόπον θανάτου καταφρονεῖν· πάντας οὖν δεῖ μοι τοὺς ἀνθρώπους Φιλοκτήτας γενέσθαι." οἱ μὲν οὖν ἀνοητότεροι τῶν ἀνθρώπων ἐδάκρυον καὶ ἐβόων "σώζου τοῖς Ἕλλησιν,"

ἔφη γὰρ...ἐπιθεῖναι = γὰρ ἔφη βούλεσθαι ἐπιθεῖναι χρυσῆν κορώνην χρυσῷ βίῳ. **βίῳ**: punning on *life* (βίῳ) and *bow* (βιῷ) with the double meaning of κορώνην. **χρῆναι**: pres. act. inf. < χρή; the inf. is governed by the previous ἔφη; τὸν, βεβιωκότα = acc. subj. of the indir. statement; βεβιωκότα: masc. acc. sing. perf. act. part. < βιόω. **ἀναμιχθῆναι**: aor. inf. pass. < ἀναμίγνυμι. **σώζου**: 2nd sing. pres. mid./pass. impera. < σώζω; the mid. is reflexive. **ὃν, τρόπον**: *which way*, i.e., *how*. **Φιλοκτήτας**: *Philocteteses*; see 20. **ἐδάκρυον, ἐβόων**: inchoative or inceptive imperfects; i.e., *they began to...*

88

Vocabulary

αἰθήρ, -έρος, ὁ, *ether, thin air, heaven; fifth element* (equivalent to fire)

ἀναμίγνυμι, ἀναμίξω, ἀνέμιξα, *commingle with, mix with*

ἀνόητος, -ον, *unintelligent, stupid, senseless, foolish*

ἀπέρχομαι, ἄπειμι, ἀπῆλθον, *go, go away, depart*

ἀποθνήσκω, ἀποθανοῦμαι, ἀπέθανον, *die*

βιόω, βιώσομαι, ἐβίωσα /ἐβίων (2nd aor.), *live*

βούλομαι, (dep.) *wish, want* (+ inf.)

βοάω, βοήσομαι, ἐβόησα, *shout*

δακρύω, *cry, lament, weep, shed tears*

δείκνυμι, δείξω, ἔδειξα, *show, point out*

διέξειμι, *go through in detail, relate*

Ἕλλην, -ηνος, ὁ, *Greek, Hellene*

ἐπακούω, ἐπακούσομαι, ἐπήκουσα, *overhear, hear distinctly; hear*

ἐπεί, conj., *since, when*

ἐπιτάφιος, ὁ, *funeral oration, eulogy*

ἐπιτίθημι, ἐπιθήσω, ἐπέθηκα, *put, place*

Ἡρακλείως, adv., *like Heracles, in the manner of Heracles*

θανατιάω, (Lucianic variant of θανατάω) *desire to die*

καταφρονέω, *despise, think lightly of* (+ gen.)

κορώνη, ἡ, *crown; tip of a bow* (on which a bowstring was hooked)

μακρός, -ά, -όν, *long; large; great*

ὀλίγος, -η, -ον, *little, small;* (pl.) *few*

πάσχω, πείσομαι, ἔπαθον, *experience; suffer, undergo*

περιίστημι, *place around;* (2nd aor., perf., pluperf. act.) *stand around*

πλῆθος, -ους, τό, *multitude*

πλήν, conj., *except, however, but*

σοφιστής, -οῦ, ὁ, *sophist*

συντρίβω, *crush*

σώζω, *save, rescue, deliver; cure, make well*

τελευτή, ἡ, *end, demise, death*

τοσοῦτος, -αύτη, -οῦτον, *so much, so great;* (pl.) *so many*

τρόπος, ὁ, *way, manner*

τύρβη, ἡ, *tumult, confusion, chaos, turmoil*

φοβέομαι, (dep.) *be frightened* or *afraid (of), fear*

φράζω, *point out, show, indicate; declare*

χαίρω, *rejoice, be glad;* χαίρειν, *farewell;* (+μακρά), *a long* or *hearty farewell*

χρυσοῦς, -ῆ, -οῦν, *golden, of gold*

ὠφελέω, *help, benefit, be of use* or *service to*

οἱ δὲ ἀνδρωδέστεροι ἐκεκράγεσαν "τέλει τὰ δεδογμένα,"
ὑφ' ὧν ὁ πρεσβύτης οὐ μετρίως ἐθορυβήθη ἐλπίζων πάντας
ἕξεσθαι αὐτοῦ καὶ μὴ προήσεσθαι τῷ πυρί, ἀλλὰ ἄκοντα
δὴ καθέξειν ἐν τῷ βίῳ. τὸ δὲ "τέλει τὰ δεδογμένα" πάνυ
ἀδόκητον αὐτῷ προσπεσὸν ὠχριᾶν ἔτι μᾶλλον ἐποίησεν,
καίτοι ἤδη νεκρικῶς τὴν χροιὰν ἔχοντι, καὶ νὴ Δία καὶ
ὑποτρέμειν, ὥστε κατέπαυσε τὸν λόγον.

ἐκεκράγεσαν: 3rd pl. pluperf. (with imperf. sense) act. indic. < κράζω;
an inchoative or inceptive "imperf." **τέλει**: 2nd sing. pres. act. impera.
< τελέω. **δεδογμένα**: neut. pl. acc. perf. mid./pass. part. < δοκῶ;
sc. *by you.* **ἄκοντα δὴ**: ἄκοντα is the masc. acc. sing. dir. obj. of
καθέξειν; the particle δὴ conveys an ironic inflection; i.e., *of course!*,
naturally! **προήσεσθαι**: fut. mid. inf. < προίημι. **ὠχριᾶν ἔτι**
μᾶλλον ἐποίησεν = ἐποίησεν (αὐτὸν) ἔτι μᾶλλον ὠχριᾶν.

[34] ἐγὼ δέ, εἰκάζεις, οἶμαι, πῶς ἐγέλων· οὐδὲ γὰρ ἐλεεῖν
ἄξιον ἦν οὕτω δυσέρωτα τῆς δόξης ἄνθρωπον ὑπὲρ ἅπαντας
ὅσοι τῇ αὐτῇ Ποινῇ ἐλαύνονται. παρεπέμπετο δὲ ὅμως ὑπὸ
πολλῶν καὶ ἐνεφορεῖτο τῆς δόξης ἀποβλέπων ἐς τὸ πλῆθος
τῶν θαυμαζόντων, οὐκ εἰδὼς ὁ ἄθλιος ὅτι καὶ τοῖς ἐπὶ τὸν
σταυρὸν ἀπαγομένοις ἢ ὑπὸ τοῦ δημίου ἐχομένοις πολλῷ
πλείους ἕπονται.

οἶμαι: parenthetical. **ἄξιον ἦν**: *it was fitting* (+ inf.). **ὑπὲρ**:
+ acc.; *beyond, more than.* **τῇ αὐτῇ Ποινῇ**: in the attributive
position (i.e., following the article), αὐτῇ means *the same*; the datives are
instrumental. **ἐχομένοις**: pass. **ἢ**: *or.* **πολλῷ πλείους**:
far more (people); πολλῷ is a dat. of degree of difference; πλείους an
alternative masc./fem. nom. pl. contracted form of πλείονες.

Vocabulary

ἀδόκητος, -ον, *unexpected*; ἀδόκητον, adv., *unexpectedly*

ἄθλιος, -α, -ον, *wretched, miserable*

ἄκων, ἄκουσα, ἆκον, *against one's will, unwilling*

ἀπάγω, ἀπάξω, ἀπήγαγον, *lead away*

ἀνδρώδης, -ες, *manly, virile*

ἀποβλέπω, *look* or *gaze steadfastly at, look to, look upon* (with love or admiration)

δήμιος, ὁ, (sc. δοῦλος, *slave, servant*) *public executioner*

δοκῶ, (uncontracted = δοκέω) *think, suppose*; (mid./pass.) *be decided* or *resolved*

δύσερως, -ωτος, ὁ, *sick in love with* (+ gen.)

εἰκάζω, *can guess / imagine*

ἐλαύνω, ἐλῶ, ἤλασα, *drive, drive away*; *persecute*

ἐλεέω, *pity, feel pity*

ἐλπίζω, *expect, hope* (frequently with a dependent clause + inf. [usually fut.])

ἐμφορέω, *pour in*; (mid./pass.) *get one's fill of* (+ gen.)

ἕπομαι, (dep.) *follow* (+ dat.)

ἔχω, ἕξω, ἔσχον, *have; hold*; (mid. + gen.) *hold onto, cling to*

θορυβέω, *trouble, throw into confusion*

καίτοι, conj. + particle, *and yet*; (later, non-Classical Greek usage) *although*

καταπαύω, *put an end to, stop*

κατέχω, καθέξω, κατέσχον, *hold fast, hold back, restrain*

κράζω, *croak, scream, shriek*

μᾶλλον, adv., *more, much more; rather, instead*

μετρίως, adv., *moderately*

νεκρικῶς, adv., *deathly, deathly pale, corpse-like*

νή, particle (of strong affirmation), νὴ Δία = *by Zeus!*

οἶμαι (uncontracted = οἴομαι), *suppose, think, expect*

παραπέμπω, *escort, attend*

πλείων, πλεῖον, (comp. of πολύς, πολλή, πολύ) *more*

Ποινή, ἡ, *Poine* (goddess of retribution and vengeance; punisher of murderers)

πρεσβύτης, -ου, ὁ, *old man*

προίημι, *send on* or *forward*; (mid.) *give up, let go, abandon; drive forward*

προσπίπτω, προσπεσοῦμαι, προσέπεσον, *fall upon, assail, attack* (+ dat.)

πῶς, adv., *how?, in what manner* or *way?*

σταυρός, ὁ, *cross*

τελέω, *finish, complete; perform; perform* (sacred rites)

ὑποτρέμω, *tremble a little, tremble slightly*

χροιά, ἡ, *complexion, color* (of the skin)

ὠχρίας, -ου, ὁ, *pale, a person of pale complexion*

[35] καὶ δὴ τὰ μὲν Ὀλύμπια τέλος εἶχεν, κάλλιστα Ὀλυμπίων γενόμενα ὧν ἐγὼ εἶδον, τετράκις ἤδη ὁρῶν. ἐγὼ δὲ — οὐ γὰρ ἦν εὐπορῆσαι ὀχήματος ἅμα πολλῶν ἐξιόντων — ἄκων ὑπελειπόμην. ὁ δὲ ἀεὶ ἀναβαλλόμενος νύκτα τὸ τελευταῖον προειρήκει ἐπιδείξασθαι τὴν καῦσιν· καί με τῶν ἑταίρων τινὸς παραλαβόντος περί μέσας νύκτας ἐξαναστὰς ἀπήειν εὐθὺ τῆς Ἁρπίνης, ἔνθα ἦν ἡ πυρά. στάδιοι πάντες οὗτοι εἴκοσιν ἀπὸ τῆς Ὀλυμπίας κατὰ τὸν ἱππόδρομον ἀπιόντων πρὸς ἔω. καὶ ἐπεὶ τάχιστα ἀφικόμεθα, καταλαμβάνομεν πυρὰν νενησμένην ἐν βόθρῳ ὅσον ἐς ὀργυιὰν τὸ βάθος.

καὶ δὴ: *And now.*   **ἦν**: *it was possible* (+ inf.); the 3rd sing. imperfect of εἰμί in this sense is from impersonal ἔστι (*it is possible*).   **ἅμα πολλῶν ἐξιόντων**: gen. abs.   **νύκτα τὸ τελευταῖον προειρήκει ἐπιδείξασθαι τὴν καῦσιν** = τὸ τελευταῖον προειρήκει νύκτα ἐπιδείξασθαι τὴν καῦσιν.   **νύκτα**: the meaning here must be one particular night, but "the Greek," as Macleod (274) notes, "is strange and may be corrupt."   **προειρήκει**: 3rd sing. pluperf. act. indic. < προλέγω.   **τῶν ἑταίρων**: partitive gen. with τινὸς. **τινὸς παραλαβόντος**: gen. abs.   **ἐξαναστὰς**: nom. masc. sing. 2nd aor. act. part. < ἐξανίστημι.   **ἀπήειν**: 1st sing. act. imperf. indic. < ἀπέρχομαι.   **τῆς Ἁρπίνης**: a town situated *c.* 2.3 miles east of Olympia on the right bank of the Alpheius river; Pausanias (6.21.8) notes that it was already in ruins when he journeyed from Arcadia to Olympia in the middle of the 2nd century CE.   **στάδιοι πάντες οὗτοι εἴκοσιν**: sc. εἰσί. πάντες conveys that the speaker thought it was quite some distance away: i.e., *it's a good twenty stadia.*   **κατὰ τὸν ἱππόδρομον**: *by* or *past the hippodrome* (which was located between the stadium and the Alpheius river, heading east/south-east out of Olympia). **ἐπεὶ τάχιστα**: *as soon as, as quickly as.*   **νενησμένην**: fem. acc. sing. perf. mid./pass. part. < νέω.   **ὅσον ἐς**: *as far as*; *about, nearly.* **τὸ βάθος**: acc. of respect.

Vocabulary

ἀεί, adv., *always*

ἄκων, ἄκουσα, ἆκον, *against one's will, unwilling*

ἅμα, adv., *at the same time*

ἀναβάλλω, ἀναβαλῶ, ἀνέβαλον, *throw* or *toss up*; (mid.) *put off, delay*

ἀπέρχομαι, ἄπειμι, ἀπῆλθον, *go, go away, depart*

Ἁρπίνα, ἡ, *Harpina*

ἀφικνέομαι, ἀφίξομαι, ἀφικόμην, (dep.) *arrive at, come to, reach*

βάθος, -ους, τό, *depth*

βόθρος, ὁ, *hole, pit*

εἴκοσιν, indecl., *twenty*

ἔνθα, adv., *where, the place where*

ἐξανίστημι, *raise up*; (2nd aor., perf., pluperf. act.) *stand up, get up (and depart)*

ἐξέρχομαι, ἔξειμι, ἐξῆλθον, *go out, depart*

ἐπιδείκνυμι, *exhibit, display*; (mid.) *display one's* X, *put on a show of one's* X

ἑταῖρος, ὁ, *comrade, companion, friend*

εὐθύ, adv. (+ gen.), *straight to* or *towards*

εὐπορέω, *procure, find available* (+ gen.)

ἕως, ἕω (gen. and acc.), ἡ, *dawn*; (direction) *east*

ἱππόδρομος, ὁ, *hippodrome* (race course for chariots)

κάλλιστος, -η, -ον, *most beautiful, finest*

κατά, prep. (+ acc.), *by*; *along*

καταλαμβάνω, καταλήψομαι, κατέλαβον, *find*

καῦσις, -εως, ἡ, *burning, cremation*

μέσος, -η, -ον, *middle, in the middle*; μέσαι νύκτες, *midnight*

νέω, *heap, pile up*

νύξ, νυκτός, ἡ, *night*

Ὀλύμπια, τά, (pl. only) *Olympic Games*

ὄργυια, ἡ, (unit of length measured by the outstretched arms) *six feet*

ὅσον, adv., *about, nearly*

ὄχημα, -ατος, τό, *carriage, transportation*

παραλαμβάνω, παραλήψομαι, παρέλαβον, *invite*

προλέγω, προερῶ, προεῖπον, *proclaim* or *declare publicly*; *foretell*

στάδιον, τό, (unit of length = 607 feet / 185 meters) *stade*

τάχιστα, (neut. pl. adj. as adv.) *most* or *very quickly*

τελευταῖος, -α, -ον, *last*; τὸ τελευταῖον, *at last, finally*; *for the last time*

τέλος, -ους, τό, *end*

τετράκις, adv., *four times*

ὑπολείπω, *leave behind* or *remaining*; (pass.) *stay behind, be left behind*

δᾷδες ἦσαν τὰ πολλὰ καὶ παρεβέβυστο τῶν φρυγάνων,
ὡς ἀναφθείη τάχιστα. [36] καὶ ἐπειδὴ ἡ σελήνη ἀνέτελλεν —
ἔδει γὰρ κἀκείνην θεάσασθαι τὸ κάλλιστον τοῦτο ἔργον —
πρόεισιν ἐκεῖνος ἐσκευασμένος ἐς τὸν ἀεὶ τρόπον καὶ
ξὺν αὐτῷ τὰ τέλη τῶν κυνῶν, καὶ μάλιστα ὁ γεννάδας
ὁ ἐκ Πατρῶν, δᾷδα ἔχων, οὐ φαῦλος δευτεραγωνιστής·
ἐδαδοφόρει δὲ καὶ ὁ Πρωτεύς. καὶ προσελθόντες ἄλλος
ἀλλαχόθεν ἀνῆψαν τὸ πῦρ μέγιστον ἅτε ἀπὸ δᾴδων καὶ
φρυγάνων. ὁ δὲ — καί μοι πάνυ ἤδη πρόσεχε τὸν νοῦν —
ἀποθέμενος τὴν πήραν καὶ τὸ τριβώνιον καὶ τὸ Ἡράκλειον
ἐκεῖνο ῥόπαλον, ἔστη ἐν ὀθόνῃ ῥυπώσῃ ἀκριβῶς.

τὰ πολλὰ: *most (of the pyre).* **παρεβέβυστο**: 3rd sing. pluperf. mid./pass. indic. < παραβύω. **ὡς**: + subju. or opt. = a final/purpose clause; i.e., *so that, in order that.* **ἀναφθείη**: 3rd sing. aor. pass. opt. < ἀνάπτω; opt. in final/purpose clause in secondary sequence. **ἡ σελήνη ἀνέτελλεν…**: although Lucian introduces the moon both as a temporal marker for the event and as a witness to Peregrinus' suicide, Macleod (274) notes that "perhaps P.[eregrinus] was influenced in this by the Pythagorean belief in the moon as recipient of good, pure souls." **κἀκείνην**: crasis of καὶ ἐκείνην. **ἐσκευασμένος**: masc. nom. sing. perf. mid./pass. part. < σκευάζω. **ἐς τὸν ἀεὶ τρόπον**: i.e., in his usual manner. **τὰ τέλη**: *the leaders.* **ὁ ἐκ Πατρῶν**: i.e., Theagenes. **οὐ φαῦλος**: possible *litotes* (see 12). **ἄλλος ἀλλαχόθεν**: *one from one place, another from another place.* **ἀποθέμενος**: masc. nom. sing. aor. mid. part. < ἀποτίθημι. **τὸ Ἡράκλειον ἐκεῖνο ῥόπαλον**: in Lucian's *The Book Collector* 14, the unnamed speaker includes among his examples of the ridiculous attempts by wealthy individuals to augment their own cultural status through the purchase of artefacts owned by celebrated writers and philosophers that someone paid a talent (*c.* $26,000) for Peregrinus' staff shortly after his suicide. **ἔστη**: 3rd sing. 2nd aor. act. indic. < ἵστημι.

Vocabulary

ἀεί, adv., *always*

ἀκριβῶς, adv., *absolutely, thoroughly*

ἀλλαχόθεν, adv., *from another place*

ἀνατέλλω, *rise*

ἀνάπτω, ἀνάψω, ἀνήψα, *attach* X *to* Y, *kindle*; (pass.) *catch fire*

ἀποτίθημι, ἀποθήσω, ἀπέθηκα, *put away*; (mid.) *lay* or *set aside one's own, put away from oneself*

ἄτε, adv., *seeing that, in as much as, since*

γεννάδας, -ου, ὁ, *noble*

δᾳδοφορέω, *carry a torch(es)*

δᾴς, δᾳδός, ἡ, *torch*, (pl.) *pine-wood, torchwood*

δευτεραγωνιστής, -οῦ, ὁ, *second lead in a drama; "second fiddle"; supporter*

δέω, *bind*; δεῖ, *it is necessary*

ἔργον, τό, *work, deed*

Ἡράκλειος, -α, -ον, *Heraclean, of Heracles, connected to Heracles*

θεάομαι, (dep.) *look on, gaze at, view (as spectator)*

ἵστημι, στήσω, ἔστησα, *make* X *stand*; *stop* X; *set* X *(up)*; (2nd aor.) ἔστην, (perf.) ἔστηκα, *stand*

κάλλιστος, -η, -ον, *most* or *very beautiful, finest* or *very fine*

κύων, κυνός, ὁ or ἡ, *dog; Cynic philosopher*

νοῦς, νοῦ, ὁ, *mind*

ὀθόνη, ἡ, *fine linen, shirt*

παραβύω, *stuff in, insert*; (pass.) *be stuffed* or *packed with* (+ gen.)

Πάτραι, -ῶν, αἱ, *Patras*

πήρα, ἡ, *leather pouch, wallet*

πρόειμι, *go* or *come forward*

προσέρχομαι, πρόσειμι, προσῆλθον, *approach; go* or *come forward*

προσέχω, προσέξω, προσέσχον, (with or without τὸν νοῦν) *pay close attention to* (+ dat.)

ῥόπαλον, τό, *club*

ῥυπάω, *be filthy* or *dirty*

σελήνη, ἡ, *moon*

σκευάζω, *prepare, make ready*; (pass.) *fully outfitted* or *dressed*

τάχιστα, (neut. pl. adj. as adv.) *most* or *very quickly*

τριβώνιον, τό, (dim. of ὁ τρίβων), *threadbare cloak, worn out garment*

τρόπος, ὁ, *way, manner*

φαῦλος, -η, -ον, *bad, inferior, poor*

φρύγανον, τό, *dry stick*; (mostly in pl.) *brush, firewood*

εἶτα ᾔτει λιβανωτόν, ὡς ἐπιβάλοι ἐπὶ τὸ πῦρ, καὶ ἀναδόντος

τινὸς ἐπέβαλέν τε καὶ εἶπεν ἐς τὴν μεσημβρίαν ἀποβλέπων

— καὶ γὰρ καὶ τοῦτ' αὐτὸ πρὸς τὴν τραγῳδίαν ἦν, ἡ

μεσημβρία — "δαίμονες μητρῷοι καὶ πατρῷοι, δέξασθέ με

εὐμενεῖς." ταῦτα εἰπὼν ἐπήδησεν ἐς τὸ πῦρ, οὐ μὴν ἑωρᾶτό

γε, ἀλλὰ περιεσχέθη ὑπὸ τῆς φλογὸς πολλῆς ἠρμένης.

λιβανωτόν: *frankincense* was burned at sacrifices.   ὡς: + subju. or
opt. = a final/purpose clause; i.e., *so that, in order that.*   ἀναδόντος
τινὸς: gen. abs.; sc. *it*, i.e., the incense, both here and as the dir. obj. of
ἐπέβαλέν.   ἐς τὴν μεσημβρίαν: the South was the region of the
dead in Indian literature, and so is another example of Peregrinus' interest in
Hindu beliefs (cf. Allinson 231; Macleod 275).   καὶ γὰρ καὶ: *and
indeed, even.*   τοῦτ' αὐτό, ἡ μεσημβρία: though neut., this
phrase refers back to τὴν μεσημβρίαν (*the south*), as the apposite ἡ
μεσημβρία (*the south, I mean*) makes clear.   δαίμονες μητρῷοι,
πατρῷοι: all voc.   εὐμενεῖς: adj. where English prefers an adv.
ἑωρᾶτό: 3rd sing. imperf. mid./pass. indic. < ὁράω.   ἠρμένης: fem.
gen. sing. perf. mid./pass. part. < αἴρω.

[37] αὖθις ὁρῶ γελῶντά σε, ὦ καλὲ Κρόνιε, τὴν καταστροφὴν

τοῦ δράματος. ἐγὼ δὲ τοὺς μητρῴους μὲν δαίμονας

ἐπιβοώμενον μὰ τὸν Δί' οὐ σφόδρα ᾐτιώμην· ὅτε δὲ καὶ τοὺς

πατρῴους ἐπεκαλέσατο, ἀναμνησθεὶς τῶν περὶ τοῦ φόνου

εἰρημένων οὐδὲ κατέχειν ἠδυνάμην τὸν γέλωτα.

καλὲ: added to a name in Attic Greek in token of love or admiration.
ἐγὼ δὲ...σφόδρα ᾐτιώμην = δὲ ἐγώ, μὰ τὸν Δί', οὐ σφόδρα
ᾐτιώμην [αὐτὸν] ἐπιβοώμενον μὲν τοὺς μητρῴους δαίμονας.
εἰρημένων: masc. gen. pl. perf. mid./pass. part. < εἴρημαι (the perf.
mid./pass. of λέγω).   ἠδυνάμην: double temporal augment (i.e., ε + ε
= η), which sometimes occurs with δύναμαι, especially in later writers.

Vocabulary

αἴρω, ἀρῶ, ἦρα, *raise (up)*

αἰτέω, *ask, ask for, demand*

αἰτιάομαι, (dep.) *censure, criticize*

ἀναδίδωμι, ἀναδώσω, ἀνέδωκα, *give, give up, hand over*

ἀναμιμνήσκω, ἀναμνήσω, ἀνέμνησα, *remind*; (pass.) *remember* (+ gen.)

ἀποβλέπω, *look* or *pay attention to, look* or *gaze steadfastly at*

αὖθις, adv., *again, once more*

γε, particle, *at least, at any rate*; *namely, that is, indeed*

γελάω, γελάσομαι, ἐγέλασα, *laugh at* (+ acc.)

δαίμων, -ονος, ὁ or ἡ, *god, goddess, divine power, spirit*

δέχομαι, (dep.) *receive*

δρᾶμα, -ατος, τό, *deed, act*; *drama, play*

δύναμαι, (dep.) *be able, can* (+ inf.)

εἶτα, adv., *then, next*; *soon, presently*; *and so, therefore, accordingly*

ἐμπηδάω, ἐμπηδήσομαι, ἐνεπήδησα, *leap in* or *into*

ἐπιβάλλω, ἐπιβαλῶ, ἐπέβαλον, *throw, cast upon*

ἐπιβοάω, ἐπιβοήσομαι, ἐπεβόησα, *call upon, cry out to*; (mid.) *invoke*; *call to aid*

ἐπικαλέω, *call upon*; (mid.) *summon*; *call in as a helper* or *ally*

εὐμενής, -ές, *gracious, kindly, with favor*

καταστροφή, ἡ, *conclusion, ending, dénouement*; *catastrophe*

κατέχω, καθέξω, κατέσχον, *hold fast, hold back, restrain*

λιβανωτός, ὁ, *frankincense, incense*

μεσημβρία, ἡ, *midday*; (direction) *south*

μήν, adv., *indeed, truly*

μητρῷος, -α, -ον, *maternal, of a mother*

ὁράω, ὄψομαι, εἶδον, *see*

ὅτε, conj., *when*

πατρῷος, -α, -ον, *paternal, of a father*

περιέχω, περιέξω, περιέσχον, *encompass, surround, embrace*

πρός, prep. (+ acc.), *engaged in, connected to*

σφόδρα, adv., *very, very much, greatly*; *strongly, violently*

τραγῳδία, ἡ, *tragedy*

φλόξ, φλογός, ἡ, *flame*

φόνος, ὁ, *murder, homicide*

οἱ Κυνικοὶ δὲ περιστάντες τὴν πυρὰν οὐκ ἐδάκρυον μέν,

σιωπῇ δὲ ἐνεδείκνυντο λύπην τινὰ εἰς τὸ πῦρ ὁρῶντες,

ἄχρι δὴ ἀποπνιγεὶς ἐπ᾽ αὐτοῖς, "ἀπίωμεν," φημί, "ὦ μάταιοι·

οὐ γὰρ ἡδὺ τὸ θέαμα ὠπτημένον γέροντα ὁρᾶν κνίσης

ἀναπιμπλαμένους πονηρᾶς. ἢ περιμένετε ἔστ᾽ ἂν γραφεύς

τις ἐπελθὼν ἀπεικάσῃ ὑμᾶς οἵους τοὺς ἐν τῷ δεσμωτηρίῳ

ἑταίρους τῷ Σωκράτει παραγράφουσιν;" ἐκεῖνοι μὲν οὖν

ἠγανάκτουν καὶ ἐλοιδοροῦντό μοι, ἔνιοι δὲ καὶ ἐπὶ τὰς

βακτηρίας ᾖξαν. εἶτα, ἐπειδὴ ἠπείλησα ξυναρπάσας τινὰς

ἐμβαλεῖν εἰς τὸ πῦρ, ὡς ἂν ἔποιντο τῷ διδασκάλῳ,

ἐπαύσαντο καὶ εἰρήνην ἦγον.

περιστάντες: masc. nom. pl. 2nd aor. act. part. < περιΐστημι.
ἀποπνιγεὶς: masc. nom. sing. aor. pass. part. < ἀποπνίγω.
ἀπίωμεν: 1st pl. pres. act. subju. < ἀπέρχομαι; the subju. is hortatory.
ὠπτημένον: masc. acc. sing. perf. mid./pass. part. < ὀπτάω.   **οὐ
γὰρ...ὁρᾶν** = γὰρ (ἐστὶν) οὐ τὸ ἡδὺ θέαμα ὁρᾶν γέροντα
ὠπτημένον.   **ἀναπιμπλαμένους**: sc. ἡμᾶς; an example of
anacolouthon (grammatical inconsistency), since ἀναπιμπλαμένους is
dependent in terms of sense (not grammar – it would need to be dat.) on οὐ
ἡδὺ.   **οἵους...παραγράφουσιν**: Lucian's language suggests that
this was a common subject for painters in the ancient world; the most
famous "modern" depiction of Socrates in prison with his companions is the
1787 painting *The Death of Socrates* by Jacques-Louis David, now in the
Metropolitan Museum of Art in New York City.   **παραγράφουσιν**:
the meaning of this word as used here (*paint* or *portray beside*) is not found
elsewhere in Greek.   **ἠπείλησα ξυναρπάσας τινὰς ἐμβαλεῖν
εἰς τὸ πῦρ**: Lucian's threat against a number of Peregrinus' disciples
seems so implausible – a single writer/orator vs. many aggrieved followers
– that one can't help but think Lucian is intentionally portraying himself in a
mock-heroic manner.   **ὡς ἂν**: ὡς + subju. or opt. = a final/purpose
clause; i.e., *so that, in order that*; the ἂν is very rare in Attic Greek prose
and does not affect the meaning.   **ἔποιντο**: 3rd pl. pres. mid./pass.
(dep.) opt. < ἕπομαι.

Vocabulary

ἀγανακτέω, *be angry*

ἄγω, ἄξω, ἤγαγον, *lead, take, bring*

αἴσσω, ἀΐξω, ᾖξα, *move quickly (to), make a dash (for), turn eagerly (to)*

ἀναπίμπλημι, *fill up*; (mid.) *fill oneself with* (+ gen.); (pass.) *be filled or infected with* (+ gen.)

ἀπεικάζω, *represent, portray, depict*

ἀπειλέω, *promise, threaten* (with dependent clauses + fut. inf.)

ἀποπνίγω, *choke, throttle*; (pass.) *be choked with rage*

ἄχρι, conj., *until*

βακτηρία, ἡ, *stick, staff*

γραφεύς, -έως, ὁ, *painter*

δακρύω, *cry, lament, weep, shed tears*

δεσμωτήριον, τό, *prison*

διδάσκαλος, ὁ, *teacher*

εἰρήνη, ἡ, *peace*; + ἄγω, *keep peace, be at peace, keep quiet*

ἐμβάλλω, ἐμβαλῶ, ἐνέβαλον, *throw in*

ἐνδείκνυμι, ἐνδείξω, ἐνέδειξα, *point out, indicate*; (mid.) *display, exhibit*

ἔνιοι, ἐνίων, *some*

ἐπέρχομαι, ἔπειμι, ἐπῆλθον, *come, come forward; make a sudden appearance*

ἐπί, prep. (+ acc.), *for*

ἕπομαι, (dep.) *follow* (+ dat.)

ἔστε, conj., (often with ἄν + subju.) *until, until such time as*

ἑταῖρος, ὁ, *comrade, companion, friend*

ἡδύς, ἡδεῖα, ἡδύ, *pleasant, agreeable, welcome, sweet*

θέαμα, -ατος, τό, *sight, spectacle*

κνῖσα, ἡ, *smell of a burnt sacrifice*

λοιδοροῦμαι, (dep.) *abuse, revile, rebuke* (+ dat.)

λύπη, ἡ, *grief*

μάταιος, -α, -ον, *vain, foolish, thoughtless, impious*

ξ/συναρπάζω, *seize and carry away, seize and pin together*

ὀπτάω, *roast*

παραγράφω, *paint or portray beside* (+ dat.)

παύω, *stop*; (mid.) *stop (oneself), cease from*

περιμένω, περιμενῶ, περιέμεινα, *wait, wait around, wait for*

περιίστημι, *place around*; (2nd aor., perf., pluperf. act.) *stand around*

πονηρός, -ή, -όν, *wicked, bad, morally deficient*

σιωπή, ἡ, *silence*; (dat. case used as adv.) *in silence, silently*

Σωκράτης, -ους, ὁ, *Socrates*

[38] ἐγὼ δὲ ἐπανιὼν ποικίλα, ὦ ἑταῖρε, πρὸς ἐμαυτὸν
ἐνενόουν, τὸ φιλόδοξον οἷόν τί ἐστιν ἀναλογιζόμενος,
ὡς μόνος οὗτος ὁ ἔρως ἄφυκτος καὶ τοῖς πάνυ θαυμαστοῖς
εἶναι δοκοῦσιν, οὐχ ὅπως ἐκείνῳ τἀνδρὶ καὶ τἄλλα
ἐμπλήκτως καὶ ἀπονενοημένως βεβιωκότι καὶ οὐκ ἀναξίως
τοῦ πυρός. [39] εἶτα ἐνετύγχανον πολλοῖς ἀπιοῦσιν ὡς
θεάσαιντο καὶ αὐτοί· ᾤοντο γὰρ ἔτι καταλήψεσθαι ζῶντα
αὐτόν. καὶ γὰρ καὶ τόδε τῇ προτεραίᾳ διεδέδοτο ὡς πρὸς
ἀνίσχοντα τὸν ἥλιον ἀσπασάμενος, ὥσπερ ἀμέλει καὶ τοὺς
Βραχμᾶνάς φασι ποιεῖν, ἐπιβήσεται τῆς πυρᾶς.

ἐπανιὼν: masc. nom. sing. pres. act. part. < ἐπάνειμι (this Attic fut. of
ἐπανέρχομαι is pres. tense in non-indic. forms).   **τὸ φιλόδοξον
οἷόν τί ἐστιν ἀναλογιζόμενος** = ἀναλογιζόμενος τί οἷόν ἐστι
τὸ φιλόδοξον.   **ὁ ἔρως ἄφυκτος**: ὁ ἔρως (ἐστιν) ἄφυκτος.
καὶ: *even.*   **τοῖς πάνυ θαυμαστοῖς εἶναι δοκοῦσιν** = τοῖς
δοκοῦσιν εἶναι πάνυ θαυμαστοῖς.   **δοκοῦσιν**: masc. dat. pl. pres.
act. part. < δοκέω.   **οὐχ ὅπως**: *to say nothing of..., let alone...*
τἀνδρὶ: crasis of τῷ ἀνδρὶ.   **τἄλλα**: crasis of τὰ ἄλλα; acc. of
respect, *in all else, in other respects.*   **βεβιωκότι**: masc. dat. sing.
perf. act. part. < βιόω.   **οὐκ ἀναξίως**: *litotes* (see 12); the same
expression is used in 21.   **ἀπιοῦσιν**: masc. dat. pl. pres. act. part. <
ἄπειμι; sc. from Olympia to Harpina.   **ὡς**: + subju. or opt. = a
final/purpose clause; i.e., *so that, in order that.*   **θεάσαιντο**: 3rd pl.
aor. mid./pass. (dep.) opt. < θεάομαι.   **καὶ**: *also, too.*   **καὶ γὰρ
καὶ**: *And in fact.*   **τόδε**: *this (report/story).*   **διεδέδοτο**: 3rd sing.
pluperf. mid./ pass. indic. < διαδίδωμι.   **ὡς** = ὅτι.

100

Vocabulary

ἀμέλει, adv., *of course*; *for instance*

ἀναλογίζομαι, (dep.) *reflect, consider*

ἀναξίως, adv., *undeserving, unworthy*

ἀνίσχω, *rise*

ἀπέρχομαι, ἄπειμι, ἀπῆλθον, *go, go away, depart*

ἀπονενοημένως, adv., *recklessly*

ἀσπάζομαι, (dep.) *greet, embrace, cling fondly to*

ἄφυκτος, -ον, *inescapable*

βιόω, βιώσομαι, ἐβίωσα / ἐβίων (2nd aor.), *live*

Βραχμᾶνες, οἱ, *Brachmanes, Bragmanni, Brahmans, Gymnosophists*

διαδίδωμι, διαδώσω, διέδωκα, *pass on, hand over*; (pass.) *be spread about, be given out, be reported*

δοκῶ, (uncontracted = δοκέω) *seem; be reputed, be held* (+ inf.)

ἐμπλήκτως, adv., *rashly, madly, foolishly, impulsively*

ἐννοέω, *think* or *reflect upon, consider*

ἐντυγχάνω, ἐντεύξομαι, ἐνέτυχον, *meet with, encounter, chance upon*

ἐπανέρχομαι, ἐπάνειμι, ἐπανῆλθον, *return, come* or *go back*

ἐπιβαίνω, ἐπιβήσομαι, ἐπέβην, *get upon, mount on*

ἔρως, -ωτος, ὁ, *love, desire, passion*

ἑταῖρος, ὁ, *comrade, companion, friend*

ζάω, (unattested hypothetical form) *live, be alive*

ἥλιος, ὁ, *sun*

θαυμαστός, -ή, -όν, *wonderful, marvelous; extraordinary*

θεάομαι, (dep.) *look on, gaze at, view (as spectator)*

καταλαμβάνω, καταλήψομαι, κατέλαβον, *find*

μονός, -ή, -όν, *alone, only, single*

οἶμαι (uncontracted = οἴομαι), *suppose, think, expect*

οἷος, οἵα, οἷον, rel. pron. *what sort / kind* (of person / thing); οἷόν τι, *what sort of thing*

ποικίλος, -η, -ον, *various, diverse, elaborate*

προτεραῖος, -η, -ον, *previous, former*; τῇ προτεραίᾳ (sc. ἡμέρᾳ), *on the day before*

φιλόδοξος, -ον, *loving fame* or *glory*; τὸ φιλόδοξον, *love of fame* or *glory*

ὡς, adv., *how*; conj., (+ subju./opt.) *so that, in order that*

ὥσπερ, adv., *just as, even as*

ἀπέστρεφον δ' οὖν τοὺς πολλοὺς αὐτῶν λέγων ἤδη τετελέσθαι

τὸ ἔργον, οἷς μὴ καὶ τοῦτ' αὐτὸ περισπούδαστον ἦν, κἂν

αὐτὸν ἰδεῖν τὸν τόπον καί τι λείψανον καταλαμβάνειν τοῦ

πυρός. ἔνθα δή, ὦ ἑταῖρε, μυρία πράγματα εἶχον ἅπασι

διηγούμενος καὶ ἀνακρίνουσιν καὶ ἀκριβῶς ἐκπυνθανομένοις.

εἰ μὲν οὖν ἴδοιμί τινα χαρίεντα, ψιλὰ ἂν ὥσπερ σοὶ τὰ

πραχθέντα διηγούμην, πρὸς δὲ τοὺς βλᾶκας καὶ πρὸς τὴν

ἀκρόασιν κεχηνότας ἐτραγῴδουν τι παρ' ἐμαυτοῦ, ὡς ἐπειδὴ

ἀνήφθη μὲν ἡ πυρά, ἐνέβαλεν δὲ φέρων ἑαυτὸν ὁ Πρωτεύς,

τετελέσθαι: perf. mid./pass. inf. < τελέω. **οἷς**: *(those) to whom*; the antecedent of the rel. pron. is τοὺς πολλούς. **τοῦτ' αὐτὸ**: although sing., a compound action (ἰδεῖν, καί, καταλαμβάνειν) is in apposition to it as a sing. idea. **κἂν**: crasis of καὶ ἄν; here, as a strengthened καί, intensifies αὐτόν; i.e., *both to see **it**, the place* (sc. where he committed suicide). **καὶ, καὶ**: *both...and*. **ἀνακρίνουσιν**: masc. dat. pl. pres. act. part.; sc. με as the dir. obj. of both this part. and ἐκπυνθανομένοις; both participles modify ἅπασι. **εἰ, ἴδοιμί, διηγούμην**: a mixed condition (past general [the protasis, or 'if' clause] + past contrary to fact [apodosis]); i.e., *If (ever) / When(ever) I saw... I would describe (in detail)*. **πραχθέντα**: neut. acc. pl. aor. pass. part. < πράττω; the article turns the part. into a noun phrase. **κεχηνότας**: masc. acc. pl. perf. act. part. < χάσκω. **παρ' ἐμαυτοῦ**: *from my own* (sc. *imagination*), *of my own*. **ὡς** = ὅτι: *(saying) that*. **ἀνήφθη**: 3rd sing. aor. pass. indic. < ἀνάπτω. **φέρων**: this part. (in all genders), is frequently joined with a verb (often of throwing + reflexive pron.); it is intransitive, with a pass. sense, and denotes unrestrained action: *full tilt, wholeheartedly*. **ἐνέβαλεν δὲ φέρων ἑαυτὸν ὁ Πρωτεύς**: this slightly exaggerated description of Peregrinus' leap into the pyre is directly modeled after the speaker's question in 25 as to the reason behind Peregrinus' plan to commit suicide. Peregrinus, in fact, as Lucian stated in 38, simply ἐπήδησεν ἐς τὸ πῦρ.

Vocabulary

ἀκριβῶς, adv., *thoroughly*

ἀκρόασις, -εως, ἡ, *thing listened to*; *lecture* (as a performance)

ἀνακρίνω, *interrogate, inquire into, examine closely*

ἀνάπτω, ἀνάψω, ἀνήψα, *attach* X *to* Y, *kindle*; (pass.) *catch fire*

ἀποστρέφω, *turn* X (acc.) *back*

βλάξ, βλακός, ὁ or **ἡ,** *stupid person, dullard, dolt, idiot* or

διηγέομαι, (dep.), *describe (in detail)*

ἐκπυνθάνομαι, (dep.) *make enquiry of, question*

ἐμβάλλω, ἐμβαλῶ, ἐνέβαλον, *throw in*

ἔνθα, adv., *then, there, in that place*; *in that situation*

ἔργον, τό, *work, deed*

ἑταῖρος, ὁ, *comrade, companion, friend*

καταλαμβάνω, καταλήψομαι, κατέλαβον, *find, take hold of, seize*

λείψανον, τό, *piece left, remnant, relic*

μυρίος, -α, -ον, *numberless, countless*

περισπούδαστος, -ον, *much desired, highly desirable*

πρᾶγμα, -τος, τό, *matter, thing, affair*; (pl.) *troubles, annoyances*

πράττω, πράξω, ἔπραξα, *do, act*

πρός, prep. (+ acc.), *for, with respect to*

τελέω, *finish, complete*; *perform*; *perform* (sacred rites)

τόπος, ὁ, *place, site*

τραγῳδέω, *tell in a tragic manner* (i.e., embellish with fantastic details)

χαρίεις, χαρίεσσα, χάριεν, (masc./neut. gen. χαρίεντος), *beautiful, nice, fine*; *smart, clever, educated, with taste and refinement*

χάσκω, χανοῦμαι, ἔχανον, *open one's mouth (in eager expectation), gape*

ψιλός, -ή, -όν, *bare, unadorned, plain*

ὥσπερ, adv., *just as, even as*

103

σεισμοῦ πρότερον μεγάλου γενομένου σὺν μυκηθμῷ τῆς γῆς,

γὺψ ἀναπτάμενος ἐκ μέσης τῆς φλογὸς οἴχοιτο ἐς

τὸν οὐρανὸν ἀνθρωπιστὶ μεγάλῃ τῇ φωνῇ λέγων

"ἔλιπον γᾶν, βαίνω δ' ἐς Ὄλυμπον."

ἐκεῖνοι μὲν οὖν ἐτεθήπεσαν καὶ προσεκύνουν ὑποφρίττοντες

καὶ ἀνέκρινόν με πότερον πρὸς ἕω ἢ πρὸς δυσμὰς ἐνεχθείη

ὁ γύψ· ἐγὼ δὲ τὸ ἐπελθὸν ἀπεκρινάμην αὐτοῖς.

σεισμοῦ...γενομένου: gen. abs. **ἀναπτάμενος, οἴχοιτο**: Homeric sounding vocabulary (cf. the common Iliadic phrase, ᾤχετ' ἀποπτάμενος: *he has taken wing and is gone*), thus imparting an "epic" inflection; οἴχοιτο: 3rd sing. pres. mid./pass. opt. < οἴχομαι; opt. in an indir. statement in secondary sequence (ἐτραγῴδουν, ὡς). **ἔλιπον, Ὄλυμπον**: note the alliterative jingle. **γᾶν** = γῆν: the spelling is Doric, used here to give the phrase a "tragic" inflection (literary Doric was employed in the choruses of Athenian tragedies). **ἐτεθήπεσαν**: 3rd pl. pluperf. (with imperf. sense) indic. act. < τέθηπα. **ἐνεχθείη**: 3rd sing. aor. pass. opt. < φέρω; opt. in an indir. question in secondary sequence.

Talking Birds

In a poem in the Palatine Anthology (7.62, date unknown), a talking eagle appears on Plato's tomb. Lucian's invented vulture may be a humorous allusion to Plato's eagle.

α. Αἰετέ, τίπτε βέβηκας ὑπὲρ τάφον; ἢ τίνος, εἰπέ,
   ἀστερόεντα θεῶν οἶκον ἀποσκοπέεις;
β. Ψυχῆς εἰμὶ Πλάτωνος ἀποπταμένης ἐς Ὄλυμπον
   εἰκών · σῶμα δὲ γῆ γηγενὲς Ἀτθὶς ἔχει.

A. "Eagle, why do you stand over a tomb? And on whose tomb?, tell me,
   and why are you gazing steadily at the starry home of the gods?"
B. "I am the image of Plato's soul, which has flown away to Olympus,
   but the land of Attica keeps his earth-born body."

Vocabulary

ἀνακρίνω, *interrogate, inquire into*

ἀναπέτομαι, ἀναπτήσομαι, ἀνεπτάμην, (dep.) *fly up* or *away, take wing*

ἀνθρωπιστί, adv., *in the language of humans, in human speech*

ἀποκρίνομαι, ἀποκρινοῦμαι, ἀπεκρινάμην, *answer, reply to* (+ dat.),

βαίνω, βήσομαι, ἔβην, *go, go away, depart*

γῆ, ἡ, *earth*

γύψ, γυπός, ὁ, *vulture*

δυσμή, ἡ, (mostly in pl.) *west*

ἐπέρχομαι, ἔπειμι, ἐπῆλθον, *come, come forward; make a sudden appearance; come into one's head, occur to one*

ἕως, ἕω (gen. and acc.), ἡ, *dawn;* (direction) *east*

λείπω, λείψω, ἔλιπον, *leave*

μέσος, -η, -ον, *middle, in the middle*

μυκηθμός, ὁ, *rumbling*

οἴχομαι, (dep., pres. with perf. sense) *have gone* (i.e., *am gone*), *went, departed*

οὐρανός, ὁ, *sky, heaven*

πότερον...ἤ, *whether...or*

προσκυνέω, *fall down on one's knees and worship, worship*

πρότερον, adv., *formerly, before, sooner, earlier, first*

σεισμός, ὁ, *shaking, shock, trembling, earthquake*

τέθηπα, (perf. with pres. sense) *be astonished, astounded,* or *amazed*

ὑποφρίττω, *shudder slightly*

φέρω, οἴσω, ἤνεγκον, *carry, bring, bear;* (pass.) *be borne along (by winds), be swept away; go*

φωνή, ἡ, *sound, noise, voice*

[40] ἀπελθὼν δὲ ἐς τὴν πανήγυριν ἐπέστην τινὶ πολιῷ ἀνδρὶ καὶ νὴ τὸν Δί᾽ ἀξιοπίστῳ τὸ πρόσωπον ἐπὶ τῷ πώγωνι καὶ τῇ λοιπῇ σεμνότητι, τά τε ἄλλα διηγουμένῳ περὶ τοῦ Πρωτέως καὶ ὡς μετὰ τὸ καυθῆναι θεάσαιτο αὐτὸν ἐν λευκῇ ἐσθῆτι μικρὸν ἔμπροσθεν, καὶ νῦν ἀπολίποι περιπατοῦντα φαιδρὸν ἐν τῇ ἑπταφώνῳ στοᾷ κοτίνῳ τε ἐστεμμένον. εἶτ᾽ ἐπὶ πᾶσι προσέθηκε τὸν γῦπα, διομνύμενος ἦ μὴν αὐτὸς ἑωρακέναι ἀναπτάμενον ἐκ τῆς πυρᾶς, ὃν ἐγὼ μικρὸν ἔμπροσθεν ἀφῆκα πέτεσθαι καταγελῶντα τῶν ἀνοήτων καὶ βλακικῶν τὸν τρόπον.

ἐπέστην: 1st sing. 2nd aor. act. indic. < ἐφίστημι.   **τὸ πρόσωπον**: acc. of respect.   **ἐπὶ**: prep. + dat.; *in addition to*.   **τά, ἄλλα**: *everything else*.   **τε, καὶ, καὶ**: *both...and...and*.   **τὸ καυθῆναι**: articular inf.; i.e., *the cremation*; καυθῆναι: aor. pass. inf. < καίω. **θεάσαιτο, ἀπολίποι**: aor. optatives in indir. statement; translate as pluperf. indic. verbs.   **ἐν λευκῇ ἐσθῆτι**: cf. Matthew 28:3, Luke 24:4.   **μικρὸν ἔμπροσθεν**: *a little while ago*.   **τῇ ἑπταφώνῳ στοᾷ**: the "seven-voiced stoa" (also called the "stoa of Echo" or "stoa of seven echoes") was a long colonnade at Olympia so named on account of its acoustic peculiarity: sounds re-echoed seven times or more in it. **ἐστεμμένον**: masc. acc. sing. perf. mid./pass. part. < στέφω. Victors at the Olympics were given crowns made of wild olive tree leaves.   **ἐπὶ πᾶσι**: *in addition to all else (he had said), finally, on top of all this* (Costa). **τὸν γῦπα**: Lucian's mention of the venerable old man's inclusion of his invented vulture omen allows him to reveal how a rationalist's attempts to mock others' irrational beliefs can backfire (and indirectly contribute to the creation of a new cult!). The next paragraph describes Lucian imagining how the cult of Peregrinus will grow postmortem, especially through the latter's pre-suicide sophisticated marketing blitz (apparently modeled, unbeknownst to Lucian, in part after what he had learned from his time with the Christians; see 41).   **ἦ μὴν**: *truly indeed, absolutely*; this adv. + particle combination often introduces an oath or a threat; after verbs of swearing it often precedes the acc. and inf. construction of an indir. statement.   **ἑωρακέναι**: perf. act. inf. < ὁράω.

106

Vocabulary

ἀναπέτομαι, ἀναπτήσομαι, ἀνεπτάμην, (dep.) *fly up* or *away, take wing*

ἀνόητος, -ον, *unintelligent, senseless, silly*; ὁ ἀνόητος, *fool*

ἀξιόπιστος, -ον, *trustworthy*

ἀπέρχομαι, ἄπειμι, ἀπῆλθον, *go, go away, depart*

ἀπολείπω, ἀπολείψω, ἀπέλιπον, *leave behind*

ἀφίημι, ἀφήσω, ἀφῆκα, *send forth, let loose; permit* (+ inf.)

βλακικός, -ή, -όν, *stupid*; ὁ βλακικός, *idiot*

γύψ, γυπός, ὁ, *vulture*

διηγέομαι, (dep.), *describe (in detail)*

διόμνυμι, διόμνυμι, διομόσω, διώμοσα, (mid. διόμνυμαι is more common, with same meaning as act.) *swear solemnly, declare on oath*

ἔμπροσθεν, adv., *before, in front*

ἑπτάφωνος, -ον, *seven-voiced*

ἐσθής, -ῆτος, ἡ, *clothing, raiment*

ἐφίστημι, ἐπιστήσω, ἐπέστησα, *set* or *place upon; stop*; (mid., pass., and perf., pluperf., and 2nd aor. act.) *come upon (suddenly* or *by surprise)* (+ dat.)

ἦ, adv., *in truth*; ἦ μὴν, *absolutely in fact*

θεάομαι, (dep.) *look on, gaze at, view (as spectator)*

καίω, καύσω, ἔκαυσα, *set on fire, burn up*

καταγελάω, *ridicule, mock, laugh at*

κότινος, -ὁ, *wild-olive tree*

λευκός, -ή, -όν, *white*

λοιπός, -ή, -όν, *remaining, rest (of)*

μήν, adv., *indeed, truly*

νή, particle (of strong affirmation), νὴ Δία = *by Zeus!*

πανήγυρις, -εως, ἡ, *assembly, festival*; *national assembly* or *festival*

περιπατέω, *walk about, stroll, walk about while teaching*

πέτομαι, (dep.) *fly*

πολιός, -ά, -όν, *gray-haired*; *venerable*

προστίθημι, προσθήσω, προσέθηκα, *add*

πρόσωπον, τό, *face*; *one's look, countenance*

πώγων, -ωνος, ὁ, *beard*

σεμνότης, -ητος, ἡ, *solemnity, dignity, seriousness, authority*

στέφω, *crown, encircle, wreath*

στοά, -ή, *portico, roofed colonnade*

τρόπος, ὁ, *manner, way*

φαιδρός, -ά, -όν, *cheerful, glad*

ὡς, adv., *how*

[41] ἐννόει τὸ λοιπὸν οἷα εἰκὸς ἐπ᾽ αὐτῷ γενήσεσθαι, ποίας

μὲν οὐ μελίττας ἐπιστήσεσθαι ἐπὶ τὸν τόπον, τίνας δέ

τέττιγας οὐκ ἐπᾴσεσθαι, τίνας δὲ κορώνας οὐκ ἐπιπτήσεσθαι

καθάπερ ἐπὶ τὸν Ἡσιόδου τάφον, καὶ τὰ τοιαῦτα. εἰκόνας

μὲν γὰρ παρά τε Ἠλείων αὐτῶν παρά τε τῶν ἄλλων

Ἑλλήνων, οἷς καὶ ἐπεσταλκέναι ἔλεγεν, αὐτίκα μάλα

οἶδα πολλὰς ἀναστησομένας. φασὶ δὲ πάσαις σχεδὸν

ταῖς ἐνδόξοις πόλεσιν ἐπιστολὰς διαπέμψαι αὐτόν,

διαθήκας τινὰς καὶ παραινέσεις καὶ νόμους· καί τινας

ἐπὶ τούτῳ πρεσβευτὰς τῶν ἑταίρων ἐχειροτόνησεν,

νεκραγγέλους καὶ νερτεροδρόμους προσαγορεύσας.

ἐννόει: 2nd sing. pres. act. imperat.; its dir. objects are οἷα, ποίας μελίττας, τίνας τέττιγας, and τίνας δὲ κορώνας.   ἐπ᾽ αὐτῷ: *for him*, i.e., *in his honor*.   γενήσεσθαι: fut. mid. inf. < γίγνομαι. ποίας μὲν οὐ μελίττας ἐπιστήσεσθαι: the first of three rhetorical questions: *what sort of bees will not settle on* = *every bee will settle on* ἐπιστήσεσθαι: fut. mid. inf. < ἐφίστημι.   τὸν Ἡσιόδου τάφον: Hesiod (*fl. c.* 700 BCE) was, along with Homer, the earliest Greek poet whose works survive. Pausanias (9.38.3) notes that when the people of Orchomenus were afflicted by a plague, they inquired of the Delphic Oracle what to do and were told to bring the bones of Hesiod from the land of Naupactus to their land, and that a crow would indicate to them the place – which it did.   εἰκόνας...ἀναστησομένας = οἶδα πολλὰς εἰκόνας ἀναστησομένας...   τε, τε: *both...and*.   ἐπεσταλκέναι: perf. act. inf. < ἐπιστέλλω.   ἀναστησομένας: fem. acc. pl. fut. mid. part. < ἀνίστημι.   φασὶ δὲ...διαπέμψαι αὐτόν = δὲ φασὶ αὐτόν διαπέμψαι ἐπιστολὰς...   ἐπὶ τούτῳ: *for this reason* or *purpose*. νεκραγγέλους, νερτεροδρόμους: neologisms created by Peregrinus, perhaps based on his knowledge of Christian operations; Harmon (47, n. 2), e.g., notes that, "In the letters of Ignatius [(c. 35 – c. 107 CE)] he recommends to the Church of Smyrna the election of a special messenger, styled "ambassador of God" (θεοπρεσβευτής: *ad Smyrn.*, 11) or "courier of God" (θεοδρόμος: *ad Polyc.*, 7), to be sent to Syria."

Vocabulary

ἀνίστημι, ἀναστήσω, ἀνέστησα, *make* X (acc.) *stand up, raise* X (acc.); (pres. imperf., and fut. mid.; 2nd aor, perf., and pluperf. act.; aor. pass.; of statues) *be set up*

αὐτίκα, adv., *at once*

διαθήκη, ἡ, *covenant, agreement; last will and testament*

διαπέμπω, *send off in different directions, send out*

εἰκός, -οτος, τό, *likely, probable, reasonable* (with or without ἐστί + inf.)

εἰκών, -όνος, ἡ, *likeness* or *image* (whether statue or painting)

ἔνδοξος, -ον, *notable, conspicuous, of high repute*

ἐννοέω, *think* or *reflect upon, consider*

ἐπάδω, ἐπάσομαι, *sing, sing to, sing to* one *so as to charm* or *soothe* him / her

ἐπιπέτομαι, ἐπιπτήσομαι, ἐπεπτάμην, (dep.) *fly to*

ἐπιστέλλω, *send a message* (especially by letter), *give written instructions to*

ἐπιστολή, -ή, *message, letter, order, commission*

ἐφίστημι, ἐπιστήσω, ἐπέστησα, *set* or *place upon*; (mid.) *settle on, stop on*

Ἠλεῖος, ὁ, *Elean* (citizen of the town of Elis)

Ἡσίοδος, ὁ, *Hesiod*

καθάπερ, adv., *just as, like*

κορώνη, ἡ, *crow*

λοιπός, -ή, -όν, *remaining, rest (of)*; τὸ λοιπὸν, *hereafter, in the future*

μέλιττα, ἡ, *bee, honey-bee*

νεκράγγελος, ὁ, *messenger of the dead*

νερτεροδρόμος, ὁ, *courier from the underworld, courier from below*

νόμος, ὁ, *law, ruling, ordinance, decree*

παρά, prep. (+ gen.), *by, from*

παραίνεσις, -εως, ἡ, *advice, counsel, recommendation; address; exhortation*

ποῖος, -α, -ον, *of what kind, what sort*

πόλις, πόλεως, ἡ, *city, city-state*

πρεσβευτής, -οῦ, ὁ, *ambassador, agent, commissioner*

προσαγορεύω, *call* so and so

σχεδόν, adv., *nearly, almost*

τάφος, ὁ, *tomb, grave*

τέττιξ, -ιγος, ὁ, *cicada, cricket*

τίς, τί, (gen. τίνος) interrog. pron. and adj., *who? which? what?*

τοιοῦτος, τοιαύτη, τοιοῦτο, *such*; τὰ τοιαῦτα, *such things as these, suchlike*

τόπος, ὁ, *place, site*

χειροτονέω, *appoint*

[42] τοῦτο τέλος τοῦ κακοδαίμονος Πρωτέως ἐγένετο,

ἀνδρός, ὡς βραχεῖ λόγῳ περιλαβεῖν, πρὸς ἀλήθειαν μὲν

οὐδεπώποτε ἀποβλέψαντος, ἐπὶ δόξῃ δὲ καὶ τῷ παρὰ τῶν

πολλῶν ἐπαίνῳ ἅπαντα εἰπόντος ἀεὶ καὶ πράξαντος, ὡς

καὶ εἰς πῦρ ἀλέσθαι, ὅτε μηδὲ ἀπολαύειν τῶν ἐπαίνων

ἔμελλεν ἀναίσθητος αὐτῶν γενόμενος.

τοῦτο τέλος...: this sentence puts a satirical spin on the final sentence of Plato's *Phaedo*, which refers to Socrates' death: ἥδε ἡ τελευτή, ὦ Ἐχέκρατες, τοῦ ἑταίρου ἡμῖν ἐγένετο, ἀνδρός, ὡς ἡμεῖς φαῖμεν ἄν, τῶν τότε ὧν ἐπειράθημεν ἀρίστου καὶ ἄλλως φρονιμωτάτου καὶ δικαιοτάτου (*This was the end, Echecrates, of our friend, a man who was, as we may say, of all those of his time of whom we had had experience, the best and also the wisest and most just.*). **τοῦ κακοδαίμονος Πρωτέως**: an echo of the text's opening words (after the epistolary greeting): ὁ κακοδαίμων Περεγρῖνος. **ὡς βραχεῖ λόγῳ περιλαβεῖν**: i.e., *to put it briefly* (Harmon). **ἅπαντα, ἀεὶ**: the first is the direct obj. of both participles; the second modifies both participles. **ἀλέσθαι**: aor. mid. (dep.) inf. < ἄλλομαι. **ἀναίσθητος**: here the lost sense is hearing; i.e., *incapable of hearing* (+ gen.). **γενόμενος**: the part. is causal; i.e., *since* or *because*...

---

[43] ἓν ἔτι σοι προσδιηγησάμενος παύσομαι, ὡς ἔχῃς ἐπὶ

πολὺ γελᾶν. ἐκεῖνα μὲν γὰρ πάλαι οἶσθα, εὐθὺς ἀκούσας

μου ὅτε ἥκων ἀπὸ Συρίας διηγούμην ὡς ἀπὸ Τρῳάδος

συμπλεύσαιμι αὐτῷ καὶ τήν τε ἄλλην τὴν ἐν τῷ πλῷ τρυφὴν

ἓν: note the aspirated breathing mark. **ἐπὶ πολύ**: *much, greatly; for a long time.* **πάλαι οἶσθα**: *you have long known.* **Συρίας**: the Roman province of Syria was Lucian's homeland. **συμπλεύσαιμι**: 1st sing. aor. act. opt. < συμπλέω; opt. in indir. question in secondary sequence.

Vocabulary

ἀεί, adv., *always*

ἀλήθεια, ἡ, *truth*

ἅλλομαι, ἁλοῦμαι, ἡλόμην (2nd aor.), (dep.) *leap*

ἀναίσθητος, -ον, *incapable of sensing* X (gen.)

ἀποβλέπω, *look* or *gaze steadfastly at, look to, look upon* (with love or admiration)

ἀπολαύω, *have enjoyment of, have the benefit of, enjoy* (+ gen.)

βραχύς, -εῖα, -ύ, *short, brief*

διηγέομαι, (dep.), *describe (in detail)*

εἷς, μία, ἕν, *one*

ἔπαινος, ὁ, *praise*

εὐθύς, adv., *immediately, at once; straight, directly*

ἔχω, ἕξω, ἔσχον, *have; hold;* (+ inf.) *can, be able*

ἥκω, (imperf.) ἧκον, (pres. = perf.; imperf. = pluperf.) *have come*

κακοδαίμων (gen., κακοδαίμονος), *possessed by an evil spirit, unlucky, wretched*

μέλλω, *be likely, have a chance* (+ inf.)

μηδέ, conj., *(and) not*; adv., *not even*

ὅτε, conj., *when*

οὐδεπώποτε, conj. and adv., *never yet at any time, never ever*

πάλαι, adv., *long ago*

παύω, *stop*; (mid.) *stop (oneself), cease from*

περιλαμβάνω, περιλήψομαι, περιέλαβον, *comprehend, grasp*

πλοῦς, πλοῦ, πλῷ, πλοῦν, ὁ, *voyage*

πράττω, πράξω, ἔπραξα, *do, act*

προσδιηγέομαι, (dep.) *narrate besides* or *in addition*

συμπλέω, *sail in company with*

Συρία, ἡ, *Syria*

τρυφή, ἡ, *luxury, self-indulgence*

Τρῳάς, -άδος, ἡ, *the Troad* (i.e., the region of Northwest Asia Minor whose principal city was Troy)

ὡς, (+ inf.) *so that, such that*; (+ subju./opt.) *so that, in order that*; adv., *how*

καὶ τὸ μειράκιον τὸ ὡραῖον ὃ ἔπεισε κυνίζειν ὡς ἔχοι

τινὰ καὶ αὐτὸς Ἀλκιβιάδην, καὶ ὡς ἐπεὶ ταραχθείημεν

τῆς νυκτὸς ἐν μέσῳ τῷ Αἰγαίῳ γνόφου καταβάντος καὶ

κῦμα παμμέγεθες ἐγείραντος, ἐκώκυε μετὰ τῶν γυναικῶν

ὁ θαυμαστὸς καὶ θανάτου κρείττων εἶναι δοκῶν. [44] ἀλλὰ

μικρὸν πρὸ τῆς τελευτῆς, πρὸ ἐννέα σχεδόν που ἡμερῶν,

πλεῖον, οἶμαι, τοῦ ἱκανοῦ ἐμφαγὼν ἤμεσέν τε τῆς νυκτὸς καὶ

ἑάλω πυρετῷ μάλα σφοδρῷ. ταῦτα δέ μοι Ἀλέξανδρος

ὁ ἰατρὸς διηγήσατο μετακληθεὶς ὡς ἐπισκοπήσειεν αὐτόν.

τὸ μειράκιον τὸ ὡραῖον: see 9 for a similar incident involving Peregrinus and an attractive boy. ὡς ἔχοι τινὰ καὶ αὐτὸς Ἀλκιβιάδην = ὡς αὐτὸς ἔχοι καὶ τινὰ Ἀλκιβιάδην; but note how the original syntax repeats the main thought twice (for emphasis): *so that he might have someone too, he himself (might have) an Alcibiades.* Ἀλκιβιάδην: Alcibiades (*c.* 450 – 404 BCE) was an Athenian politician and general famous for his physical beauty and aggressive, imperialistic agenda (Thucydides 6.15-19); in his youth he tried to seduce the middle-aged Socrates, but failed (Plato, *Symposium* 217a-219e). Since it was customary for older males to pursue younger males, Alcibiades' attempts to woo Socrates were considered highly unusual. Peregrinus' pursuit of a μειράκιον was more of the norm, though less common in Lucian's day than in fifth-century BCE Athens. ὡς: adv., *how.* ταραχθείημεν: 1st pl. aor. pass. opt. < ταράττω; ἐπεὶ can sometimes take the opt. in temporal clauses. τῆς νυκτὸς: gen. of time within which; *at night, during the night.* γνόφου καταβάντος: gen. abs. γνόφου: the regular meaning of this word is *darkness*. Here it must refer to a *squall, storm* or *tempest.* κῦμα παμμέγεθες ἐγείραντος: gen. abs. θανάτου κρείττων εἶναι δοκῶν = δοκῶν εἶναι κρείττων θανάτου. θανάτου: gen. of comparison. ἐμφαγὼν: masc. nom. sing. aor. act. < ἐνέφαγον. τοῦ ἱκανοῦ: gen. of comparison. τε, καὶ: *both... and.* ἑάλω: 3rd sing. aor. act. indic. < ἁλίσκομαι. μετακληθεὶς: masc. nom. sing. aor. pass. part. < μετακαλέω. ἐπισκοπήσειεν: 3rd sing. aor. act. opt. < ἐπισκοπέω.

Vocabulary

Αἰγαῖος, ὁ, (sc. πόντος) *the Aegean (Sea)*

ἁλίσκομαι, ἁλώσομαι, ἑάλων/ἥλων, (defective pass.) *be caught* or *seized*; (of illness or disease) *come down with*

Ἀλκιβιάδης, -ου, ὁ, *Alcibiades*

γνόφος, ὁ, (Aeolic; in later Greek used for ὁ δνόφος) *squall, tempest, storm*

γυνή, γυναικός, ἡ, *woman*

δοκῶ, (uncontracted = δοκέω) *appear, seem*; *be reputed, have the reputation for, held* or *thought* (+ εἶναι)

ἐγείρω, *awaken, rouse, stir up, raise*

ἐμέω, *vomit, throw up*; *be sick*

ἐνέφαγον (2nd aor.; no pres. – ἐνέσθιω – in use), *eat quickly* or *greedily*

ἐννέα, indecl., *nine*

ἐπισκοπέω, *examine*

ἡμέρα, ἡ, *day*

θάνατος, ὁ, *death*

θαυμαστός, -ή, -όν, *wonderful, marvelous*

ἰατρός, ὁ, *doctor, physician, surgeon*

ἱκανός, -ή, -όν, *enough*

καταβαίνω, καταβήσομαι, κατέβην, *go* or *come down, descend*

κρείττων, -ον, (gen. -ονος), *stronger, mightier*

κῦμα, -ατος, τό, *wave*

κυνίζω, *play the dog*; *live like a Cynic, become a Cynic*

κωκύω, *shriek, wail*

μειράκιον, τό, (diminutive of μεῖραξ) *boy, young man* (under the age of 21)

μέσος, -η, -ον, *middle, in the middle (of)*

μετακαλέω, *summon, call in* (e.g., a doctor or a midwife)

μικρός, -ά, -ό, *little, small*; μικρόν, adv., *a little time*

νύξ, νυκτός, ἡ, *night*

παμμεγέθης, -ες, *very great, immense*

πείθω, πείσω, ἔπεισα, *persuade, convince*

πλείων, πλεῖον, (comp. of πολύς, πολλή, πολύ) *more*; πλεῖον (adv.), *more*

που, adv., *possibly, perhaps, I suppose*

πρό, prep. (+ gen.), *before*

πυρετός, ὁ, *fever*

σφοδρός, -ή, -όν, *strong, violent*

σχεδόν, adv., *nearly, about*

ταράττω, *disturb, trouble, agitate*

ὡραῖος, -α, -ον, *ripe*; *bursting with life*; *beautiful*

113

ἔφη οὖν καταλαβεῖν αὐτὸν χαμαὶ κυλιόμενον καὶ τὸν φλογμὸν

οὐ φέροντα καὶ ψυχρὸν αἰτοῦντα πάνυ ἐρωτικῶς, ἑαυτὸν δὲ

μὴ δοῦναι. καίτοι εἰπεῖν ἔφη πρὸς αὐτὸν ὡς εἰ πάντως θανάτου

δέοιτο, ἥκειν αὐτὸν ἐπὶ τὰς θύρας αὐτόματον, ὥστε καλῶς

ἔχειν ἕπεσθαι μηδὲν τοῦ πυρὸς δεόμενον· τὸν δ' αὖ φάναι, "ἀλλ'

οὐχ ὁμοίως ἔνδοξος ὁ τρόπος γένοιτ' ἄν, πᾶσιν κοινὸς ὤν."

μὴ = οὐ in Attic Greek.   **δοῦναι**: aor. act. inf. < δίδωμι.   **εἰπεῖν**
ἔφη: *he said (to me) that he had said.*   **ὡς** = ὅτι: *that.*   **δέοιτο**:
pres. opt. in a mixed condition (past general [the protasis, or 'if' clause] +
indir. statement [apodosis]); i.e., *if (ever) he wanted...*   **αὐτὸν**: i.e.,
Death (the subj. of the indir. statement).   **ὥστε καλῶς ἔχειν**
ἕπεσθαι: *with the result that it would be a good idea (for him) to follow*
(Death).   **δεόμενον**: modifies the understood subj. (*him*) of the
preceding inf. ἕπεσθαι.   **τὸν**: common in Attic prose for αὐτὸν; it is
the subj. of the indir. statement; i.e., *and (sc. he said) that he (i.e.*
Peregrinus) in turn said.   **φάναι**: aor. act. inf. < φημί.   **γένοιτ'** =
γένοιτο: 3rd sing. aor. mid. (dep.) opt. < γίγνομαι; a potential opt.

[45] ταῦτα μὲν ὁ Ἀλέξανδρος. ἐγὼ δὲ οὐδ' αὐτὸς πρὸ

πολλῶν ἡμερῶν εἶδον αὐτὸν ἐγκεχρισμένον, ὡς ἀποδακρύσειε

τῷ δριμεῖ φαρμάκῳ. ὁρᾷς; οὐ πάνυ τοὺς ἀμβλυωποῦντας

ὁ Αἰακὸς παραδέχεται. ὅμοιον ὡς εἴ τις ἐπὶ σταυρὸν

ταῦτα μὲν ὁ Ἀλέξανδρος: sc. *said.*   **οὐδ', πρὸ πολλῶν**
ἡμερῶν: *(and) not many days before*; i.e., *a few days before.*
ἐγκεχρισμένον: masc. acc. sing. mid./pass. perf. part. < ἐγχρίω.
ἀποδακρύσειε: 3rd sing. aor. act. opt. < ἀποδακρύω.   **τῷ δριμεῖ**
φαρμάκῳ: instrumental datives.   **ὁ Αἰακὸς**: in mythology, Aeacus
was the son of Zeus and the nymph Aegina, and the father of three sons:
Telamon, Peleus, and Phocus. After his death he became one of the three
judges of the underworld.

Vocabulary

Αἰακός, ὁ, *Aeacus*

αἰτέω, *ask, beg*

ἀμβλυωπέω, *be dim-sighted, have poor sight, have sick* or *sore eyes*

ἀποδακρύω, *weep much, be made to weep*

αὖ, adv., *again, once more, in turn*

αὐτόματος, -η, -ον, *acting of one's own will, of one's own accord, spontaneous*; αὐτόματος θάνατος, *natural death*

δέομαι, (dep.) *be in need of, want* (+ gen.)

δίδωμι, δώσω, ἔδωκα, *give*

δριμύς, -εῖα, -ύ, *sharp, acrid, pungent*

ἐγχρίω, *anoint, rub, smear*

ἔνδοξος, -ον, *notable, conspicuous, of high repute*

ἔπομαι, (dep.) *follow*

ἐρωτικῶς, adv., *passionately*

ἥκω, (imperf.) ἧκον, (pres. = perf.; imperf. = pluperf.) *have come, be present*

θύρα, ἡ, *door*

καίτοι, conj. + particle, *and indeed, and further, furthermore, moreover*

καλῶς, adv., *well, rightly, happily*; καλῶς ἔχειν, *to be well* (i.e., a good thing or idea)

καταλαμβάνω, καταλήψομαι, κατέλαβον, *find, take hold of, seize*

κοινός, -ή, -όν, *common*

κυλίω, (later form of κυλίνδω) *roll*

μηδείς, μηδεμία, μηδέν, *not one, nobody, nothing*; μηδέν, adv., *not at all*

ὅμοιος, -α, -ον, *like, resembling; the same*; ὅμοιον, adv. (+ ὡς), *the same as, like, just as, just like*

ὁμοίως, adv., *equally*

πάντως, adv., *absolutely, altogether*

πάνυ, adv., *very, exceedingly*; οὐ πάνυ, *not at all; hardly, scarcely*

παραδέχομαι, (dep.) *receive, admit, accept*

πρό, prep. (+ gen.), *before*

σταυρός, ὁ, *cross*

φάρμακον, τό, *drug, salve*

φέρω, οἴσω, ἤνεγκον, *bear, endure, put up with*

φλογμός, ὁ, *feverish heat*

χαμαί, adv., *on the ground*

ψυχρός, -ά, -όν, *cold*; ψυχρόν (sc. ὕδωρ) *cold water*

ἀναβήσεσθαι μέλλων τὸ ἐν τῷ δακτύλῳ πρόσπταισμα

θεραπεύοι. τί σοι δοκεῖ ὁ Δημόκριτος, εἰ ταῦτα εἶδε; κατ᾽

ἀξίαν γελάσαι ἂν ἐπὶ τῷ ἀνδρί; καίτοι πόθεν εἶχεν ἐκεῖνος

τοσοῦτον γέλωτα; σὺ δ᾽ οὖν, ὦ φιλότης, γέλα καὶ αὐτός, καὶ

μάλιστα ὁπόταν τῶν ἄλλων ἀκούῃς θαυμαζόντων αὐτόν.

ἀναβήσεσθαι: fut. mid. (dep.) inf. < ἀναβαίνω.   **θεραπεύοι**: 3rd
sing. pres. act. opt. < θεραπεύω; opt. in a comparative clause (ὅμοιον ὡς
εἴ) with τις as subj.   **τί σοι δοκεῖ ὁ Δημόκριτος**: sc. ποιῆσαι
ἄν; this implied inf. + ἄν is the apodosis of a past contrary-to-fact
conditional sentence in indir. statement; i.e., *what do you think Democritus
(would have done)?*   **ὁ Δημόκριτος**: for Democritus and why he was
known for his laughter, see 7 and note ad loc.   **γελάσαι ἂν**: the inf. +
ἄν is the apodosis of a past contrary-to-fact conditional sentence in implied
indir. statement; i.e., *(don't you think that he) would have laughed...?*
πόθεν εἶχεν ἐκεῖνος τοσοῦτον γέλωτα: i.e., even the person
famous for his unending laughter couldn't laugh at Peregrinus as much as
he deserved.   **γέλα**: 2nd sing pres. act. impera. < γελάω.   **ὁπόταν**:
ὁπότε + ἄν; *when(ever)* (+ subju.).   **τῶν ἄλλων**: *all other people, the
rest (of mankind)*.   **θαυμαζόντων αὐτόν**: although in these final
sentences Lucian launches a triple assault of laughter (γελάσαι, γέλωτα,
γέλα) against his victim, the text ends with words that would have been
music to Peregrinus' ears.

Vocabulary

ἀναβαίνω, ἀναβήσομαι, ἀνέβην, *go up, mount*

ἀξία, ἡ, *worth, value*; κατ' ἀξίαν, *as he/she deserves, deservedly*

γελάω, γελάσομαι, ἐγέλασα, *laugh*

γέλως, -ωτος, ὁ, *laughter*

δάκτυλος, ὁ, *finger*; *toe*

Δημόκριτος, ὁ, *Democritus*

δοκῶ, (uncontracted = δοκέω) *think, suppose, imagine*; (3rd sing.) *it seems*

θαυμάζω, *marvel, be amazed, wonder at*; *admire, honor, worship*

θεραπεύω, *take care of, nurse, treat medically*

καίτοι, conj. + particle, *and yet*; *and indeed, and further, furthermore, moreover*

μάλιστα, adv., *most of all, especially*

μέλλω, *be going to* X, *be about to* X (+ fut. inf.)

πόθεν, adv., *from where?*

πρόσπταισμα, -ατος, τό, *whitlow* (an abscess in the soft tissue near a fingernail or toenail); *bump, bruise*

φιλότης, ἡ, *friendship, love, affection*; ὦ φιλότης, *my friend*

Appendix: Another Indian Self-Immolation

In addition to Calanus' self-immolation before Alexander the Great in Susa in 323 BCE (see *Peregrinus* 25), another Indian self-immolation of more recent memory would have been available to Peregrinus as an example of Brahman "fortitude." This Indian sage, called either Zarmanochegas or Zarmarus, committed suicide in Athens before the emperor Augustus in 20 BCE. Two accounts of his suicide survive, one by Strabo (64/63 BC – *c*. 24 CE) and the other by Cassius Dio (*c*. 155 – 235 CE).

Strabo 15.1.73:

> "...and they were accompanied also, according to him, by the man who burned himself up at Athens; and that whereas some commit suicide when they suffer adversity, seeking release from the ills at hand, others do so when their lot is happy, as was the case with that man; for, he adds, although that man had fared as he wished up to that time, he thought it necessary then to depart this life, lest something untoward might happen to him if he tarried here; and that therefore he leaped upon the pyre with a laugh, his naked body anointed, wearing only a loin-cloth; and that the following words were inscribed on his tomb: "Here lies Zarmanochegas, an Indian from Bargosa, who immortalised himself in accordance with the ancestral customs of Indians."" (Horace Leonard Jones, trans.)

Cassius Dio 54.9.10:

> "One of the Indians, Zarmarus, for some reason wished to die, — either because, being of the caste of sages, he was on this account moved by ambition, or, in accordance with the traditional custom of the Indians, because of old age, or because he wished to make a display for the benefit of Augustus and the Athenians (for Augustus had reached Athens);— he was therefore initiated into the mysteries of the two goddesses, which were held out of season on account, they say, of Augustus, who also was an initiate, and he then threw himself alive into the fire." (Earnest Cary, trans.)

GLOSSARY

A α

ἀβελτερία, ἡ, *silliness, stupidity*

Ἀγαθόβουλος, ὁ, *Agathoboulos*

ἄγαλμα, τό, *glory, delight; gift (pleasing to the gods); sacred image/statue*

ἄγαν, adv., *too much, excessive*

ἀγανακτέω, *be angry*

ἀγορεύω, *speak* (in public)

ἀγρός, ὁ, *field, farm, land*

ἄγω, ἄξω, ἤγαγον, *lead, take, bring*

ἀγῶν, -ῶνος, ὁ, *contest*

ἀδελφός, ὁ, *brother*

ἀδιάφορον, τό, *indifference, Stoic indifference*

ἀδόκητος, -ον, *unexpected*; ἀδόκητον, adv., *unexpectedly*

ἀδύνατος, -ον, *impossible*

ἄδυτον, τό, *innermost sanctuary, "holy of holies"*

ἀεί, adv., *always*; ὁ ἀεί χρόνος, *eternity, forever*

ἀθάνατος, -ον, *immortal*

ἄθεος, -ον, *without god, godless*; (as substantive) *atheist, godless person*

ἀθλητής, -οῦ, ὁ, *athlete*

ἄθλιος, -α, -ον, *wretched, miserable*

Αἰακός, ὁ, *Aeacus*

Αἰγαῖος, ὁ, (sc. πόντος) *the Aegean (Sea)*

Αἴγυπτος, ἡ, *Egypt*

αἰδέομαι, (dep.) *stand in awe of, fear, respect, revere*

αἰδοῖον, τό, *private parts, sexual organ, penis* (literally, *the shameful thing*)

αἰθήρ, -έρος, ὁ, *ether, thin air, heaven; fifth element* (equivalent to fire)

αἴθω, *light, kindle*; (pass. often) *burn, blaze*

αἷμα, -ατος, τό, *blood*

αἱρέω, αἱρήσω, εἷλον, *take*; (mid.) *choose*

αἴρω, ἀρῶ, ἦρα, *raise (up)*

ἀίσσω, ἀίξω, ᾖξα, *move quickly (to), make a dash (for), turn eagerly (to)*

αἰτέω, *ask, ask for, demand, beg*

αἰτία, ἡ, *reason, cause*

αἰτιάομαι, (dep.) *blame, accuse, censure, criticize*

ἀκαρής, -ές, *small, tiny*; ἐν ἀκαρεῖ (χρόνου), *in a moment (of time)*

ἀκίνητος, -ον, *motionless*

121

ἀκούω, ἀκούσομαι, ἤκουσα, *hear* (+ gen. of person)

ἀκριβής, -ές, *exact, accurate, precise; definite*

ἀκριβῶς, adv., *accurately, thoroughly, absolutely*

ἀκρόασις, -εως, ἡ, *thing listened to; lecture* (as a performance)

ἀκροατής, -οῦ, ὁ, *listener, hearer*

ἄκων, ἄκουσα, ἄκον, *against one's will, unwilling*

Ἀλέξανδρος, ὁ, *Alexander*

ἀλήθεια, ἡ, *truth*

ἁλίσκομαι, ἁλώσομαι, ἑάλων/ἥλων, (defective pass; + part.) *be caught* or *seized* (doing a thing); *be detected* (doing a thing); (of illness or disease) *come down with*

Ἀλκιβιάδης, -ου, ὁ, *Alcibiades*

ἀλλαχόθεν, adv., *from another place*

ἀλλήλων, *of one another*

ἄλλομαι, ἀλοῦμαι, ἡλόμην (2nd aor.), (dep.) *leap, jump*

ἄλλός, -ή, -ό, *another, other*

ἄλλοτε, adv., (+ ἄλλος, -η, -ο) *sometimes to this, sometimes to that*

ἄλλως, adv., *in another way* or *manner, otherwise*; ἄλλως τε, *and besides*

ἅμα, adv., *together, at the same time*; prep. (+ dat.), *together with*

ἀμβλυωπέω, *be dim-sighted, have poor sight, have sick* or *sore eyes*

ἀμείβω, *pass, cross, leave, exchange*

ἀμείνων, -ον, *better*; ἄμεινόν (ἐστι), *it is better*

ἀμέλει, adv., *of course; for instance*

ἀμελέω, *disregard, pay no attention to*

ἀμέτρως, adv., *excessively, immoderately*

ἀμήχανος, -ον, *difficult, hard, impossible; extraordinary, incredible*

ἄμιλλα, ἡ, *contest, contest for superiority*

ἀμπέχω, ἀμφέξω, ἤμπεσχον, *put on/round*; (mid.) *put round oneself, wear*

ἀναβαίνω, ἀναβήσομαι, ἀνέβην, *go up, mount (the speaker's platform)*

ἀναβάλλω, ἀναβαλῶ, ἀνέβαλον, *throw* or *toss up*; (mid.) *put off, delay*

ἀναβοάω, ἀναβοήσομαι, ἀνεβόησα, *shout, cry out*

ἀνάγκη, ἡ, *necessity*; ἀνάγκη ἐστί(ν), *it is necessary* (+ inf.)

ἀναδύομαι, ἀναδύσομαι, ἀνέδυν (2nd aor.), (dep.) *draw back, withdraw, back out*

ἀναίσθητος, -ον, *incapable of sensing* X (gen.)

ἀνακαίω, ἀνακαύσω, ἀνέκαυσα, *kindle, light (a fire)*

ἀνακράζω, *cry out, shout*

ἀνακρίνω, *interrogate, inquire into, examine closely*

ἀναλογίζομαι, (dep.) *reflect, consider*

ἀναμίγνυμι, ἀναμίξω, ἀνέμιξα, *commingle with, mix with*

ἀναμιμνήσκω, ἀναμνήσω, ἀνέμνησα, *remind*; (pass.) *remember* (+ gen.)

ἄναξ, ἄνακτος, ὁ, *lord*

ἀνάξιος -α, -ον, *unworthy, undeserved*

ἀναξίως, adv., *undeserving, unworthy*

ἀναπέτομαι, ἀναπτήσομαι, ἀνεπτάμην, (dep.) *fly up* or *away, take wing*

ἀναπηδάω, ἀναπηδήσομαι, ἀνεπήδησα, *jump out (in haste* or *fear)*

ἀναπίμπλημι, *fill up*; (mid.) *fill oneself with* (+ gen.); (pass.) *be filled* or *infected with* (+ gen.)

ἀνάπτω, ἀνάψω, ἀνῆψα, *attach* X *to* Y, *kindle*; (pass.) *catch fire*

ἀνασκολοπίζω, *fix on a pole* or *stake, impale; crucify*

ἀνατέλλω, *rise*

ἀναφέρω, ἀνοίσω, ἀνήνεγκα, *ascribe, attribute*

ἀναφλάω, *masturbate* (literally, *crush* or *pound up*)

ἀνδροφόνος, ὁ, *murderer*

ἀνδρώδης, -ες, *manly, virile*

ἀνέρχομαι, ἄνειμι, ἀνῆλθον, *go up*

ἄνευ, prep. (+ gen.), *without*

ἀνέχω, ἀνέξω, ἀνέσχον, *hold up*; (mid.) *endure, hold out; allow, tolerate* (+ part.)

ἀνεψιός, ὁ, *first cousin*

ἀνήρ, ἀνδρός, ὁ, *man, gentleman*

ἀνθρωπιστί, adv., *in the language of humans, in human speech*

ἄνθρωπος, ὁ, *man, human being*

ἀνίημι, ἀνήσω, ἀνῆκα, *let go, give up*

ἀνίστημι, ἀναστήσω, ἀνέστησα, *make* X *stand up, raise* X; (pres., imperf., and fut. mid.; 2nd aor, perf., and pluperf. act.; aor. pass.; of statues) *be set up*

ἀνίσχω, *rise*

ἀνόητος, -ον, *unintelligent, stupid, senseless, foolish, silly*; ὁ ἀνόητος, *fool*

ἀνοίγνυμι, ἀνοίξω, ἀνέῳξα, *open*

ἀνταγωνίζομαι, (dep.) *prove a match for, vie with; be set against*

ἀνταίρω, ἀνταρῶ, ἀντῆρα, (act./mid.) *raise* X (acc.) *against* Y (dat.)

ἀντιπρεσβεύομαι, (dep.) *send counter-ambassadors*

ἀξία, ἡ, *penalty, just desserts; worth, value*; κατ' ἀξίαν, *as he/she deserves, deservedly*

ἀξιόπιστος, -ον, *trustworthy*

ἄξιος, -α, -ον, *worth, worthy of, deserving of, fitting* (+ gen. or inf.)

ἀξιόω, *think, deem worthy; think one has the right, think it right* or *fit; consent expect* (+ inf.)

ἀξίωμα, -ατος, τό, *reputation, honor; rank, position*

ἀπαγγέλλω, ἀπαγγελῶ, ἀπήγγειλα, *report, announce, relate*

ἀπάγω, ἀπάξω, ἀπήγαγον, *lead away*

ἀπαιτέω, *demand back*

ἀπαλλάττω, *set free, release*; (mid./pass.) *recover from* (+ gen.); *be set free or released from (life), die*

ἀπανθρακόω, *burn to a cinder, carbonize*

ἀπαντάω, ἀπαντήσομαι, ἀπήντησα, *go to meet, present oneself, turn out.*

ἅπαξ, adv., *once, once for all*

ἀπαξαπλῶς, *in general*

ἀπαρνέομαι, (dep.) *deny, deny utterly*; *reject*

ἅπας, ἅπασα, ἅπαν, *all*; *every*; *whole*

ἀπεικάζω, *represent, portray, depict*

ἀπεικώς, -υῖα, -ός, *unlikely, unreasonable*

ἀπειλέω, *promise, threaten* (with dependent clauses + fut. inf.)

ἀπέρχομαι, ἄπειμι, ἀπῆλθον, *go, go away, depart*

ἄπλαστος, -ον, *not moulded, unformed*; *in its natural state*

ἀπό, prep. (+ gen.), *from, away from*; *by*

ἀποβαίνω, ἀποβήσομαι, ἀπέβην, *disembark, step off of / from* (+ gen.)

ἀποβλέπω, *look or pay attention to, gaze steadfastly at, look at / upon* (with love or admiration)

ἀποδακρύω, *weep much, be made to weep*

ἀποδείκνυμι, ἀποδείξω, ἀπέδειξα, *appoint, name, create*

ἀποδειλιάω, *play the coward, be terrified*

ἀποδημία, ἡ, *being abroad, being away*

ἀποθνήσκω, ἀποθανοῦμαι, ἀπέθανον, *die*

ἀποίχομαι, (dep.) *have departed, be absent*; *be dead and gone*

ἀποκρίνομαι, ἀποκρινοῦμαι, ἀπεκρινάμην, *answer, reply to* (+ dat.),

ἀπολαύω, *have enjoyment of, have the benefit of, enjoy* (+ gen.)

ἀπολείπω, ἀπολείψω, ἀπέλιπον, *leave behind*

ἀπόλλυμι, ἀπολῶ, ἀπώλεσα, *destroy utterly, kill, slay*; *lose*; (mid.) *die*; *be lost, perish*

ἀπολογία, -ας, ἡ, *defense*

ἀπομνημονεύω, *relate or quote (from memory), recount*

ἀπονενοημένως, adv., *recklessly*

ἀπόνοια, ἡ, *loss of all sense*; *madness*; *recklessness*; *rebellion*; *desperation*

ἀποπέμπω, ἀποπέμψω, ἀπέπεμψα, *send off or away*; *get rid of*

ἀποπνίγω, *strangle, choke, throttle*; (pass.) *be choked with rage*

ἀπορέω, (mid. often in same sense as act.) *be at a loss, be without means or resource*

ἀπόρρητος, -ον, *forbidden*

ἀποστρέφω, *turn* X (acc.) *back*

ἀποτίθημι, ἀποθήσω, ἀπέθηκα, *put away*; (mid.) *lay* or *set aside one's own, put away from oneself*

ἀποτίνω, ἀποτείσω, ἀπέτεισα, *pay, repay, pay in full*

ἀποφαίνω, ἀποφανῶ, ἀπέφηνα, *make clear that* X (acc.) *(is)* Y (acc.), *render* or *make* X (acc.) *so and so* (acc) *by example*

ἄρα, particle, *after all, so; therefore, then, as it seems*

ἆρα, particle introducing a question

ἀρετή, ἡ, *excellence, goodness, virtue*

ἄριστος, -η, -ον, *best, finest, most excellent*

ἁρμοστής, -οῦ, ὁ, *governor*

ἄρουρα, ἡ, *tilled land, ploughland, fields*

Ἀρπίνα, ἡ, *Harpina*

Ἄρτεμις, -ιδος, ἡ, *Artemis*

ἄρτι, adv., *presently*

ἀρχή, ἡ, *beginning*

ἄρχω, *begin; rule, govern*; (mid.) *begin*

ἄρχων, -οντος, ὁ, *governor*

ἀσεβῶς, adv., *impiously*

Ἀσία, ἡ, *Asia* (i.e., modern-day Western Asia Minor)

ἄσκησις, ἡ, *practice, training; training in asceticism; mode of life*

Ἀσκληπιός, ὁ, *Asclepius*

ἀσπάζομαι, (dep.) *greet, embrace, cling fondly to*

ἀσφαλής, -ές, *safe, secure*

ἀσφαλῶς, adv., *safely, without any risk* or *danger*

ἄτε, adv., *seeing that, in as much as, since*

αὖ, adv., *further, moreover, besides; again, once more, in turn*

αὖθις, adv., *again, once again, once more*

αὐξάνω, αὐξήσω, ηὔξησα, *make large, increase, strengthen*; (pass.) *increase, grow*

αὐτίκα, adv., *immediately, at once*

αὐτόματος, -η, -ον, *acting of one's own will, of one's own accord, spontaneous*; αὐτόματος θάνατος, *natural death*

αὐτός, -ή, -ό, (intensive adj.) *-self, -selves*; (adj.) *same*; (pron. in gen., dat., acc.) *him, her, it, them*

ἀφειδέω, *do not spare, lavish* (+ gen.)

ἄφθονος, -ον, *without envy; plentiful*; (pl.) *wealth, prosperity, comfort*

ἀφίημι, ἀφήσω, ἀφῆκα, *let go, set free, relinquish, bequeath, leave alone*; ; *permit* (+ inf.)

ἀφικνέομαι, ἀφίξομαι, ἀφικόμην, (dep.) *arrive at, come to, reach*

ἄφυκτος, -ον, *inescapable*

Ἀχαιοί, οἱ, *Achaeans* (in Homer the name most commonly used for the Greeks)
ἄχθομαι, (dep.) *be annoyed, be angry*
ἄχρι, conj., *until*

Β β

βάθος, -ους, τό, *depth*
βαθύς, βαθεῖα, βαθύ, *deep*
βαίνω, βήσομαι, ἔβην, *go, go away, depart*
Βάκις, -ιδος, ὁ, *Bacis*
βακτηρία, ἡ, *stick, staff*
βάκτρον, τό, *staff, walking stick*
βάλλω, βαλῶ, ἔβαλον, *hit, strike*
βασιλεύς, -έως, ὁ, *king, emperor*
βέλτιστος, -η, -ον, *best, very good*; (as mode of address) *(my) good friend*;
    ὁ βέλτιστος, *very fine/excellent gentleman*
βίβλον, τό, *roll, scroll, book*
βίος, ὁ, *life, manner of living*; *career*; *the world, the world we live in*
βιόω, βιώσομαι, ἐβίωσα/ἐβίων (2nd aor.), *live*
βλακικός, -ή, -όν, *stupid*; ὁ βλακικός, *idiot*
βλάξ, βλακός, ὁ or ἡ, *stupid person, dullard, dolt, idiot*
βλασφημία, ἡ, *slander, defamation, libel*; *abuse*
βοάω, βοήσομαι, ἐβόησα, *shout*
βοή, ἡ, *shout(ing), loud cry(ing)*
βοηθέω, *help, aid, assist*
βόθρος, ὁ, *hole, pit*
βόσκημα, -ατος, τό, *cattle*
βόσκω, *feed, nourish, support*; *maintain*
βουλεύω, *plan, decide*; *deliberate, consider*; (mid.) *determine, resolve*
βούλομαι, *wish, want, be willing* (+ inf.); *mean*
Βραχμᾶνες, οἱ, *Brachmanes, Bragmanni, Brahmans, Gymnosophists*
βραχύς, -εῖα, -ύ, *short, brief*; ἐν βραχεῖ, *in a short time, in no time*; *in few
    words, briefly*
βύω, *stuff, plug*; (pass.) *be stuffed* or *plugged, have one's* X (acc.) *plugged* or
    stopped (with, + dat.)
βωμός, ὁ, *altar*

Γ γ

γάρ, *for, for you see.*

γε, particle, *at least, at any rate; namely, that is, indeed*

γειτνιάω, *be a neighbor, be adjacent, border on*

γελάω, γελάσομαι, ἐγέλασα, *laugh; laugh at* (+ acc.)

γέλοιος, -α, -ον, *ridiculous, laughable*

γελοίως, adv., *ridiculously, laughably*

γέλως, -ωτος, ὁ, *laughter*

γεννάδας, -ου, ὁ, *noble*

γενναῖος, -α, -ον, *noble, excellent*

γέρων, -οντος, ὁ, *old man;* (as adj. with masc. nouns) *old*

γῆ, ἡ, *earth*

γῆρας, γήρως, τό, *old age*

γηράω (alternative pres. of γηράσκω), *grow old*

γίγνομαι, γενήσομαι, ἐγενόμην, (dep.) *become, be*

γνόφος, ὁ, (Aeolic; in later Greek used for ὁ δνόφος) *squall, tempest, storm*

γνώμη, ἡ, *disposition, purpose; character; mind, will, purpose, resolve, intent*

γνωρίζω, γνωριῶ, *be acquainted with, recognize*

γόης, -ητος, ὁ, *charlatan, con artist; sorcerer, wizard*

γονεύς, γονέως, ὁ, *father;* (pl.) *parents*

γοῦν, particle, *at any rate, to be sure, at least*

γράδιον, τό, (diminutive of γραῖα) *(little) old woman*

γραμματεῖον, τό, *petition*

γραμματεύς, -έως, ὁ, *scribe, clerk; scholar*

γραφεύς, -έως, ὁ, *painter*

γυμνάσιον, τό, *training ground, public place where athletic exercises were practiced (and philosophers and sophists would gather to peddle their "wares")*

γυνή, γυναικός, ἡ, *woman*

γύψ, γυπός, ὁ, *vulture*

Δ δ

δαδουχία, ἡ, *torchlight parade, torch-bearing festival/ceremony*

δαίμων, -ονος, ὁ or **ἡ,** *god, goddess, divine power, spirit*

δάκρυον, τό, *tear*

δακρύω, *cry, lament, weep, shed tears*

δάκτυλος, ὁ, *finger; toe*

δανείζω, *lending money out at interest*

δᾷς, δᾳδός, ἡ, *torch*, (pl.) *pine-wood, torchwood*

δείκνυμι, δείξω, ἔδειξα, *show, point out*

δειλός, -ή, -όν, *cowardly, vile, worthless*

δεῖμα, -ατος, τό, *fear, terror, horror*

δεινός, -ή, -όν, *mighty, powerful, incredible; terrible, fearful*

δεῖπνον, τό, *meal, food*

δέομαι, (dep.) *be in need of, want* (+ gen.)

δεσμός, ὁ, *bond, chain;* (pl.) *bonds, chains, imprisonment*

δεσμοφύλαξ, -ακος, ὁ, *prison guard*

δεσμωτήριον, τό, *prison*

δέχομαι, (dep.) *take, accept, receive; prefer* (+ inf.)

δέον, (neut. part. of the impersonal δεῖ) *it being necessary*

δευτεραγωνιστής, -οῦ, ὁ, *second lead in a drama; "second fiddle";
supporter*

δεύτερος, -α, -ον, *second;* τὸ δεύτερον, *a second time*

δέω, *lack, be in need of* (+ gen.); *bind, tie, enchain; put in prison;* δεῖ, *it is
necessary;* δεῖν, *to be necessary*

δή, particle, *indeed; in fact; then, therefore, now*

δηλαδή, adv., *quite clearly*

δῆλος, -η, -ον, *clear, obvious, evident*

δήμιος, ὁ, (sc. δοῦλος, *slave, servant*) *public executioner*

δημιουργέω, *fabricate, fashion, construct*

δημιούργημα, -ατος, τό, *work of art; masterpiece*

Δημόκριτος, ὁ, *Democritus*

δῆμος, ὁ, *the people, the common people;* (Lucian) *crowd* (made up of
commoners)

δημόσιος, -ον, *common, shared, belonging to the people*

διά, prep. (+ gen.), *by, through;* (+ acc.) *because of, on account of*

διαβοάω, διαβοήσομαι, διεβόησα *proclaim, publish;* (pass.) *be made
public, be well known*

διαγιγνώσκω, διαγνώσομαι, διέγνων, *resolve, determine, decide* (+ inf.)

διαδίδωμι, διαδώσω, διέδωκα, *spread (abroad); pass on, hand over;* (pass.)
be spread about, be given out, be reported

διαθήκη, ἡ, *covenant, agreement; last will and testament*

διακαρτερέω, *endure to the end, put up with, bear patiently/steadfastly*

διακρίνω, διακρινῶ, διέκρινα, *separate* or *distinguish one from the other,
draw a distinction, decide*

διαλανθάνω, διαλήσω, διέλαθον, *escape notice*

διαλύω, *disband, break up;* (pass., of a gathering/assembly) *break up, disperse*

128

διανομή, ἡ, distribution, largess

διαπέμπω, send off in different directions, send out

διαρπάζω, carry off, seize as plunder

διαρρήγνυμι, break through, cleave asunder; (pass.) burst (with passion)

διασαφέω, make quite clear, explain clearly

διασκευή, ἡ, stage setting, mise-en-scène; theatrical performance; rhetorical elaboration (of a topic)

διασκέω, deck out; (pass.) train, practice

διασπάω, tear apart, tear to pieces

διαφεύγω, διαφεύξομαι, διέφυγεν, escape

διαφθείρω, διαφθερῶ, διέφθειρα, corrupt with bribes, bribe

διδάσκαλος, ὁ, teacher, master

διδάσκω, teach

δίδωμι, δώσω, ἔδωκα, give

διέξειμι, expound, set forth, relate in detail, go through in detail, recount in full

διεξέρχομαι, διέξειμι, διεξῆλθον, expound, set forth, relate in detail, go through in detail, recount in full

διηγέομαι, (dep.), set out in detail, describe in detail, describe in full

δίκη, ἡ, custom; justice; right; judgment; penalty

Διογένης, -ους, ὁ, Diogenes

διόμνυμι, διομόσω, διώμοσα, (mid. διόμνυμαι is more common, with same meaning as act.) swear solemnly, declare on oath that

διότι, conj., because

διψάω, be thirsty

δίψος, -εος, τό, thirst

Δίων, -ονος, ὁ, Dio or Dion

δοκῶ, (uncontracted = δοκέω) seem; be reputed, have the reputation for, be held or thought (+ εἶναι); think; expect; imagine; δοκῶ μοι, I think; I intend; I am determined, I have resolved (+ inf.); (3rd sing.) it seems (good); (mid./pass.) be decided or resolved

δόξα, ἡ, reputation, honor, glory; notion, expectation; opinion, judgment

δοξάριον, τό, (diminutive of ἡ δόξα) a little estimation / reputation / honor / glory

δοξοκοπία, ἡ, thirst / hunger for fame or popularity

δορυφορέω, attend, attend as a bodyguard

δρᾶμα, -ατος, τό, deed, act; drama, play

δραπετεύω, run away

δράω, do, do some great thing (good or bad)

δριμύς, -εῖα, -ύ, fierce, sharp, keen; acrid, pungent

δύναμαι, (dep.) be able, can (+ inf.)

δυνατός, -ή, -όν, possible

δύο, (indecl.) *two*

δύσερως, -ωτος, ὁ, *sick in love with* (+ gen.)

δυσμή, ἡ, (mostly in pl.) *west*

Ε ε

ἑαυτοῦ, ἑαυτῆς, ἑαυτοῦ, (reflex. pron. in gen., dat., acc.) *himself, herself, itself*

ἐάω, *let alone, let be, permit, allow* (+ acc. of person and inf.)

ἐγείρω, *awaken, rouse, stir up, raise*

ἐγκαρτερέω, *endure, be strong in, remain steadfast in the face of* (+ dat.)

ἔγκλημα, -ατος, τό, *legal complaint; accusation, charge*

ἐγχάσκω, ἐγχανοῦμαι, ἐγχανεῖν, *laugh* or *scoff at* (+ dat.)

ἐγχρίω, *anoint, rub, smear*

ἐγώ, ἐμοῦ / μου, ἐμοί / μοι, ἐμέ / με, *I, me.*

ἔδω, (Epic pres. for which Attic uses ἐσθίω) *eat*

ἐκεῖθεν, adv., *from there*

εἰ, conj., *if*

εἰκάζω, *compare, liken* X (acc.) *to* Y (dat.); *can guess / imagine*

εἰκός, -οτος, τό, *likely, probable, reasonable* (with or without ἐστί + inf.)

εἴκοσιν, indecl., *twenty*

εἰκών, -όνος, ἡ, *likeness* or *image* (whether statue or painting)

εἰμί, ἔσομαι, ἦν, *be; exist*

εἴπερ, conj., *if really, if indeed*

εἰρήνη, ἡ, *peace*; + ἄγω, *keep peace, be at peace, keep quiet*

εἰς, prep. (+ acc.), *into; to; at*; (of time) *for*

εἷς, μία, ἕν, *one*

εἰσάγω, εἰσάξω, εἰσήγαγον, *lead* or *bring in / into, introduce*

εἰσκομίζω, *bring in*

εἶτα, adv., *then, next; soon, presently; and so, therefore, accordingly*

εἴωθα, (perf. with pres. meaning) *be accustomed, be in the habit*

ἐκ, ἐξ, prep. (+ gen.), *from, out of*

ἐκβάλλω, ἐκβαλῶ, ἐξέβαλον, *throw* or *cast out*

ἐκεῖνος, -η, -ο, *that*; (pl.) *those*

ἐκκλησία, ἡ, *assembly of the citizens, legislative assembly*

ἐκμανθάνω, ἐκμαθήσομαι, ἐξέμαθον, *learn thoroughly, master completely*

ἐκπλήσσω, *amaze, astound* (literally, *strike out of [one's senses]*) ἐκπυνθάνομαι, (dep.) *make enquiry of, question*

ἐκφέρω, ἐξοίσω, ἐξήνεγκον, *deliver; exhibit, display, publish*

ἐκών, ἐκοῦσα, ἐκόν, *willingly, of free will, readily, voluntarily*

ἐλαύνω, ἐλῶ, ἤλασα, *drive, drive away; persecute*

ἐλεέω, *pity, feel pity*

ἐλευθερία, ἡ, *freedom, liberty, license*

ἕλκω, *pull, tear*

Ἑλλανοδίκαι, -ῶν, οἱ, the chief judges / officials at the Olympic Games

Ἑλλάς, -άδος, ἡ, *Greece, Hellas*

Ἕλλην, -ηνος, ὁ, *Greek, Hellene*

Ἑλληνικός, -ή, -όν, *Greek, Hellenic*

ἐλπίζω, *expect, hope* (frequently with a dependent clause + inf. [usually fut.])

ἐλπίς, -ίδος, ἡ, *hope, expectation*

ἐμβάλλω, ἐμβαλῶ, ἐνέβαλον, *throw in*

ἐμέω, *vomit, throw up; be sick*

ἐμμένω, ἐμμενῶ, ἐνέμεινα, *abide by* (+ dat.)

ἐμπηδάω, ἐμπηδήσομαι, ἐνεπήδησα, *leap in* or *into*

ἐμπίμπρημι, ἐμπρήσω, ἐνέπρησα, *set on fire, burn*

ἐμπίπτω, ἐμπεσοῦμαι, ἐνέπεσον, *fall into*; (of prison or punishment with pass. sense) *be thrown into*

ἐμπλήκτως, adv., *rashly, madly, foolishly, impulsively*

ἔμπροσθεν, adv., *before, earlier, previous; in front*

ἐμφορέω, *pour in*; (mid./pass.) *get one's fill of* (+ gen.)

ἐν, prep. (+ dat.), *in, by, by means of, among*; (later Greek) *into, on*

ἔναγχος, adv., *just now, lately, recently*

ἐναντίος, -η, -ον, *opposite, over against, contrary*

ἐναποπνίγομαι, (mid./pass.; a Lucianic coinage) *be suffocated in, asphyxiate oneself*

ἐνδείκνυμι, ἐνδείξω, ἐνέδειξα, *point out, indicate*; (mid.) *display, exhibit*

ἔνδον, adv., *within, inside*

ἔνδοξος, -ον, *famous, well-known, notable, conspicuous, of high repute*

ἔνειμι, *be in a place, be among*; ἔνεστι, *it is possible, one can*

ἕνεκα, prep. (+ preceding gen.), *for the sake of, because of*

ἐνέφαγον (2nd aor.; no pres. – ἐνέσθιω – in use), *eat quickly* or *greedily*

ἔνθα, adv., *where, a / the place where; then, there, in that place; in that situation*

ἔνιοι, ἐνίων, *some*

ἐννέα, indecl., *nine*

ἐννοέω, *think* or *reflect upon, consider*

ἐντελής, -ές, *finished, completed*

ἐντήκω, *pour in while molten*; (perf. act. = pass. sense) *sink deep in, be absorbed by, penetrate to the core* (+ dat.)

ἐντρέπω, *turn about*; *change, alter*

ἐντρυφάω, *revel in, delight in, indulge in*; *treat contemptuously* (+ dat.)

ἐντυγχάνω, ἐντεύξομαι, ἐνέτυχον, *meet with, encounter, chance upon* (+ dat.)

ἐξάγω, ἐξάξω, ἐξήγαγον, *lead out, take from*

ἐξαερόω, *make into air, aerify*

ἐξανίστημι, *raise up*; (2nd aor., perf., pluperf. act.) *stand up, get up (and depart)*

ἐξαρπάζω, *rescue*

ἐξελαύνω, ἐξελῶ, ἐξήλασον, *drive out*

ἐξέρχομαι, ἔξειμι, ἐξῆλθον, *go out, go away, depart*

ἐξευρίσκω, ἐξευρήσω, ἐξεῦρον, *discover, invent*

ἐξηγέομαι, (dep.) *expound, interpret*

ἐξήκοντα, indecl., *sixty*

ἐξῆς, adv., *future, next*

ἐξωνέομαι, (dep.) *buy off* (+ gen. of price paid and acc. or παρά + gen. of person paid)

ἔοικα, (perf. with pres. sense) *be like*; *seem* (+ inf.); ἔοικε(ν), (often impersonal) *it seems* (+ inf.)

ἐπάγω, ἐπάξω, ἐπήγαγον, *bring to*

ἐπᾴδω, ἐπᾴσομαι, *sing, sing to, sing to* one *so as to charm* or *soothe* him / her

ἐπαινέω, *praise*

ἔπαινος, ὁ, *praise, panegyric*

ἐπακούω, ἐπακούσομαι, ἐπήκουσα, *listen, hear* (+ gen. of person); *overhear, hear distinctly*

ἐπανέρχομαι, ἐπάνειμι, ἐπανῆλθον, *return, come* or *go back*

ἐπανατείνω, ἐπανατενῶ, ἐπανέτεινα, *stretch out and hold up, hold out*; (mid.) *hold over as a threat, threaten* someone (dat.) *with* something (acc.)

ἐπανίστημι, ἐπαναστήσω, ἐπανέστησα, *set up again*; (mid./pass.) *rise up against* (+ dat.)

ἐπαντλέω, *pour a flood (of words) over*

ἐπεί, conj., *after, since, when*; (+ τάχιστα) *as soon as*

ἐπέρχομαι, ἔπειμι, ἐπῆλθον, *come, come forward*; *make a sudden appearance*; *come into one's head, occur to one*

ἐπί, prep. (+ gen.), *before, in the presence of*; (+ gen. with verbs of motion) *for, towards*; (+ dat.), *on, upon, on to*; *in reference to*; *for*; (in later Greek) *at*; (+ acc.), *to, towards, up to*; *before*; *for*

ἐπιβαίνω, ἐπιβήσομαι, ἐπέβην, *get upon, mount on*

ἐπιβάλλω, ἐπιβαλῶ, ἐπέβαλον, *throw, cast upon*

ἐπιβοάω, ἐπιβοήσομαι, ἐπεβόησα, *cry* or *shout out (to)*; *call upon*; (mid.) *cry* or *shout out* X (acc.) *over* Y (dat.); *invoke*; *call to aid* ἐπιγράφω, *inscribe* ; (mid.) *have one registered as*

ἐπιδείκνυμι, ἐπιδείξω, ἐπέδειξα, (mid. is more common, with same meaning) *exhibit, show, display, show off, give a specimen of, exhibit one's powers of, display one's X, put on a show of one's* X (+ acc.)

ἐπιδίδωμι, ἐπιδώσω, ἐπιέδωκα, *give freely; give into (another's hands), deliver; file, submit*

ἐπιθυμέω, *lust after, long for, desire* (+ gen.)

ἐπικαλέω, *call upon*; (mid.) *summon; call in as a helper* or *ally*

Ἐπίκτητος, ὁ, *Epictetus*

ἐπιλέγω, ἐπιλέξω, ἐπεῖπον, *say in connection with, say besides* or *afterwards, utter, pronounce, say in apposition*

ἐπινοέω, *think of, plan, intend*

ἐπιπέτομαι, ἐπιπτήσομαι, ἐπεπτάμην, (dep.) *fly to*

ἐπιπολάζω, *be prevalent, be rife, run riot*

ἐπίσημος, -ον, *notable, remarkable; notorious*

ἐπισκοπέω, *examine*

ἐπισπάω, (act. or mid.) *draw* or *drag; bring on, cause*

ἐπιστέλλω, *send a message* (especially by letter), *give written instructions to*

ἐπιστολή, -ή, *message, letter, order, commission*

ἐπιστρέφω, *turn about/around*; (mid.) *turn oneself around, change, recover*

ἐπιτάφιος, ὁ, *funeral oration, eulogy*

ἐπιτηρέω, *keep an eye on, watch carefully*

ἐπιτίθημι, ἐπιθήσω, ἐπέθηκα, *put, place*

ἐπιτρέπω, *commit, entrust*; (pass.) *be entrusted with* (+ acc.)

ἐπιτρέχω, ἐπιδραμοῦμαι, ἐπέδραμον, *rush upon/at* (to attack)

ἐπιτυγχάνω, ἐπιτεύξομαι, ἐπέτυχον, *attain, achieve, gain* (+ gen.)

ἐπιφαίνω, ἐπιφανῶ, ἐπέφηνα, *display*; (pass.) *come suddenly into view, present oneself, show oneself, appear* (often of divine epiphanies)

ἐπιχειρέω, *try to, attempt to* (+ inf.)

ἐπιχέω, *pour (water) over*

ἐπιών, -οῦσα, -όν (participles < ἔπειμι), *following, coming, approaching*

ἕπομαι, (dep.) *follow* (+ dat.)

ἔπος, -ους, τό, *word*; (pl.) *words, verses*

ἑπτάφωνος, -ον, *seven-voiced*

ἐράω, *love* or *desire (passionately)* (+ gen.); + ἔρωτα, *have a consuming passion for* (+ gen.)

ἐργάζομαι, (dep.) *do, accomplish*

ἔργον, τό, *work, deed*

ἐρίγδουπος, -ον, (Homeric epithet of Zeus) *loud-sounding, thundering*

ἐρινύς, -ύος, ἡ, *frenzy, fury* ; ἡ Ἐρινύς, *Fury*

ἔρομαι (not found in pres. ind), ἐρήσομαι, ἠρόμην, *ask, inquire, question*

ἔρχομαι, εἶμι, ἦλθον, *come, go*

ἐρῶ, (fut., along with λέξω, of λέγω) *will say, tell, speak*

ἔρως, -ωτος, ὁ, *love, desire, passion (for* + gen.)

ἐρωτικῶς, adv., *passionately*

ἐς, εἰς, prep. (+ acc.), *(ended) in/with*; *against*

ἐσθής, -ῆτος, ἡ, *clothing, raiment*

ἐσθίω, ἔδομαι, ἔφαγον, *eat*

ἔστε, conj., (often with ἄν + subju.) *until, until such time as*

ἑταῖρος, ὁ, *comrade, companion, friend*

ἕτερος, -α, -ον, *other, another*

ἔτι, adv., *still, yet, as yet*; + οὐ or οὐδὲ, *no longer*

ἔτος, -ους, τό, *year*

εὖ, adv., *well*

εὔδενδρος, -ον, *well-wooded, covered in trees*

εὐθύ, adv. (+ gen.), *straight to* or *towards*

εὐθύς, adv., *immediately, at once*; *straight, directly*; (later Greek) *then*

εὐμενής, -ές, *gracious, kindly, with favor*

εὐπορέω, *procure, find available* (+ gen.)

εὑρίσκω, εὑρήσω, ηὗρον/εὗρον, *find*; (mid.) *find out* or *discover how to* (+ inf.)

Ἐφέσιος, -α, -ον, *Ephesian, of Ephesus*

ἐφίστημι, ἐπιστήσω, ἐπέστησα, *set* or *place upon*; *stop*; (mid.) *settle on, stop on*; (mid., pass., and perf., pluperf., and 2nd aor. act.) *come upon (suddenly or by surprise)* (+ dat.)

ἐφόδιον, τό, (usually pl.) *supplies for travelling, money and provisions*

ἐχθρός, ὁ, *enemy*

ἔχω, ἔξω, ἔσχον, *have*; *hold*; (+ inf.) *can, be able*; (mid. + gen.) *hold onto, cling to*

ἔωθεν, adv., *at earliest dawn, from the break of dawn*

ἕως, ἕω (gen. and acc.), ἡ, *dawn*; (direction) *east*

Z ζ

ζάω, (unattested hypothetical form) *live, be alive*

Ζεύς, Διός, Διΐ, Δία, ὁ, *Zeus*

ζῆλος, ὁ, *imitation, emulation, following (a leader)*

ζηλόω, *zealously follow, imitate*

ζηλωτής, -οῦ, ὁ, *follower, zealous follower, imitator*; *rival*

Ζῆν, Ζηνός, Ζηνί, Ζῆνα, ὁ, (Epic and tragic alternative spelling of) *Zeus*

H η

ἤ, conj., *or*; (with comparatives) *than*

ἦ, adv., *in truth*; ἦ μὴν, *absolutely in fact*

ἡγέομαι, (dep.) *believe, consider*

ἡδέως, adv., *gladly, sweetly, pleasantly*

ἤδη, adv., *already, now; by this time, by now*

ἡδύς, ἡδεῖα, ἡδύ, *pleasant, agreeable, welcome, sweet*

ἥκω, (imperf.) ἧκον, (pres. = perf.; imperf. = pluperf.) *have come*

Ἠλεῖος, ὁ, *Elean (citizen of the town of Elis)*

ἡλίκος, -η, -ον, *as big as, as great as*; (in indir. questions) *how big/great*; neut. pl. as adv., *how greatly*

ἥλιος, ὁ, *sun*; Ἥλιος, ὁ, *Helios (the sun-god), sun*

Ἦλις, -ιδος, ἡ, *Elis*

ἡμεῖς, ἡμῶν, ἡμῖν, ἡμᾶς, (pl.) *we, us*

ἡμέρα, ἡ, *day*

ἥμερος, -ον, *gentle*

ἥμισυς, -εια, -υ, *half*

ἡμίφλεκτος, -ον, *half-burnt*

Ἡράκλειος, -α, -ον, *Heraclean, of Heracles, connected to Heracles*

Ἡρακλείως, adv., *like Heracles, in the manner of Heracles*

Ἡρακλῆς, -έους, ὁ, *Heracles*

ἥρως, ἥρωος, ὁ, *hero*

Ἡσίοδος, ὁ, *Hesiod*

Ἥφαιστος, ὁ, *Hephaestus*

Θ θ

θάλαττα, ἡ, *sea*

θανατιάω, (Lucianic variant of θανατάω) *desire to die*

θάνατος, ὁ, *death*

θάπτω, *bury*

θαρσέω, *be confident, have no fear*

θαυμάζω, *marvel, be amazed, wonder at; admire, honor, worship*

θαυμαστός, -ή, -όν, *wonderful, marvelous; extraordinary; strange, absurd*

θαυματοποιέω, *do hocus-pocus, perform tricks, play the miracle-mongering game, play the mountebank*

Θεαγένης, -ου, ὁ, *Theagenes*

θέαμα, -ατος, τό, *sight, spectacle*

θεάομαι, (dep.) *look on, gaze at, view (as spectator)*

θεατής, -οῦ, ὁ, *spectator*

θέλω, *wish, desire, want* (+ inf.)

θεός, ὁ, *god*

θεραπεία, ἡ, *attention, care, service*

θεραπεύω, *take care of, nurse, treat medically*

θερμηγορέω, *make a fiery speech in public*

θερμός, -ή, -όν, *hot, warm; still warm, fresh*

θιασάρχης, -ου, ὁ, *cult-leader* (originally, *leader of the Bacchic revel*)

θνήσκω, θανοῦμαι, ἔθανον, *die*; τέθνηκα (perf.), *have died, i.e., be dead*

θορυβέω, *trouble, throw into confusion*

θρίξ, τριχός, ἡ, *hair*

θυμός, ὁ, *soul, spirit, heart, mind*

θύρα, ἡ, *door*

I ι

ἰατρός, ὁ, *doctor, physician, surgeon*

ἰαχή, ἡ, *cry, shout, wail, shriek* (usually of men in battle, both victors and vanquished)

ἴδιος, -η, -ον, *one's own, personal, peculiar*

ἰδιώτης, -ου, ὁ, *simple, average,* or *ignorant person/citizen*

ἰδρώς, -ῶτος, ὁ, *sweat*

ἱερεῖον, τό, *sacrifice, sacrificial victim*

ἱερεύς, -έως, ὁ, *priest*

ἱερός, -ά, -όν, *holy, sacred*

ἱερόσυλος, ὁ, *sacrilegious person, temple robber*

ἱκανός, -ή, -όν, *sufficient, adequate, enough*

ἵναπερ, adv., *where*

Ἰνδικός, -ή, -όν, *Indian*

Ἰνδός, ὁ, *Indian*

ἱππόδρομος, ὁ, *hippodrome* (race course for chariots)

ἴσος, -η, -ον, *equal, the same*; ἐξ ἴσης, *equally*

ἵστημι, στήσω, ἔστησα, *make X stand; stop X; set X (up)*; (2nd aor.) ἔστην, (perf.) ἕστηκα, *stand*

Ἰταλία, ἡ, *Italy*

K κ

καθάπερ, adv., *just as, just like, like*

καί, (conj.) *and, also, but, even*

καινός, -ή, -όν, *new; innovative; novel; weird* (in a pejorative sense)

καινουργέω, *make something new* or *novel*

καίτοι, conj. + particle, *and yet; and indeed, and further, furthermore, moreover;* (later, non-Classical Greek usage) *although*

καίω, καύσω, ἔκαυσα, *set on fire, burn up*

κακοδαίμων (gen., κακοδαίμονος), *possessed by an evil spirit, unlucky, wretched*

κακός, -ή, -όν, *bad, evil, malicious*

κακοῦργος, ὁ, *criminal*

κακῶς, adv., *badly, wretchedly*

Κάλανος, ὁ, *Calanus*

καλέω, *call, call in, summon;* (pres. pass. part.) *being called, so-called*

κάλλιστος, -η, -ον, *most* or *very beautiful, finest* or *very fine*

καλός, -ή, -όν, *beautiful, fine*

καλῶς, adv., *well, rightly, happily;* καλῶς ἔχειν, *to be well* (i.e., a good thing or idea)

κανών, -όνος, ὁ, *canon, rule, standard, model; Polycleitan sculpture* and *treatise*

καρπός, ὁ, *crops, produce, fruit*

καρτερία, ἡ, *fortitude, endurance; act* or *display of fortitude / endurance*

καπνός, ὁ, *smoke*

κατά, prep. (+ gen.), *down from;* (+ acc.), *in the manner of; with regard to, concerning, in relation to, according to, with respect to, in accordance with; in, in the region of; by; along*

καταβαίνω, καταβήσομαι, κατέβην, *go* or *come down, descend*

καταγελάω, *ridicule, mock, laugh at*

καταδικάζω, *condemn* person X (gen.) *to punishment* Y (acc.)

καταδίκη, ἡ, *judgment given against one, judicial sentence*

καταθηλύνω, *make* X (acc.) *effeminate, turn* X *into a woman/women, soften*

κατάκλισις, -εως, ἡ, *lying down, way* or *position of lying down*

καταλαμβάνω, καταλήψομαι, κατέλαβον, *find, take hold of, seize; learn*

καταλείπω, καταλείψω, κατέλιπον, *leave, leave behind, desert*

καταλεύω, *stone to death*

καταλήγω, *end, stop*

καταναγκάζω, *coerce, force*

καταπαύω, *end, bring an end to, put an end to, stop, conclude*
κατάπτυστος, -ον, *be spat upon, despicable, contemptible*
κατάρατος, -ον, *accursed, abominable*
καταστροφή, ἡ, *conclusion, ending, dénouement; catastrophe*
καταφεύγω, καταφεύξομαι, κατέφυγον, *flee for refuge* or *protection*
καταφρονέω, *despise, think lightly of* (+ gen.)
κατεσθίω, κατέδομαι, κατέφαγον, *eat up, devour*
κατέχω, καθέξω, κατέσχον, *hold fast, hold back, restrain*
κατηγορέω, *speak against, denounce* (+ gen.)
κατηγορία, ἡ, *accusation, charge*
κατόπιν, adv. (+ gen.), *after*
καῦσις, -εως, ἡ, *burning, cremation*
καυτήριον, τό, *branding iron*
κε, Homeric equivalent of the modal particle ἄν
κελεύω, *command, order*
κέλομαι, (dep.) *urge, exhort, command*
κενοδοξία, ἡ, *vanity, conceit*
κενόδοξος, -ον, *vainglorious, conceited*
Κενταύρειος, -α, -ον, *of the Centaur, Centaur's*
κεραυνός, -οῦ, *thunderbolt*
κεφάλαιον, τό, *culmination, crowning act, completion (of a thing)*
κεφαλή, ἡ, *head*; ἐπὶ κεφαλήν, *headlong, head first*
κῆρυξ, -υκος, ὁ, *herald*
κινδυνεύω, *venture, hazard; run* or *take a/the risk*
κίνδυνος, ὁ, *danger, risk*
κινέω, *move, set in motion*; + πάντα, *move heaven and earth, leave nothing undone*
κλεινός, -ή, -όν, *well known, famous,*
κνῖσα, ἡ, *smell of a burnt sacrifice*
κοινός, -ή, -όν, *shared, common*; τὸ κοινόν, *shared* or *common funds*
κολάζω, *punish*
κόλασις, -εως, ἡ, *punishment*
κομάω, *wear long hair, let one's hair grow long*
κομίζω, *get back, recover*; (mid.) *get back for oneself, recover*
κορμός, ὁ, *log*
κόρυζα, -ης, ἡ, *running nose, nasal discharge; stupidity*
κορώνη, ἡ, *crown; tip of a bow* (on which a bowstring was hooked); *crow*
κότινος, -ὁ, *wild-olive tree*
κράζω, *scream, shriek, croak*
κρατήρ, -ῆρος, ὁ, (pl. often = sing.) *crater, mouth of a volcano*

Κράτης, -ητος, ὁ, *Crates*
κρείττων, -ον, (gen. -ονος), *stronger, mightier*
κτῆμα, -ατος, τό, *possession, piece of property*
κυβερνήτης, -ου, ὁ, *pilot, navigator*
κυβιστάω, *tumble head foremost, turn somersaults*
κυλίω, (later form of κυλίνδω) *roll*
κῦμα, -ατος, τό, *wave*
κυναλώπηξ, -εκος, ἡ, *mongrel between dog and fox, dog-fox*
κυνίζω, *play the dog; live like a Cynic, become a Cynic*
Κυνικός, ὁ, *Cynic*, i.e., a follower of the philosopher Antisthenes
κύων, κυνός, ὁ or ἡ, *dog; Cynic philosopher*
κωκύω, *shriek, wail*

Λ λ

λᾶας, ου, ὁ, *stone*
λαμβάνω, λήψομαι, ἔλαβον, *take*
λανθάνω, λήσω, ἔλαθον, *escape notice*
λέγω, ἐρῶ, εἶπον, *say, speak, tell*
λείπω, λείψω, ἔλιπον, *leave*
λείψανον, τό, *piece left, remnant, relic*
λευκός, -ή, -όν, *white*
λιβανωτός, ὁ, *frankincense, incense*
λίθος, ὁ, *stone*
λογοποιέω, *invent stories, fabricate tales*
λόγος, ὁ, *word, speech; story, narrative; report*
λοιδοροῦμαι, (dep.) *abuse, revile, rebuke* (+ dat.)
λοιπός, -ή, -όν, *remaining, rest (of)*; τὸ λοιπόν, *hereafter, in the future*; τὰ λοιπὰ, *the rest*
λύζω, *sob violently*
λύκος, ὁ, *wolf*
λύπη, ἡ, *grief*

Μ μ

μά, particle (used in protestations and oaths), *by*
μαθητής, -οῦ, ὁ, *student, disciple*

μακαρίτης, ὁ, *one blessed*, i.e., *dead* (especially of one lately dead); (+ πατήρ, functions as an adj.) *recently deceased, late*

μακρός, -ά, -όν, *long; large; great*; (fem. acc. sing. as adv.) *long time*

μάλα, adv., *very, very much, exceedingly*

μάλιστα, adv., *most, most of all, very much, especially, too much*

μᾶλλον, adv., *more, much more; rather, instead*

μαντικός, -ή, -όν, *prophetic, oracular, like a prophet*

μαρτύρομαι, μαρτυροῦμαι, ἐμαρτυράμην, (dep.) *testify, solemnly declare*

μάρτυς, μάρτυρος, ὁ, *witness*

μάστιξ, -ιγος, ἡ, *whip*

μάταιος, -α, -ον, *vain, foolish, thoughtless, impious*

μέγας, μεγάλη, μέγα, *large, great*; (of sounds) *loud*

μέγιστος, -η, -ον, *biggest, largest, greatest*

μειράκιον, τό, (diminutive of μεῖραξ) *boy, young man* (under the age of 21)

μέλιττα, ἡ, *bee, honey-bee*

μέλλω, *be likely, have a chance; be going to X, be about to X* (+ fut. inf.)

μέλω, (most often impersonal 3rd sing., with the obj. in the gen. and the person in the dat.) (to whom) *there is care* or *thought for* (+ gen.), i.e, *he/she cares about* or *gives thought to* (+ gen.)

μένος, -ους, τό, *might, force*

μέντοι, particle, *indeed, to be sure, of course; however*

μεσημβρία, ἡ, *midday*; (direction) *south*

μέσος, -η, -ον, *middle, in the middle*; μέσον, adv., *in the middle*; διὰ μέσου, *in the interim, intervening*; μέσαι νύκτες, *midnight*

μεστός, -ή, -όν, *full, full of, filled with* (+ gen.)

μέτα, prep. (+ acc.), *after*

μεταβάλλω, μεταβαλῶ, μετέβαλον, *turn about, change, alter*; (mid.) *change one's mind*

μετακαλέω, *summon, call in* (e.g., a doctor or a midwife)

μεταξύ, prep. (+ gen.), *between, among*; (adv.) *in the midst/middle of* (+ part.).

μετονομάζω, *call by a new name*; (+ reflexive pron. + acc.) *change one's name to*

μετρίως, adv., *moderately*

μέχρι, adv., *until*

μηδέ, conj., *(and) not*; adv., *not even*

μηδείς μηδεμία, μηδέν, *not one, not even one, nobody, nothing*; μηδέν, adv., *not at all*

μηκέτι, adv., *no longer, no more*

μήν, adv., *indeed, truly*

μητρῷος, -α, -ον, *maternal, of a mother*

μηχανάομαι, μηχανήσομαι, ἐμηχανησάμην, (dep.) *construct, build; contrive, devise*

μιαίνω, defile, pollute (morally)
μιαρός, -ή, -όν, foul, repulsive; unclean, ritually impure
μικρός, -ά, -ό, little, small; μικροῦ, adv., almost; μικρόν, adv., a little time
μιμέομαι, (dep.) imitate
μιμνήσκω, remind; (mid./pass.) mention, make mention of (+ gen.)
μοιχεύω, commit adultery (with a woman)
μονονουχί, adv., all but, practically
μονός, -ή, -όν, alone, only, single; μόνον, adv., only μόνον οὐκ, all but, practically, virtually
Μουσωνίος, ὁ, Musonius
μυκηθμός, ὁ, rumbling
μυρίος, -α, -ον, numberless, countless
μωρός, -ά, -όν, dull, stupid, foolish; (as substantive) fool, moron

N ν

νάρθηξ, -ηκος, ὁ, stalk of fennel; cane
ναῦς, νεώς, ἡ, ship
νεανικός, -ή, -όν, adolescent; vigorous, violent, excessive; insolent
νειόθεν, adv., from the bottom (of his heart), heartily
νεκράγγελος, ὁ, messenger of the dead
νεκρικῶς, adv., deathly, deathly pale, corpse-like
νερτεροδρόμος, ὁ, courier from the underworld, courier from below
Νέστωρ, -ορος, ὁ, Nestor
νέω, heap, pile up
νεώς, νεώ, ὁ, temple
νή, (particle of strong affirmation) νὴ Δία = by Zeus!
νομοθέτης, -ου, ὁ, lawgiver
νόμος, ὁ, law, ruling, ordinance, decree
νόσος, ἡ, sickness, disease, affliction
νοῦς, νοῦ, ὁ, mind
νυκτέριος, -η, -ον, nocturnal, by night
νυκτιπόλος, -ον, night-roaming
νυκτοφύλαξ, -ακος, ὁ, guardian of the night
νύκτωρ, adv., at night
νῦν, adv., now
νύξ, νυκτός, ἡ, night

Ξ ξ

ξηρός, τό, *dryness*

ξ/συγγίγνομαι, ξ/συγγενήσομαι, ξ/συνεγενόμην, (dep.) *associate
with*; (of disciples), *converse (with a master)*

ξύλον, τό, *piece of wood, staff*

ξύν, σύν, prep. (+ dat.), *with*

ξ/συναγωγεύς, -έως, ὁ, *convener, uniter*; *Head of the synagogue*

ξ/συναρπάζω, *seize and carry away, seize and pin together*

ξυρέω, *shave*; (mid./pass.) *shave oneself, have oneself shaved*

Ο ο

ὀθόνη, ἡ, *fine linen, shirt*

οἱ or οἷ, (3rd sing. dat. masc. pron. = αὐτῷ) *to / for him*

οἶδα, (perf. with pres. meaning) *know*

οἰκεῖος, -α, -ον, *in* or *of the house*; *one's own*

οἶμαι (uncontracted = οἴομαι), *suppose, think, expect*

οἷος, οἵα, οἷον, *such as, like, for example*; *what sort / kind* (of person / thing);
οἷόν τι, *what sort of thing*

οἴχομαι, (dep., pres. often with perf. sense) *have gone* (i.e., *be gone*), *went,
have departed*; *go, go away, depart*

ὀλίγος, -η, -ον, *little, small*; (pl.) *few*; (neut. acc. sing. as adv.) *little*

ὅλος, -η, -ον, *whole, entire*; τὸ ὅλον, *wholly, entirely*

Ὀλύμπια, τά, (pl. only) *Olympic Games*

Ὀλυμπιάς, -άδος, ἡ, *Olympic Games*

Ὀλυμπίασι(ν), adv., *at Olympia*

Ὀλύμπιος, -ον, *Olympian*; ὁ Ὀλύμπιος, *Zeus*

Ὄλυμπος, ὁ, *Olympus*

ὅλως, adv., *on the whole, generally speaking, in short*

Ὁμηρικός, -ή, -όν, *Homeric*

ὁμιλητής, -οῦ, ὁ, *disciple, follower*

ὅμοιος, -η, -ον, *like, resembling*; *the same*; ὅμοιον, adv. (+ ὡς), *the same as,
like, just as, just like*; τὸ ὅμοιον, *the same thing*

ὁμοίως, adv., *similarly, in the same way*

ὅμως, conj., *nevertheless*; *together, alike, equally*

ὄνειρον, τό, *dream*; (ὀνείρατα is the common neut. nom./acc. pl. form)

Ὀνησίκριτος, ὁ, *Onesicritus*

142

ὀνομάζω, name, *call*
ὀξύς, -εῖα, -ύ, *quick, swift*
ὀπισθόδομος, ὁ, *rear porch* or *chamber (of a temple)*
ὅπλον, τό, *tool, implement*; (mostly in pl.) *arms, weapons*
ὅπου, adv., *when, since*
ὀπτάω, *roast*
ὅπως, adv., *how*
ὁράω, ὄψομαι, εἶδον, *see*
ὄργυια, ἡ, (unit of length measured by the outstretched arms) *six feet*
ὀρίνω, *stir, move, excite, rouse*
ὄρνεον, τό, *bird*
ὄρος -ους, τό, *mountain, hill*
ὀρύττω, *dig*
ὀρφανός, -ή, -όν, *orphan*
ὅς, ἥ, ὅ, rel. pron., *who, whose, whom, which, that*
ὅσιος, -η, -ον, *hallowed, sanctioned by religious law*; ὅσιόν or ὅσιά (ἐστι),
    + inf., *it is sanctioned by religious law, it is lawful*
ὅσον, adv., *so far as, as much as*; *about, nearly*
ὅσος, -η, -ον, *as great as, as much as*; (pl.) *as many as*
ὅσπερ, ἥπερ, ὅπερ, rel. pron., emphatic forms, *who, whose, whom, which, that*
ὅστις, ἥτις, ὅ τι, rel. pron., *anyone who, who, anything that, that, which*
ὅτε, conj., *when*
ὅτεπερ, (intensive form of ὅτε) *at which time, at that time*
ὅτι, conj., *that, because*; (+ superlative) *as X as possible*
οὐδέ, *(and/but) not*; ἀλλ' οὐδὲ, *and not even*
οὐδείς, οὐδεμία, οὐδέν, *no one, nobody, nothing*; *no*
οὐδέπω, adv., *(and) not yet, not as yet*
οὐδεπώποτε, conj. and adv., *never yet at any time, never ever*
οὐκέτι, adv., *no longer*
οὐρανός, ὁ, *sky, heaven*
οὐσία, ἡ, *property*
οὗτος, αὕτη, τοῦτο, *this*; (pl.) *these*
οὕτω, οὕτως, adv., *so, thus; as follows*
ὄχα, adv., *far*; ὄχ' ἄριστος, *far the best*
ὀχέω, *carry*; (mid.) *have oneself carried, be carried* or *borne*
ὄχημα, -ατος, τό, *carriage, transportation*
ὀψέ, adv., *late, late in the day*

Π π

παγγέλοιος, -ον, *utterly ridiculous*

παιδεία, ἡ, *culture, learning, education; accomplishments*

παιδίον, τό, (diminutive of παῖς) *(little or young) child*

παῖς, παίδος, ὁ or ἡ, *boy, girl, son, daughter, child*

παίω, *strike, beat*

πάλαι, adv., *long ago*

παλαιός, -ά, -όν, *ancient*

Παλαιστίνος, -η, -ον, *of or from Palestine, Palestinian*

παλινῳδία, ἡ, *palinode, recantation*

παμμεγέθης, -ες, *very great, immense*

πανευδαίμων, -ον, *absolutely happy, eternally blissful*

πανήγυρις, -εως, ἡ, *assembly, festival; national assembly or festival*

πανηγυριστής, -οῦ, ὁ, *one who attends a festival in honor of a national god*

πάντως, adv., *at all costs, absolutely, altogether*

πάνυ, adv., *altogether, entirely; very, exceedingly, too much*; οὐ πάνυ, *not at all; hardly, scarcely*

παρά, prep. (+ gen.), *by, from*; (+ dat.) *at, near, by*; (+ acc.), *except; beside, near, by; along the whole course of, during, throughout*

παραβαίνω, παραβήσομαι, παρέβην, *transgress, sin against*

παραβάλλω, παραβαλῶ, παρέβαλον, *compare* X (acc.) *with* Y (dat.)

παραβύω, *stuff in, insert*; (pass.) *be stuffed or packed with* (+ gen.)

παραγράφω, *paint or portray beside* (+ dat.)

παραδέχομαι, (dep.) *receive, admit, accept; recognize as correct*

παραίνεσις, -εως, ἡ, *advice, counsel, recommendation; address; exhortation*

παραλάμβανω, παραλήψομαι, παρέλαβον, *take, receive, accept, take charge of; invite*

παραμυθέομαι, (dep.) *console, comfort*

παρανομέω, *transgress the law, commit a crime or outrage*

παραπέμπω, *escort, attend*

παραρτάομαι, (dep.) *have* X (acc.) *hung by one's side*

παρασκευάζω, *get ready, prepare*

παρασκευή, ἡ, *equipment, belongings*

παραφυλάττω, παραφυλάξω, παρεφύλαξα, *watch or observe carefully*

παρέργως, adv., *desultorily, halfheartedly*

παρέρχομαι, πάρειμι, παρῆλθον, *come (among); come forward to speak to, arrive*; (+ ἐς/εἰς,) *arrive at*

Παριάνος, -α, -ον, *Parian*

παρίστημι, παραστήσω, (1st aor.) παρέστησα, present, show;
(2nd aor.) παρέστην, (perf.) παρέστηκα, stand by, be present

παροπτάω, roast slightly, toast, singe

παρορμάω, urge on, incite

παρρησία, ἡ, outspokenness, frankness

πᾶς, πᾶσα, πᾶν, all, every, whole

πάσχω, πείσομαι, ἔπαθον, experience; suffer, undergo

πατήρ, πατρός, ὁ, father

Πάτραι, -ῶν, αἱ, Patras

πατραλοίας, -α / -ου, ὁ, parricide, one who murders his father

πατρίς, πατρίδος, ἡ, one's fatherland / country

πατρῷος, -η, -ον, paternal, of one's father, hereditary

παύω, stop; (mid.) stop (oneself), cease from

πείθω, πείσω, ἔπεισα, persuade, convince

πειράομαι, πειράσομαι, ἐπειράθην, (mid more common than act.
πειράω) try, attempt, endeavor (often + inf.)

πένης, -ητος, ὁ, poor person; as adj. (when preceding another noun), poor

πενθέω, mourn for, lament

πεντακισχίλιοι, -αι, -α, five thousand

πέντε, indecl., five

πεντεκαίδεκα, indecl., fifteen

περί, prep. (+ gen.), about, concerning, on (the topic / matter of); (+ dat.)
concerning; (+ acc.) in, about, around

περίβλεπτος, -ον, admired by many

περιέχω, περιέξω, περιέσχον, encompass, surround, embrace

περιίστημι, περιστήσω, περιέστησα, place around; (2nd aor.)
περιέστην, (perf.) περιέστηκα, stand around

περιλαμβάνω, περιλήψομαι, περιέλαβον, comprehend, grasp

περιμένω, περιμενῶ, περέμεινα, wait, await, wait for, wait around for

περιπατέω, walk about, stroll, walk about while teaching

περιποιέω, procure, secure, achieve

περισκοπέω, look around or about, consider carefully

περισπούδαστος, -ον, much desired, highly desirable

περίστασις, -εως, ἡ, situation, circumstances, state of affairs

πέρνημι / πιπράσκω (later form found in Lucian), sell

πέτομαι, (dep.) fly

πηδάω, πηδήσομαι, ἐπήδησα, leap

πηλός, ὁ, clay, mud

πήρα, ἡ, leather pouch, wallet

πιναρός, -ά, -όν, dirty, squalid

πίνω, πίομαι, ἔπιον, drink (+ gen.)

πίστις, -εως, ἡ, proof

πλανάω, make to wander; lead astray; (pass.) wander, roam about

πλάσμα, -ατος, τό, figure, image; counterfeit, forgery, fiction

πλάστης, -ου, ὁ, sculptor, creator

Πλέθριον, τό, Plethrium

πλεῖστος, -η, -ον, most, greatest, largest; τὰ πλεῖστα, the vast majority

πλείων, πλεῖον, (comp. of πολύς, πολλή, πολύ) more; πλεῖον (adv.), more

πλέω, πλεύσομαι, ἔπλευσα, sail

πληγή, ἡ, blow, strike, beating

πλῆθος, -ους, τό, number, multitude, crowd, throng

πλήθω, (intransitive form of πίμπλημι, mostly in pres. part) be full, be at its height

πλήν, conj., except, however, but; (+ ἀλλά is a Koine Greek construction) however, but, as it happened

πλησίον, adv., near, close

πλοῦς, πλοῦ, πλῷ, πλοῦν, ὁ, voyage

πλούσιος, -α, -ον, wealthy

πόθεν, adv., from where?

ποιέω, make, produce, create; do; (mid.) regard, consider, reckon X (acc.) (as) Y (acc.); make X (acc.) (one's) Y (acc), procure for oneself; gain

ποιητής, -οῦ, ὁ, poet, writer; playwright

ποικίλος, -η, -ον, various, diverse, elaborate

Ποινή, ἡ, Poine (goddess of retribution and vengeance; punisher of murderers)

ποῖος, -α, -ον, of what kind, what sort

πολιός, -ά, -όν, gray-haired; venerable

πολίτης, -ου, ὁ, citizen, fellow-citizen

πόλις, πόλεως, ἡ, city, city-state

πολλάκις, many times, often

πολυάνθρωπος, -ον, crowded, much-visited

πολύς, πολλή, πολύ, much, great; (pl.) many; (as substantive) the majority

πολυώνυμος, -ον, having many names; of great name, famous

πονηρός, -ή, -όν, worthless, bad, wicked, morally deficient

πόρρω, adv., far off, far away

πορρωτάτω, adv., furthest, very far

ποταμός, ὁ, river

ποτε, adv., at some time, ever

πότερον...ἤ, whether...or

πότμος, ὁ, doom, fate, destiny; death

που, adv., somewhere, around; possibly, perhaps, I suppose

πρᾶγμα, -τος, τό, matter, thing, affair; (pl.) circumstances, situation; troubles, annoyances

πρᾶος, -ον, mild, gentle

πράττω, πράξω, ἔπραξα, do, act; achieve, accomplish

πρεσβύτης, -ου, ὁ, old man; ambassador, agent, commissioner

πρό, prep. (+ gen.), before

προαίρεσις, -εως, ἡ, choice, purpose; character, reputation

προβαίνω, προβήσομαι, προὔβην, go forward, advance

πρόειμι, go or come forward

προερῶ (fut. in Attic; present is from different stems: προλέγω and προαγορεύω), προεῖπον (aor.), foretell, make a prediction

προίημι, send on or forward; (mid.) give up, let go, abandon; drive forward

προλέγω, προερῶ, προεῖπον, proclaim or declare publicly; foretell

προπάτωρ, -ορος, ὁ, ancestor, progenitor

πρός, prep. (+ acc.), to, in reference or relation to, with respect to; with; for; in the presence of, before; engaged in, connected to

προσαγορεύω, call so and so

προσδιηγέομαι, (dep.) narrate besides or in addition

προσελαύνω, προσελῶ, προσήλασον, drive towards, arrive at, reach (+ dat.)

προσέχω, προσέξω, προσέσχον, (with or without τὸν νοῦν) pay close attention to (+ dat.)

προσίημι, send to or towards; (mid.) admit, accept, allow to come near one

προσκυνέω, fall down on one's knees and worship, worship

πρόσοδος, ἡ, revenue, income

προσπίπτω, προσπεσοῦμαι, προσέπεσον, fall upon, assail, attack (+ dat.)

πρόσπταισμα, -ατος, τό, whitlow (an abscess in the soft tissue near a fingernail or toenail); bump, bruise

προστάτης, -ου, ὁ, ruler, leader, patron, president; champion, protector

προστίθημι, προσθήσω, προσέθηκα, add

πρόσωπον, τό, face; one's look, countenance

προτεραῖος, -η, -ον, previous, former; τῇ προτεραίᾳ (sc. ἡμέρᾳ), on the day before

πρότερον, adv., formerly, before, earlier, sooner, first

πρότερος, -η, -ον, former, prior, previous

προὔχω (uncontracted = προέχω), be preeminent / superior / outstanding

πρόφασις, -εως, ἡ, pretext; cause; ἐπὶ προφάσει, because of, on account of

προφήτης, -ου, ὁ, prophet

πρῶτος, -η, -ον, first; τὸ πρῶτον (adv.), first, first of all, in the first place

πυγή, ἡ, ass, buttock(s)

πυνθάνομαι, learn by hearsay or inquiry

πῦρ, πυρός, τό, *fire*
πυρά, ἡ, *pyre, funeral-pyre*
πυρετός, ὁ, *fever*
πώγων, -ωνος, ὁ, *beard*
πως, adv., *in any way, at all, by any means; somehow;* ὧδέ πως, *somehow so/ thus/in this way*
πῶς, adv., *how?, in what manner* or *way?*

Ρ ρ

ῥᾴδιος, -α, -ον, *easy*
ῥαφανίς, -ῖδος, ἡ, *radish*
ῥῆμα, -ατος, τό, *word*
ῥῆσις, -εως, ἡ, *saying, speech*
ῥόπαλον, τό, *club*
ῥυπάω, *be filthy* or *dirty*
Ῥωμαῖος, -α, -ον, *Roman*

Σ σ

σάττω, *fill quite full, pack, stuff* X (acc.) *with* Y (gen. or dat.)
σέβω, *worship*
σεισμός, ὁ, *shaking, shock, trembling, earthquake*
σελήνη, ἡ, *moon*
σεμνός, -ή, -όν, *revered, august, awe-inspiring*
σεμνότης, -ητος, ἡ, *solemnity, dignity, seriousness, authority*
Σίβυλλα, ἡ, *Sibyl*
σιγή, ἡ, *silence*
Σινωπεύς, -έως, ὁ, *an inhabitant of Sinope, a Sinopean*
σιωπή, ἡ, *silence;* (dat. case used as adv.) *in silence, silently*
σκέπτομαι, σκέψομαι, ἐσκεψάμην, (dep.) *consider* or *examine (carefully)*
σκευάζω, *outfit, dress up;* (pass.) *be outfitted, dressed up,* or *fully accoutred*
σκηνή, ἡ, *stage*
σοφία, ἡ, *wisdom, insight, intelligence, knowledge; philosophy*
σοφιστής, -οῦ, ὁ, *sophist*
σοφός, -ή, -όν, *subtle, ingenious, clever; wise*
σπονδή, ἡ, *libation, drink-offering* (poured out to the gods)

σπουδή, ἡ, *zeal, effort, passion, eagerness, assiduousness, haste*

στάδιον, τό, (unit of length = 607 feet / 185 meters) *stade*

σταυρός, ὁ, *cross*

στέλλω, στελῶ, ἔστειλα, *equip; send*

στέφω, *crown, encircle, wreath*

στοά, -ἡ, *portico, roofed colonnade*

στόμα, -ατος, τό, *mouth*

σύ, σοῦ / σου, σοί / σοι, σέ / σε, (sing.) *you*

συγγράφω, *compose, write*

συγκαθεύδω, συγκαθευδήσω, (no aor. in Attic Greek), *sleep with*

συγκατασπάω, *pull down with himself*

συγκομίζω, *gather, collect, bring together*

σύκινος, -η, -ον, *of the figtree, fig wood*

συλλαμβάνω, συλλήψομαι, συνέλαβον, *arrest, seize*

συμπλέω, *sail in company with*

συμφορά, ἡ, *disaster, catastrophe*

σύν, prep. (+ dat.), *with*

συναγορεύω, *support, speak on behalf of someone*

συναρπάζω, *seize and carry off*

σύνειμι, *attend, be with*; οἱ συνόντες, *associates, disciples*

συνεμπίπτω, συνεμπεσοῦμαι, συνενέπεσον, *fall in together* or *also*

συνήθης, -ες, *habitual, customary, usual, ordinary*

σύνθρονος, -ον, *enthroned with*

συνίημι, συνήσω, συνῆκα, *perceive, hear; understand*

συνίστημι, συνστήσω, συνέστησα, *combine, associate*; (pass.) *form, be organized* or *put together; arise, take shape, come into existence*

συνοδεύω, *travel together with, accompany* (+ dat.)

συντίθημι, συνθήσω, συνέθηκα, *put together, compose, build, make*

συντρίβω, *crush*

συνωθέω, *push* or *shove together / as one*

Συρία, ἡ, *Syria*

σφόδρα, adv., *very, very much, greatly; strongly, violently*

σφοδρός, -ἡ, -όν, *strong, violent*

σχεδόν, adv., *nearly, almost, about*

σχῆμα, -ατος, τό, *form, shape, figure, appearance; bearing, comportment*

σώζω, *save, rescue, deliver; cure, make well*

Σωκράτης, -ους, ὁ, *Socrates*

T τ

τάλαντον, -ου, τό, *talent* (a weight and a sum of money = 6,000 drachmas)

ταράττω, *disturb, trouble, agitate*

ταῦρος, ὁ, *bull*

τάφος, ὁ, *tomb, grave*

τάχα, adv., *quickly, at once, without delay*

τάχιστος, -η, -ον, *quickest, swiftest*; τάχιστα (neut. pl. adj. as adv.), *most or very quickly*

τάχος, -ους, τό, *speed, quickness*

τέγος, -ους, τό, *roof*

τέθηπα, (perf. with pres. sense) *be astonished, astounded*, or *amazed*

τελετή, ἡ, *mystic rite, initiation ceremony, initiation into the mystery religions, cult*

τελευταῖος, -α, -ον, *last*; τὰ τελευταῖα (adv.), *at last, finally, in the end; for the last time*

τελευτή, ἡ, *end, demise, end of life* (i.e., *death*)

τελέω, *finish, complete*; *perform*; *perform* (sacred rites); (+ εἰς) *belong to, become, reach the state of*

τέλος, -ους, τό, *end, consummation*; *end of life, death*; *magistracy, office*; οἱ ἐν τέλει, *magistrates, officials*; (acc. sing. often as adv.) *finally, at last*

τέμενος, -ους, τό, *sacred precinct*

τερατεία, ἡ, *charlatanism, performing hocus-pocus, the art of clap-trap*

τερατουργία, ἡ, *hocus-pocus, flimflammery*

τέσσαρες (m./f.), τέσσαρα (n.), (τεττάρων gen.), *four*

τεταρταῖος, -η, -ον, *on the fourth day*; τεταρταῖος [πυρετός], *quartan fever*

τετράκις, adv., *four times*

τέττιξ, -ιγος, ὁ, *cicada, cricket*

τέχνη, ἡ, *art, craft, profession*

τεχνίτης, -ου, ὁ, *artisan, craftsman; trickster*

τέως, adv., *up to then*

τηρέω, *watch for, wait for*

τίλλω, *tear* or *pull out (one's hair)*; (mid.) *tear of pull out one's hair in sorrow*

τιμάω, *honor, revere, show reverence to*

τις, τι, (gen. τινος) (indefinite adj.) *a certain*; *some*; *a, an*; (indefinite pron.) *someone*; *something*; *anyone*; *anything*

τίς, τί, (gen. τίνος) interrog. pron. and adj., *who? which? what?*

τοίνυν, particle, *therefore, accordingly*; *moreover*

τοιόσδε, τοιάδε, τοιόνδε, *of such a kind* (as follows)

τοιοῦτος, τοιαύτη, τοιοῦτο, *such*; τὰ τοιαῦτα, *such things as these, suchlike*

τολμάω, *dare, be brave* or *bold enough* (to do something terrible or difficult)

τόλμημα, -ατος, τό, *venture, adventure, enterprise, deed of daring, daring* or *shameless act*

τολμηρός, -ή, -όν, *daring, bold*

τόπος, ὀ, *place, site*

τοσοῦτος, -αύτη, -οῦτον, *so much, so great*; (pl.) *so many*

τότε, adv., *then, at that time*

τραγικῶς, adv., *in tragic style* or *getup*

τραγῳδέω, *put on an elaborate performance* (in the style of ancient tragedy); *tell in a tragic manner* (i.e., embellish with fantastic details)

τραγῳδία, ἡ, *tragedy*

τραχύς, -εῖα, -ύ, *rough, sharp, harsh*; *hoarse*

τρέπω, τρέψω, ἔτρεψα, (Epic and Ionic have 2nd aor. ἔτραπον), *turn* X; (mid.) *turn* X *(for oneself / one's own benefit), turn oneself*

τριάκοντα, indecl., *thirty*

τρίβων, -ωνος, ὁ, *threadbare cloak, worn out garment*

τριβώνιον, τό, (dim. of ὁ τρίβων), *threadbare cloak, worn out garment*

τρίοδος, ἡ, *street corner, a meeting of three roads*; *trite, hackneyed, everyday, trivial*

τρίς, indecl., *three times, thrice*

τρισχίλιοι, -αι, -α, *three thousand*

τρίτος -η, -ον, *third*

τροπή, ἡ, *turn, turning*; *change, transformation*

τρόπος, ὁ, *manner, means, way*

τρυφή, ἡ, *luxury, self-indulgence*

Τρῳάς, -άδος, ἡ, *the Troad* (i.e., the region of Northwest Asia Minor whose principal city was Troy)

τυγχάνω, τεύξομαι, ἔτυχον, *happen* (+ supplementary participle)

τύρβη, ἡ, *tumult, confusion, chaos, turmoil*

Υ υ

ὕδωρ, ὕδατος, τό, *water*

ὑπεκκάω, ὑπεκκαύσω, ὑπεξέκαυσα, *inflame, excite, provoke*

ὑπέρ, prep. (+ gen.), *on, concerning; for, in defense of, on behalf of, for the sake of*; (+ acc.), *over, above, exceeding, beyond, more than*

ὑπερβολή, ἡ, *hyperbole*

ὑπισχνέομαι, ὑποσχήσομαι, ὑπεσχόμην, *promise (to do* or *undertake)*

ὑπό, prep. (+ gen. of the agent, with pass. verbs), *by*

ὑποδύομαι, *creep under; put on a character* (because ancient actors wore masks)

ὑπολαμβάνω, ὑπολήψομαι, ὑπέλαβον, *consider, suppose*

ὑπολείπω, ὑπολείψω, ὑπέλιπον, *leave behind* or *remaining;* (pass.) *stay behind, be left behind*

ὑπομένω, ὑπομενῶ, ὑπέμεινα, *endure, submit to*

ὑποτρέμω, *tremble a little, tremble slightly*

ὑποφείδομαι, (dep.) *spare a little; be moderate* or *restrained*

ὑποφρίττω, *shudder slightly*

Φ φ

φαιδρός, -ά, -όν, *cheerful, glad*

Φάλαρις, -ιδος, ὁ, *Phalaris*

φάρμακον, τό, *drug, salve*

φαῦλος, -η, -ον, *low (in rank), mean, common; bad, poor;* (comparative) *inferior*

φέρω, οἴσω, ἤνεγκον, *carry, bring, bear; endure, put up with;* (pass.) *be borne along (by winds), be swept away; go*

φεύγω, φεύξομαι, ἔφυγον, *flee, run away*

φημί, φήσω, ἔφην (imperf.), ἔφησα (aor., rare), *say*

φιλόδοξος, -ον, *loving fame* or *glory;* τὸ φιλόδοξον, *love of fame* or *glory*

φιλοκίνδυνος, -ον, *adventurous, reckless, fond of danger* or *risk*

Φιλοκτήτης, -ου, ὁ, *Philoctetes*

φιλόπατρις, -ιδος, (acc. φιλόπατριν) ὁ or ἡ, *patriot*

φιλοσοφία, ἡ, *philosophy*

φιλόσοφος, ὁ, *philosopher*

φιλότης, ἡ, *friendship, love, affection;* ὦ φιλότης, *my friend*

φιμόω, *muzzle, make silent*

φλεγμαίνω, *be heated, inflamed, fester*

φλογμός, ὁ, *feverish heat*

φλόξ, φλογός, ἡ, *flame*

φοβέομαι, (dep.) *be frightened* or *afraid (of), fear*

φοῖνιξ, -ικος, ὁ, *phoenix (mythological bird of India-Arabia-Egypt)*

Φοῖνιξ, -ικος, ὁ, *Phoenix*

φόνος, ὁ, *murder, homicide*

φράζω, *point out, show, indicate; declare*

φρύγανον, τό, *dry stick;* (mostly in pl.) *brush, firewood*

φυγή, ἡ, *banishment, exile; flight, hasty departure, running away, escape*

φυλάσσω, φυλάξω, ἐφύλαξα, *keep*

φύσις, -εως, ἡ, *nature, being, essence*

φωνή, ἡ, *sound, noise, voice*

X χ

χαίρω, χαιρήσω, ἐχάρην, *rejoice, be glad;* (+ pres. part.) *be in the habit of, accustomed to; take pleasure in* (+ dat.); χαίρειν, *farewell;* (+μακρά), *a long or hearty farewell*

χαρίεις, χαρίεσσα, χάριεν, (masc./neut. gen. χαρίεντος), *beautiful, nice, fine; smart, clever, educated, with taste and refinement*

χαμαί, adv., *on the ground*

χάσκω, χανοῦμαι, ἔχανον, *open one's mouth (in eager expectation), gape*

χείρ, χειρός, ἡ, *hand*

χειροτονέω, *appoint* **χήρα, ἡ,** *widow*

χλωρός, -ά, -όν, *pale-green, green*

χρεών, (indecl.) *necessity, fate;* mostly in the phrase χρεών (sc. ἐστι), *it is necessary*

χρή, (imperf. ἐχρῆν), *it is necessary, one must* (+ inf.)

χρῆμα, -ατος, τό, *thing;* (pl.) *money, goods*

χρησμολόγος, -ον, *uttering oracles, expounder of oracles; soothsayer*

χρησμός, ὁ, *oracle, oracular response*

χρηστήριον, τό, *oracular shrine*

χρηστός, -ή, -όν, *good, honest, worthy*

Χριστιανός, ὁ, *Christian*

χρίω, *rub, smear,* or *anoint with;* (mid.) *rub, smear,* or *anoint oneself with*

χροιά, ἡ, *complexion, color (of the skin)*

χρόνος, ὁ, *time*

χρυσός, ὁ, *gold*

χρυσοῦς, -ῆ, -οῦν, *golden, of gold*

χρῶμαι (uncontracted = χράομαι), **χρήσομαι, ἐχρησάμην,** *make use of* (+ dat.)

χωρίον, τό, *place*

Ψ ψ

ψιλός, -ή, -όν, *bare, unadorned, plain*

ψυχρός, -ά, -όν, *cold, frigid; vain; heartless; silly;* ψυχρόν (sc. ὕδωρ) *cold water*

Ω ω

ὧδε, adv., *in this way, so, thus*; **ὧδέ πως**, *somehow so/thus/in this way*

ὥρα, ἡ, *time, right time*

ὡραῖος, -α, -ον, *beautiful, youthful*; *ripe*; *bursting with life*

ὡς, adv., *as, like*; *so*; *how*; conj., (= ὅτι) *that*; (+ aor. indic.) *when, after*; (+ subju./opt.) *so that, in order that*

ὥσπερ, adv., *as, like, just as (if), even as*

ὥστε, conj., *so that, that, with the result that*; *and so, therefore, consequently*

ὠφελέω, *help, benefit, be of benefit, use*, or *service to, assist*

ὠφέλιμος, -ον, *helpful, useful, beneficial, profitable, advantageous*

ὠχρίας, -ου, ὁ, *pale, a person of pale complexion*

NOTES

NOTES

NOTES

CPSIA information can be obtained
at www.ICGtesting.com
Printed in the USA
LVHW050038030723
751382LV00003B/334

9 781500 303099